The Quest for Mental Health

This is the story of one of the most far reaching human endeavors in modern history: the quest for mental well-being. From its origins in the eighteenth century to its wide scope in the early twenty-first, this search for emotional health and welfare has cost billions. In the name of mental health, millions around the world have been tranquilized, institutionalized, psychoanalyzed, sterilized, lobotomized, and even euthanized. Yet at the dawn of the new millennium, reported rates of depression and anxiety were unprecedentedly high. Drawing on years of field research, Ian Dowbiggin argues that if the quest for emotional well-being has reached a crisis point in the twenty-first century, it is because mass society is enveloped by cultures of therapism and consumerism, which increasingly advocate bureaucratic and managerial approaches to health and welfare. Over time, stakeholders such as governments, medicine, researchers, industry, schools, the media, the courts, families, and a public whose taste for treatment seems insatiable have transformed the campaign to achieve mental health into a movement that has come to mean all things to virtually all people. As Dowbiggin shows, if current trends continue, the quest for mental health is likely to make people more miserable before they become happier.

Ian Dowbiggin has taught history at the University of Rochester, the University of Dallas, the University of Toronto, and the University of Prince Edward Island. The author of six books on the history of medicine, he has also published in the *American Historical Review*, the *Journal of Contemporary History*, the *Journal of Policy History*, the *Canadian Historical Review*, the *Canadian Journal of Psychiatry*, and the *Bulletin of the History of Medicine*. He is on the editorial board of the *History of Psychiatry*.

CAMBRIDGE ESSENTIAL HISTORIES

Series Editor
Donald Critchlow, *St. Louis University*

Cambridge Essential Histories is devoted to introducing critical events, periods, or individuals in history to students. Volumes in this series emphasize narrative as a means of familiarizing students with historical analysis. In this series leading scholars focus on topics in European, American, Asian, Latin American, Middle Eastern, African, and world history through thesis-driven, concise volumes designed for survey and upper-division undergraduate history courses. Each book contains an introduction that acquaints readers with the historical events and reveals the book's thesis; narrative chapters that cover the chronology of the event or problem; and a concluding summary that provides the historical interpretation and analysis.

Titles in the Series

Edward D. Berkowitz, *Mass Appeal: The Formative Age of the Movies, Radio, and TV*
John Earl Haynes and Harvey Klehr, *Early Cold War Spies: The Espionage Trials That Shaped American Politics*
James H. Hutson, *Church and State in America: The First Two Centuries*
Maury Klein, *The Genesis of Industrial America, 1870–1920*
John Lauritz Larson, *The Market Revolution in America: Liberty, Ambition, and the Eclipse of the Common Good*
Charles H. Parker, *Global Interactions in the Early Modern Age, 1400–1800*

The Quest for Mental Health

A Tale of Science, Medicine, Scandal, Sorrow, and Mass Society

IAN DOWBIGGIN

The University of Prince Edward Island

CAMBRIDGE UNIVERSITY PRESS

CAMBRIDGE UNIVERSITY PRESS
Cambridge, New York, Melbourne, Madrid, Cape Town,
Singapore, São Paulo, Delhi, Tokyo, Mexico City

Cambridge University Press
32 Avenue of the Americas, New York, NY 10013-2473, USA

www.cambridge.org
Information on this title: www.cambridge.org/9780521688680

First published 2011

Printed in the United States of America

A catalog record for this publication is available from the British Library.

Library of Congress Cataloging in Publication data
Dowbiggin, Ian Robert, 1952–
   The quest for mental health : a tale of science, medicine, scandal,
   sorrow, and mass society / Ian Dowbiggin.
      p.   cm. – (Cambridge essential histories)
   Includes bibliographical references and index.
   ISBN 978-0-521-86867-9 (hardback) – ISBN 978-0-521-68868-0 (paperback)
   1. Mental health.   2. Personality.   3. Emotions.   I. Title.   II. Series.
   RA790.D69   2011
   362.196'89–dc22   2010054413

ISBN 978-0-521-86867-9 Hardback
ISBN 978-0-521-68868-0 Paperback

Contents

Acknowledgments

This book is the culmination of research, writing, and teaching over thirty years in the field of the history of mental health care. It has been my pleasure during this period to have met and chatted with many of the outstanding historians who have tilled this field. My first training in the history of mental health came at the University of Rochester from the psycho-historian William J. McGrath and the historian of medicine Theodore M. Brown, both exceptional scholars. The list also includes German Berrios, Joel Braslow, Edward M. Brown, John Burnham, Bill Bynum, Eric Engstrom, Toby Gelfand, Cyril Greenland, Gerald Grob, Paul Lerner, Mark Micale, George Mora, Michael Neve, Patricia Prestwich, Roy Porter, Andrew Scull, Edward Shorter, Nancy Tomes, Trevor Turner, and David Wright. In 2002, to my great pleasure, James Moran moved into the office across the hall and became my valued colleague. To all these superb scholars, I dedicate this book.

Like my earlier books, this one would have been next to impossible to write if it had not been for the generous support of the Social Sciences and Humanities Research Council of Canada, the Associated Medical Services, and the University of Prince Edward Island's Senate Committee on Research Grant. I also owe a deep debt of gratitude to Don Critchlow and Lew Bateman for encouraging me in this book project, as well as the many librarians and archivists who have aided me unstintingly over the years at locations such as the Canadian Archives for the History of Psychiatry, the Wellcome Institute for the History of Medicine, the University of Michigan's Bentley Historical Library, the Social Welfare History Archives at the University of Minnesota, Harvard University's Schlesinger Library on the History of Women in America, and the Harvard

Medical School's Francis A. Countway Library of Medicine. Last but not least, my student assistant, Peter Rankin, pitched in with some invaluable online research.

Part of this book appeared previously in altered form in "High Anxieties: The Social Construction of Anxiety Disorders," *Canadian Journal of Psychiatry*, 54, no. 7, July 2009: 429–36. I am grateful to the *Canadian Journal of Psychiatry* for permission to reproduce copyrighted material.

Introduction

"Mental health issues are huge," exclaimed a Canadian official in 2008, an assertion that may prove to be one of the greatest understatements of the twenty-first century. In 2001 the World Health Organization (WHO) announced its intention to "raise awareness of mental health issues at the highest level of decision and policy making." The WHO's aim was "to mark the beginning of a new era in the field of mental health care."

In 2002 former U.S. president George W. Bush created the New Freedom Commission on Mental Health. In 2004 (with Bush's endorsement) the Commission recommended extensive screening of every child in the United States for mental disorders, to be followed by widespread medicating of those diagnosed with psychological problems.

Europe, too, appeared to be caught up in the quest for mental health. In 2005 the European Union (UN) announced a new and urgent strategy to promote mental health. To the twenty-seven countries of the EU, mental illness rivaled cancer as a deadly threat to public health.[1] In 2006 a Canadian Senate committee issued *Out of the Shadows at Last*, a report that called for a massive overhaul of national mental health policy aimed at helping people with mental disabilities get the services they need and deserve.

The WHO's announcement, EU's strategy, the U.S. president's initiative, and the Canadian report are just some indications that at the beginning of the new century national and international governments on both sides of the Atlantic Ocean seem as dedicated as ever to making mental health one of the most significant policy issues looming over the twenty-first century. Yet the new century's quest for mental health has a long, contested, complex, and colorful history. Over the past two hundred years the struggle to achieve psychological wellness has been a key chapter of modern history, resulting in the emergence of a loose but burgeoning coalition of stakeholders in mental health care policy, including government, professions, researchers, the media, the courts, drug companies, the insurance industry, unions, schools, families, and those who used to be called patients but are now referred to as "consumers."[2] Though sometimes at cross-purposes, these vested interest groups have been united on the basis of an evolving consensus emphasizing the virtues of bureaucracy, welfare, education, science, professional expertise, and public administration. This consensus is sometimes referred to as "therapism," the doctrine which states that a growing number of people in the early twenty-first century suffer from a bona fide medical condition beyond their control and require treatment from a wide range of healers and caregivers, including psychiatrists, psychologists, counselors, nurses, educators, workshoppers, and life coaches.[3] By the new millennium the doctrine of therapism had spread throughout society, into schools, offices, hospitals, and homes.[4] The search for sanity had culminated in a widespread belief that everyone is entitled to mental health, people are sicker than they realize, and government's mandate is to empower people to enjoy a right to emotional well-being. The early years of the twenty-first century suggest that therapism shows no sign of flagging anytime soon.

The widespread enthusiasm for therapism in the early twenty-first century might suggest that previous generations scarcely tried to improve mental health, but nothing could be further from the truth. Throughout history, and in the name of psychological well-being, millions of people the world over have been hospitalized, psychoanalyzed, tranquilized, sterilized, lobotomized, or even euthanized. They have undergone testing, screening, counseling, and lecturing, to say nothing of a variety of shock therapies, all in the hope of feeling better. Over the years governments, industries, professions, schools, families, and private citizens have spent untold billions of dollars to make people less troubled.

The quest for mental health has not been without some successes. At the turn of the twenty-first century, researchers knew more than ever before about the ways in which the brain's chemical and physiological processes affected mood and mental functioning. New technologies of neuro-imaging enabled scientists to scan for the first time abnormalities in blood flow and anatomical structure. The field of evolutionary neurobiology had made impressive strides. Therapists possessed unprecedentedly effective drugs for a range of psychological conditions. Studies showed that forms of cognitive behavioral therapy were effective in combating depression. The stigma surrounding mental illness may not have disappeared, but increasingly the public appeared willing to acknowledge that people with mental disabilities were not responsible for their conditions and were as deserving of medical assistance as anyone else.

Yet these advances have been offset by other, troubling trends. In the early twenty-first century, rates of psychological distress had never been higher. The working manual of psychiatric illnesses published by the American Psychiatric Association listed hundreds of mental disorders. A 2004 U.S. psychiatric survey found that one in ten Americans had an addiction disorder, nearly 20 million Americans suffered from mood disorders, and another 23 million met the criteria for anxiety disorders. A 2007 study reported that up to 30 percent of people worldwide will suffer from a clear-cut mental illness each year, making psychiatric disease a bigger threat to public health than cancer or heart disease. The WHO recently announced that one in four Europeans will suffer from a mental illness at least once in their life, and one in five children or adolescents experience serious developmental, cognitive, or emotional problems.

Yet all this grim news appears to have had little impact on the widespread belief that mental health is an achievable goal. Current society is unprecedentedly saturated with psychological ways of thinking. Bookstore shelves groan under the weight of countless volumes dedicated to understanding and solving emotional issues. Day and night the media broadcast the message that everyone can feel better with pills, counseling, information, and public education.

As the diagnosis of social anxiety illustrates, the threshold for emotional pain appears to be dropping steadily. Reports of anxiety, including shyness and stage fright, stretch back to classical antiquity, but before the nineteenth century the majority view was that most social anxiety was normal and even an asset in some situations that called for vigilance. Within cultures that prized bashfulness as a mark of modesty, shyness was widely praised in women. It may be little consolation for people wracked with anxiety, for whom it is a genuinely painful experience, to learn how history has affected the public perception of anxiety, but the fact remains that over time everyday feelings have been transformed into symptoms of illness. The same goes for commonplace sorrow, which now is defined as depression. In this process of medicalization, more and more people have concluded that life is impossible without the guidance of state-certified experts.

This book's account of how the quest for mental health has culminated in therapism begins in Chapter 1 with an examination of the first stirrings of mental health care reform during the years straddling the American Revolution and the U.S. Civil War. It was no coincidence that antecedents of modern-day mental health policies showed up in locations such as eighteenth-century England, revolutionary France, the young American republic, and late-eighteenth-century Tuscany, where the shift toward constitutionalism, republicanism, and popular sovereignty and away from rule by autocratic monarchs was most noticeable. Although much of the impetus for reform came from the efforts of religious activists motivated by the teachings of the social gospel, the most significant result of the ferment of these years was the emergence of the medical specialty of psychiatry, the study and treatment of diseases of the mind. Over the next two hundred years the psychiatric profession played a vital leadership role in the quest for mental health, molding and in turn adapting to shifts in popular values and expectations. Although psychiatrists have been targets of intermittent criticism since the founding of their profession, their viewpoint that psychological disorders are certifiable medical conditions rather than moral failings or the outcome of sin had become widely accepted by the turn of the twenty-first century.

Chapter 2 charts the search for sanity against the backdrop of the growth of centralizing nation-states and the rise of mass society in the late nineteenth century. The chief feature of this era from the perspective of mental health was the building and administration of publicly funded mental hospitals, or "asylums." As asylum heads, psychiatrists wielded a power and authority that the rest of organized medicine envied. At the same time, and for the first time in history, governments assumed responsibility for mental health care policy making by providing their populations with welfare in the form of taxpayer-funded asylums, as well as incipient versions of state-funded insurance for illness and disability, thereby stimulating popular demand and taste for psychological wellness.

On other fronts, mental health was becoming more and more democratized as families exerted influence over the profession of asylum medicine and people were attracted to spiritualism and other forms of popular mental healing, including Freudian psychoanalysis. Freudianism never ceased to be controversial, yet in its popularized versions it helped spread the theory that almost everyone was a fit candidate for psychological therapy. Freud's views and other egalitarian trends in the psychological sciences signaled that by the early twentieth century an increasingly broad-based quest for mental health was under way.

A major turning point in the struggle for psychological well-being was the era of the two world wars, the topic of Chapter 3. Just as centralizing state power expanded in other fields and jurisdictions, so governments increasingly viewed mental health as a key cause of national prosperity and power. Mental hygiene, race hygiene, intelligence testing, the eugenics movement: all these currents thrived during the 1914–45 period and stressed government interest in the early detection and prevention of mental weakness. Meanwhile, psychiatry – bedeviled by challenges to its professional authority – resorted to physicalist treatments such as lobotomy, electro-convulsive therapy, and insulin coma. Some of these treatments proved more useful than others, but they all were linked to the frustrations psychiatrists felt trying to help patients and their families cope with mental disabilities. Despite the highly mixed results of such therapies, public faith in medical approaches, far from ebbing, tended to rise throughout this period.

Chapters 4 and 5 chart the main events in the search for sanity in the post-1945 era, a time of tremendous ferment and flux in the quest for mental health. Five outstanding developments affecting mental health policy, marking the period from Yalta to Y2K, bequeathed a wide-reaching and mixed legacy to the twenty-first century.

The first was the rise of the discipline of psychology, many of whose leaders taught that they possessed the solutions to a wide range of personal and social problems.

The second was the process called deinstitutionalization, the shift away from hospitalization to community living as the main form of treatment for people with mental disabilities. Deinstitutionalization signaled that in the eyes of experts and the public at large, the definition of emotional sickness had expanded to include the entire community. Just because you were not in a hospital did not mean you were not sick.

The third crucial development was researchers' discoveries in the field of pharmaceutical medicine. Beginning in the 1950s, industry introduced a series of drugs that promised to relieve the anxiety, depression, delusions, and phobias that tormented people in day-to-day life. Amid the hoopla surrounding the new medications, pharmaceutical companies forged partnerships with government, organized medicine, and health insurance companies, thus adding to the considerable clout they derived from the multi-billion-dollar global market for prescription drugs.

The fourth development was the emergence of a full-fledged movement dedicated to patients' rights and more collaborative relationships among doctors, patients, and the families of people with mental disabilities. This movement overturned the customary hierarchy that had ruled health care, based on the belief that licensed medical professionals knew what was best for patients.

The fifth was the growth of the media, which, beginning with print journalism, went on to include radio, television, and digital technology, and stimulated keen interest in mental health over the second half of the twentieth century.

These five developments combined with the rise of a post-1945 consumerist culture and what one author has dubbed "affluenza" – a late-twentieth-century malaise linked to rising levels of material prosperity – to produce an ever-widening democratization of mental health care policy and practice, including a growing reliance on psychiatric medications to raise levels of personal happiness.⁵ The mass consumption of psychiatric pills has deeply affected many aspects of life, such as consumer trends, definitions of health, and conceptions of well-being. Expanding markets for prescription drugs have helped to make mental health a vital and far-reaching concern, encouraging more and more people to rely on psychological concepts to interpret the full range of human behavior, emotions, and thoughts. At the close of the twentieth century, for the first time in history, serious credence was given to the notion that human beings were entitled to feel "better than well." New medications have also shaped clinical psychiatry by expanding existing categories of mental illness or creating new ones, what psychiatrist Peter Kramer calls "diagnostic bracket creep."⁶ The escalating rates of psychiatric drug use have placed heavy financial burdens on governments, which increasingly have to scramble to pay for state health care programs. Yet in the early twenty-first century, despite daunting fiscal challenges, most stakeholders insisted that no price could be fixed on emotional well-being.⁷

This book, then, reconstructs the winding road the world has followed since the French Revolution in the populist pursuit of psychological wellness. This unresolved quest is a tale of soaring expectations, dashed hopes, wasted opportunities, sporadic successes, incalculable suffering, and all too human careerism and self-interest. It is also the story of the resilient belief that the combined forces of science, medicine, government, public education, and professional expertise can make populations feel better about themselves. The historical quest for mental health, buffeted repeatedly by the winds of politics, business, science, and social change, was never inevitable, nor has it been uncontested. Its many stakeholders have periodically disagreed over tactics and goals. Governments that assumed leadership roles have had to perform delicate balancing acts, trying, on the one hand, to placate those who argued that greater governmental involvement threatens civil liberties and, on the other, to satisfy those who contended that governments were not doing enough to ease the burdens of families and patients who lived with crushing emotional pain every day of their lives. In the twenty-first century, as governments declare their determination to launch major reform efforts, many decry the prospect of millions of people receiving stigmatizing diagnoses and swallowing expensive and potentially dangerous drugs, but policy makers, health care providers, mental health advocacy organizations, and the pharmaceutical industry tend to believe that such programs would be a major step forward.

Above all, by preaching the importance of achieving mental health as a way of fulfilling individual and collective needs, governmental bodies have discovered time and again that the public is disposed to accept such messages. Governments routinely reward entire groups who claim victim status on the basis of (often dubious) psychiatric theories. The EU's 2005 call for an "authentic commitment to the human rights of people with mental health problems" suggests that, as globalization spreads in the early twenty-first century, millions around the world will seek to exercise such rights.[8] To quote historian Jacques Barzun, we live in "demotic times" characterized less by representative government than by rule "of the people," embodied in the welfare state with its bureaucratic promises of security, emancipation, material gratifications, and managerial solutions.[9] As this book shows, the questions facing society in the new century remain the same as those facing French political observer Alexis de Tocqueville in 1837: will the principle of democratic equality in everything from politics to mental health lead to "servitude or freedom ..., prosperity or wretchedness?"[10] This book argues that unless a historically grounded approach is taken, the consensus necessary to back concrete solutions will not be easier to find, demands for the right to psychological well-being will continue to multiply, and on the whole "wretchedness" and "servitude" will be likelier than "freedom" from the terrible ravages of mental disease as the new millennium unfolds.

I

A New Egalitarianism

The late eighteenth century was a time of vast changes throughout the Western world, so it was no coincidence that the modern quest for mental health began in the same era. As political revolutions wracked governments on both sides of the Atlantic Ocean, as the industrial revolution spread throughout Europe, and as an unprecedented wave of sentiment for reform swept through England, western Europe, and North America, approaches and attitudes toward mental health were also in flux.

The origins of these shifts in mental health care sometimes pre-dated the late eighteenth century. Yet it is equally true that what emerged from the turmoil and ferment of the years between the American Revolution and the death of Napoleon was so different from what had gone before that contemporaries in the nineteenth century readily acknowledged that a major watershed in the history of mental health care had occurred. A new idea was born: that psychological well-being was not just an aim whose realization governments and their citizens increasingly desired, but – thanks to the march of science, the expansion of expert knowledge, and the right level of state support – an achievable and laudable goal. By the mid–nineteenth century, more and more people within industrializing societies had concluded that mental disabilities could best be treated in an institutional setting under the watchful eyes of licensed physicians. But in the meantime a new understanding of what it means to be emotionally unwell began to emerge.

THE ENGLISH MALADY

The first stirrings of the modern quest for mental health occurred in England, whose government and economy in the eyes of its admirers were the most advanced in the world. To the French thinker Charles-Louis de Secondat, baron de Montesquieu (1689–1755), England in the eighteenth century, though ruled by a king, was "a republic concealed under the form of a monarchy."[1] Montesquieu was impressed by England's comparatively brisk industrial and commercial development, but most of all praised its division of powers among Parliament, the monarchy, and the courts, which, he claimed, gave its people the greatest freedom of all the nations of the world. According to Montesquieu's countryman François-Marie Arouet, better known as Voltaire (1694–1778), the English people "share[d] in the government without confusion."[2] Such comments overlooked the corruption and class-bound nature of England's system of government, but to those who lived in countries ruled by absolute monarchs England was comparatively self-governing.

Out of this historically unique political background emerged eighteenth-century England's "trade in lunacy," an unprecedented proliferation of licensed, privately owned and run "madhouses." Nowhere else did private asylums thrive so well as in eighteenth-century England with its buoyant "laissez-faire" economy. It had the highest standard of living in Europe and a rapidly growing population. Private madhouse proprietors provided a service that a society enjoying rising levels of disposable income first learned it could afford and gradually concluded it could not do without. In other words, for the first time in history, leisure, affluence, and surplus wealth begat demand for mental health care services. A consumer society, with disposable income and rising standards of living, was born.[3]

Private asylums, with or without resident physicians, housed inmate populations that ranged in size from a handful of patients to several hundred, and conditions varied widely according to the training, knowledge, and compassion of the keepers who ran them. The physician Francis Willis, best known for treating Britain's King George III during the monarch's bouts with porphyria-induced mental troubles, was one doctor who ran a private asylum. Willis's home in Lincolnshire drew raves from visitors. The poet William Cowper spent eighteen months in a single private asylum after several suicide attempts. Once recovered, he had nothing but praise for his doctor.[4] Patients at other madhouses did not fare as well, and the absence of regulation, combined with the all too human pursuit of profit, guaranteed that in 1815, when Parliament investigated the treatment of people with mental disabilities, allegations of cruelty, neglect, over-crowding, and physical brutality were rife. The British government eventually stepped in to curb abuses, marking a fateful stage in the evolution of mental health care toward greater state involvement.

William Cowper's battle with depression and suicide reflected the
fact that by the eighteenth century melancholy was a common affliction
of the times, and nowhere was interest in it and other forms of mental
illness keener than in England. The plays of William Shakespeare (1564–
1616) contained reference after reference to the ease with which mental
illness could play tricks on the mind. Robert Burton's *The Anatomy of
Melancholy* (1621) was probably the most renowned of the many texts
on depression that appeared in the early modern era. By the eighteenth
century the tendency of English people to suffer from depression was so
well known that in 1733 the British doctor George Cheyne dubbed melancholy the "British malady." The noted author Samuel Johnson (1709–84),
just one of many Englishmen tormented by depression, saw himself as
the victim of a "vile melancholy" and on several occasions startled his
acquaintances with his spasms, tics, phobias, hypochondria, and debilitating indolence. Quoting Shakespeare, Johnson asked his physician:

> Canst thou not minister to a mind diseased;
> Pluck from the memory a rooted sorrow;
> And with some sweet oblivious antidote
> Cleanse the stuffed bosom of that perilous stuff
> Which weighs upon the breast?

However, Johnson knew enough about the quality of medicine in his day
to realize his doctor would not be of much help.[5]

Samuel Johnson's reflections on his depression were an example of the
mounting interest in matters relating to mental health in the eighteenth
century. England's reputation as the homeland of madness during this
period may have been due to a combination of genetics and the country's
climate, which struck other Europeans as uncommonly gloomy, but it
most likely also derived from England's fledgling consumerist economy
and its political evolution as a nation in which, according to Alexis de
Tocqueville, the "doctrine of the sovereignty of the people had been introduced into the bosom of the monarchy."[6]

NERVOUSNESS

In the eighteenth century the quest for mental health reached another
milestone that has shaped the way people perceive their own emotional
health to the present day. During the eighteenth century it became possible for the first time in history to say that one suffered from nerves.

As the eighteenth century dawned, physicians reported over and
over again seeing patients without any glaring sickness, but medical

terminology to describe such patients remained mired in the past. In 1702 the London physician John Purcell remarked that "vapours, otherwise called hysteric fits and improperly, fits of the mother, is a distemper which more generally afflicts humankind than any other whatsoever." Among the symptoms of this "distemper," Purcell listed belching, vomiting, heaviness in the chest, difficulty in breathing, weak pulse, and fainting, what then and in later eras would be labeled the classic signs of hysteria. Purcell's comments suggested that the old theory, dating back to classical antiquity, that hysteria was a disease of the womb, was falling out of favor among physicians.[7] Yet the language used to describe nervous illnesses in general was still frozen in time.

The thaw in terminology started with George Cheyne's 1733 *English Malady*. Cheyne introduced the reading public to a personality type marked by "weak, loose and feeble or relax'd nerves" and suffering from "low spirits," poor digestion, diarrhea, shortness of breath, and sensitivity to cold and heat. Cheyne linked this kind of patient to the over-eating, luxury-loving, and sedentary habits of England's emerging affluent classes. After Cheyne, the usage of "nervous" as a medical and lay term expanded, and in 1777 Cheyne's fellow Scot William Cullen coined the word "neurosis" to refer to a disease of the nervous system. Neurosis and its meanings caught on swiftly. In 1807 a student of Cullen wrote that "at the beginning of the nineteenth century, we do not hesitate to affirm, that *nervous disorders* have now taken the place of fevers, and may be justly reckoned two thirds of the whole, with which civilized society is afflicted."[8]

Over the course of the next two centuries it became increasingly fashionable to interpret a broad range of everyday, non-lethal complaints, both physical and mental, as signs of bona fide illness. Some conditions turned out to be symptoms of genuine physical disease, but in a huge number of cases the symptoms were "psycho-somatic," that is, originating in patients' minds and in the surrounding cultural climate. Over time the tendency of exhausted women to take to their beds for long periods has ebbed and flowed in the same way that fashions in clothing and diet have waxed and waned. What has been much less cyclical is the overall tendency among wider and wider segments of society to perceive bodily and psychological sensations as indicators of a bona fide medical condition. Initially, this new type of patient was rare, and it was not until the late twentieth century that the familiar "post-modern patient" – suspicious of medical authority, inclined to try self-help approaches, with an unprecedentedly low threshold of pain – began to attract attention. Whether they have resorted to orthodox medical care or alternative healers, "post-modern" patients have demanded good health, including mental well-being, as a kind of civil right, and have relentlessly sought out access to treatment.[9] The origins of this post-modern patient lie in the eighteenth century, when a heightened sensitivity toward one's emotions and bodily sensations among England's leisured classes first became noticeable.

THE SOLITARY WALKER

The quest for mental health may have reached its apex in the twentieth century, but its beginnings can be traced back to the Geneva-born philosopher Jean-Jacques Rousseau (1712–78). Rousseau could be called the first true democrat in history, if by democracy we mean a form of government in which sovereignty resides in the people alone. In his writings, which included the best-selling *New Héloïse* (1761), *The Social Contract* (1762), *Émile: Or, On Education* (1762), and *Reveries of the Solitary Walker* (1776), Rousseau celebrated the behavior, instincts, and feelings of the common people. At the same time, he angrily accused high society of vice, corruption, artificiality, and self-indulgence. In these and other writings, Rousseau taught readers a new sensibility, a revolutionary way for human beings to regard their own feelings and thoughts. "I always feel before I think," he wrote in 1761. "I am the most sensitive animal upon this earth."[10] Later, similarly minded generations eagerly identified with this self-proclaimed "solitary walker" and his belief that the time had come for people to get in touch with their inner, natural selves.

Over the course of his itinerant life, Rousseau dabbled as a musician, tutor, secretary, and essayist, enjoying the protection of patrons such as King Frederick the Great of Prussia. For the most part Rousseau was quarrelsome, accusing friends and foes of plotting against him. His fears of persecution were liberally sprinkled throughout his *Confessions* (posthumously published in 1782), perhaps the first tell-all autobiography in modern history. By the time he died in 1778, no one disputed Rousseau's brilliance. Some, following Rousseau's own cue, called him the most honest man of his century, but many thought he was a self-centered, self-pitying hypochondriac. The writer Madame de Staël (1766–1817) said that Rousseau "inflamed everything, but discovered nothing."[11]

Rousseau's influence on history was slim while he was alive, but it began to soar almost immediately after his death. In a remarkable turn of events, his grave site just outside Paris quickly became a shrine, attracting visitors by the thousands, including France's Queen Marie Antoinette.

Statues of Rousseau were erected, busts were modeled, and portraits were painted, all celebrating his accomplishments in the fields of music, literature, and drama. His books enjoyed mass and adoring audiences.[12] A veritable cult grew up around his name, thanks to his blossoming reputation as a solitary and unjustly maligned genius. His tomb rested on a small island in the middle of a lake surrounded by trees, fostering the perception that Rousseau could teach people how to reconnect with their real selves by obeying the dictates of nature.

Rousseau was a leading proponent of the theory that human beings were naturally innocent, not tainted with original sin as taught by Christianity. Individual unhappiness, in other words, was society's fault. Rousseau helped to engender the belief that civilized existence destroyed individual authenticity, which could best be recovered by relying on emotions, instincts, and sentiments while jettisoning convention, propriety, and manners, all of which, Rousseau argued, were unnatural and thus dangerous to health. He insisted that he was unhappy because others made him so; the solution, therefore, was to make him and his fellow citizens feel better by overturning respectable society. Revolution could be therapeutic, a message not lost on his admirers in revolutionary France. According to one French observer in 1790, "People can be heard to say, 'I feel better since the Revolution.'"[13]

Rousseau's impact on the quest for sanity was not limited to his advice that people should try to feel and behave more honestly. Society had an obligation to make its citizens happier. "Man is born free, and everywhere he is in chains!" Rousseau famously stated in the opening sentence of *The Social Contract*. The task at hand was to construct a society and a form of government that conformed to human nature. Rousseau believed there was such a thing as the "general will," which expressed the collective belief of a community. Policy had to be designed to serve this "general will." Those who disagreed with the principles of the "general will" labored under a false consciousness, according to Rousseau. They had to be "forced to be free," he wrote. Rousseau preferred equality to personal freedom.

When Rousseau uttered his comments about humankind languishing in chains, he did not have the mentally ill uppermost in his mind, but in the eyes of some his words applied to that social group. By the end of the eighteenth century the view that as a group people with mental disabilities were being held in cruel bondage, though far from accurate, was gaining momentum in some elite circles, as was the growing belief that the mentally ill were more curable than customarily thought. Rousseau's thesis that the underprivileged were victims of an unjust social order echoed the notion that the time had come to right a grievous wrong inflicted on these helpless and innocent people.

As the nineteenth century dawned, efforts in pursuit of this goal were under way, revolutionizing the care and treatment of the mentally ill. A new approach to mental health was gathering momentum, one that demanded that the treatment of people with mental disabilities become more humane. Such people were not incorrigible, reformers argued, but had simply lost their reason temporarily. Yet just as Rousseau's theory did not countenance liberation for the sheer sake of individual freedom, so cutting-edge approaches to improving the lot of the mentally ill were often tinged with value-laden expectations of how model citizens should behave and think. In the eyes of many nineteenth-century mental health advocates, the cause of liberating people with mental disabilities was as much a political as a medical undertaking.

UNIVERSAL MEDICINE

Rousseau's ideas about the severe conflict between health and society surfaced in another fad from late-eighteenth-century Europe, the tremendous popularity among the literate classes of Franz Anton Mesmer's theory of animal magnetism, what contemporaries dubbed mesmerism. The German-born Mesmer (1734–1815) introduced terms that are still used today, such as "mesmerized." Later, in the nineteenth century, interest in mesmerism led to the development of hypnotism, which countless therapists have since used in their attempts to relieve patients of neurological complaints and painful memories. Scientists dismissed most of mesmerism as quackery, but its historical impact has proved to be hefty.

Mesmer studied and practiced medicine in Vienna, where he befriended the brilliant young composer Wolfgang Amadeus Mozart. In 1777 Mesmer left Vienna, by which time he was preaching the doctrine that space was full of a special invisible fluid that penetrated and surrounded all bodies, a primeval natural agent that, when harnessed, could be employed to cure patients of sicknesses that ranged from scurvy, deafness, and blindness to boredom and depression. Illness, Mesmer maintained, was caused by a blockage in the flow of the fluid through the body. Treatment consisted of massaging the body's "poles" where the fluid might collect, thereby restoring the balance of fluids.

Mesmer soon found that his services were in high demand. No elitist, he treated rich and poor patients alike. Often he gathered the sick around a tub with movable iron rods and ropes designed to channel the magnetic fluid to the affected parts of the body. Though proclaimed the next Isaac Newton by his disciples, Mesmer frequently found himself the target of satirists who gleefully pointed out it was mainly bored, high-society women with vague complaints who flocked to mesmerist sessions. Rumors of financial swindles and wild orgies swirled around mesmerism. Accused of being a trumped-up form of sexual mischief, mesmerism was popular enough to make the king of France fret about its effect on his kingdom's morals.

Mesmer arrived in Paris in 1778, then a hotbed of enthusiasm for the latest discoveries in science and technology. Parisians mobbed Benjamin Franklin, the noted experimenter with electricity, and marveled at Étienne Montgolfier's balloons as they drifted across the sky. Hailed as a comparable sage of science, Mesmer soon became the talk of the kingdom. To one contemporary, in the early 1780s mesmerism was an "epidemic" that was sweeping all of France.[14] In 1784 a commission made up of France's most eminent scientists decreed that there was no such thing as Mesmer's magnetic fluid, and he fled Paris the next year, returning in 1801 but living a shadowy existence in later years.

In the meantime, however, Mesmer's theories grew more and more popular, capturing the interests of literate French people and in the last years of Louis XVI's reign dovetailing with both the mounting rage for Rousseau and the epoch's political unrest. Most of Mesmer's followers were attracted to his theory because it seemingly offered a dramatically new and effective cure for a vast range of physical and mental ills. One contemporary called mesmerism the "sole universal medicine."[15] Mesmerists celebrated their theory as a return to the "natural" medicine of Hippocrates in classical antiquity, when the aim was to live in harmony with the environment. Patients who disliked the drugs and bleedings routinely prescribed by regular doctors saw in mesmerism a benign form of therapy that did not leave them feeling debilitated.

Mesmerism's appeal, however, was not limited to medicine. It quickly took on the trappings of a radical, anti-establishment theory, especially after its condemnation at the hands of the nation's top scientists. Mesmerists interpreted elite society's rejection as a sign that the theory was onto something after all, that its acceptance threatened the vested interests and socially exclusive institutions of the time, notably organized medicine. Little wonder that mesmerists pounced on the similarities between Rousseauism and Mesmer's ideas. Mesmerism was Rousseauism in action: it reportedly helped to restore the natural balance of forces in the body that society with its harmful customs and mores continually jeopardized. Allegiance to mesmerism became a moral duty and a symbol of faith in the notion that challenging the established order could produce a new egalitarianism. As one mesmerist exclaimed, "Mesmerism is a way to bring social classes closer together."[16]

Mesmerism's popularity throughout pre-revolutionary France and its infusion with Rousseauian elements showed that attitudes toward health were shifting dramatically as Louis XVI's monarchy began its death throes. Mesmerism's immediate impact on the history of mental health care was limited. Yet wherever it thrived, it whetted the public's taste for more egalitarian and innovative approaches to health. Mesmerism reinforced the belief that the old regime's institutions and ideologies were barriers to progress and emotional wellness. Mesmerism helped to infuse the topic of medicine with a new populism and stimulated a mounting demand for better methods of making people happier and healthier. This demand would become more evident in the twentieth century, when the quest for mental health reached its zenith, yet its foundations had been laid within the revolutionary environment that enveloped France at the end of the eighteenth century.

MEDICAL POLICE

As literate French people on the eve of the Revolution and under the influence of Rousseau and mesmerism increasingly viewed health as a matter of political virtue, governments also began showing the first distinct signs that they considered health a vital policy concern. Rousseau's gospel that civilized society was bad for human health found a sympathetic listener in the German Johann Peter Frank (1745–1821), author of a landmark, multi-volume treatise that advocated the many ways governments could legislate "healthy minds in healthy bodies." Frank, a university professor and personal physician to the bishop of Speyer from 1775 to1784, was perhaps the most renowned of a wave of eighteenth-century experts who contended that overall health in general and mental health in particular ought to be of keen interest to ruling elites. Although he did not coin the term "medical police," his popularization of the concept had a long-lasting impact on public policy, the ripples from which would still be felt in the twentieth century. If Rousseau taught that people should desire emotional health and if mesmerism taught people how to seek it, the theory of medical police taught governments that mental and physical health was too important to leave to either the public or its doctors.

Everywhere Frank looked around eighteenth-century Europe he saw appalling suffering and an enormous waste of human life. Like many thinkers during the eighteenth-century Enlightenment, Frank was highly impressed with the potential of science, technology, and public education to improve living conditions, yet he complained that standing in the way were established customs, morals, classes, and institutions. Citing Rousseau, Frank lambasted organized medicine for doing more harm than good, insisting that the healthiest states were actually the ones where the number of licensed physicians was lowest. Instead of reliance on organized medicine to cure diseases, Frank advocated prevention, notably public health innovations such as inoculation for smallpox, regulation of the food industry, and the draining of moats and other stagnant bodies of water, which he correctly linked to mass outbreaks of fever.

Frank was likewise alarmed about the incidence of depression, suicide, and nervous diseases, which, he lamented, "today flourish practically everywhere." This epidemic of mental and emotional problems he blamed on the failure to live according to the laws of nature, and no institution, Frank maintained, did more to thwart nature than the Roman Catholic Church. Through its defense of exorcism, celibacy, and monasticism, and its command to fear the punishments of hell, the Church, Frank averred, "reign[ed] contrary to Nature." Long before Freud and twentieth-century sexology, Frank linked psychological disorders to sexual repression. "How many [mental] ailments would not be cured by the opening of the virgin uterus and the granting of freedom to the Brothers to discard their vows?" he asked rhetorically. His message was straightforward: public education and legislation based on the advice of scientific sages like himself would make people mentally healthier.[17]

The theory that the state had a vital interest in the health of its citizens and should legislate accordingly grew in popularity during the late eighteenth century, chiefly in the various independent jurisdictions of central Europe. The roots of state interest in public health can be traced back to the Thirty Years' War (1618–48/59), which caused an immense loss of life and damage to property throughout the German lands. The staggering depopulation of these territories, combined with their vulnerability to invasion by foreign powers, led their rulers to pursue policies aimed at stimulating the economy, boosting birthrates and preventing disease, disability, and overall misery.

The general idea that governments should attempt to maximize their subjects' health and productivity was adopted by the Austrian rulers Maria

Theresa and Joseph II, and even spread to Catherine the Great's Russia (r. 1762–96). All of these monarchs had been influenced by the ideas of eighteenth-century thinkers such as Voltaire, Montesquieu, Diderot, and Cesare Beccaria, who like Frank blamed the Roman Catholic Church and its doctrines for most of the inefficiency, sickness, and injustice that characterized European society. Bent on modernizing their domains, eighteenth-century rulers were receptive to policies that purported to make their subjects healthier, more robust, and more numerous.

The idea that governments should do their utmost to ensure that all aspects of life served the interests of the state became known as cameralism, or the science of public administration. Cameralism, including Frank's version, steadily found a home in various German universities over the course of the eighteenth century. According to cameralists, the healthiest and most populous states were the strongest and most prosperous. It was rarely clear what aim was uppermost in the minds of cameralists: state security or the welfare of individuals. What is undeniable is that cameralists believed that governments had a vested interest in everything from morals to mortality.

Frank's pioneering writings established a paternalist blueprint for later governments that similarly wanted to make their citizens healthier. The view that governments should maintain and promote the health of their citizens included applying the lessons learned by animal breeders to the reproduction of human beings. Frank's advice that people with hereditary diseases should be prevented by law from marrying adumbrated twentieth-century eugenic laws that similarly outlawed the procreation of those deemed to be biologically inferior.

In the short term, Frank's influence was felt most keenly in the German states. Over time the statist theory of medical police fared better there and in Italy than it did in English-speaking countries, where its inherent authoritarianism and paternalism tended to conflict with long-standing traditions of individual liberty. Yet its essential message that governments could increase state security by preventing misery, disease, and death thrived in nineteenth-century France in particular under the name "political medicine" and was a major inspiration behind the French 1838 law that established the nation's modern asylum system.[18] The notion of medical police lingered into the twentieth century in the form of public health or "social medicine." In his frequent, Rousseau-like invocations of Nature, Frank paved the way for changes in the prevention and treatment of mental illness. The origins of twentieth-century "womb to tomb" or "cradle to grave" public welfare policies, including mental health care services, were firmly planted in the soil of late-eighteenth-century cameralism and medical police.

MORAL RESTRAINT

Governmental interest in the health of subjects and citizens may have been stirring in the late eighteenth century, but it was overshadowed by the rise of a grassroots movement to radically improve conditions for people with mental disabilities. A handful of activists on both sides of the Atlantic Ocean, heavily motivated by Christianity's social gospel, agitated for the abolition of slavery, the suppression of prostitution, and the reform of schools and prisons. Swept up in this movement to rid society of injustice and ignorance was a campaign to introduce better means for treating people and families living with mental disabilities. Taking their cue from attempts at the same time to improve schools and prisons, mental health reformers advocated institutionalization as the best way to help people regain their senses. The view that people with mental disabilities were better off in institutions than at home or in the community swiftly caught on and held sway for the next 150 years.

In England this reform movement was due chiefly to the efforts of Quakers and evangelical Christians. Evangelicals, led by parliamentarian William Wilberforce (the subject of the 2007 feature film *Amazing Grace*), accused the Anglican Church and the governing classes of corruption, complacency, and moral aimlessness, specifically a thoughtless toleration of a host of outrages inflicted on the poor and other disadvantaged groups. The rich, in Wilberforce's words, had let the "success of their commercial speculations" breed a "more relaxed morality."[19] Evangelicals emphasized the performance of "good works," or acts of public charity, as a key step toward salvation. Wilberforce himself plunged into projects to curb prostitution, assist the poor, ban cruelty to animals, and end the slave trade. His biggest success occurred in 1807 when Parliament abolished the slave trade. In 1833 all slaves in the British Empire were emancipated.

Evangelicals' social activism was similar to the reformist fervor of the Quaker community. Quakerism (the Society of Friends) began in the seventeenth century as a radical Puritan sect. Over the next century the Quakers became some of England's most successful bankers and industrialists, along the way gaining the enviable reputation for being scrupulously honest businesspeople. Yet by the end of the eighteenth century many Quakers were worried that they were becoming "wholly immersed in Mammon" and shifted their attention to rehabilitating criminals and relieving the distress of the poor.[20] Elizabeth Fry and John Howard were perhaps the two best-known Quakers associated with the effort to curb corporal punishment and other forms of physical brutality in prisons.

The exertions of Quakers with a social conscience overlapped the field of mental health reform. A milestone was reached in 1792 when tea merchant William Tuke, along with local Quakers, founded the York Retreat. Run by a non-physician, the Retreat minimized the use of restraints, such as muffs, manacles, and chains, and within its walls patients and staff members were expected to live together as one big, happy family. The ethos of the Retreat was decidedly non-medical – if not overtly anti-medical – in that it discouraged the employment of typical bodily therapies such as bleeding and purging. Instead, the Retreat's staff encouraged "moral treatment," an institutional approach in which the patient was treated "as much in the manner of a rational being as the state of mind will possibly allow."[21] By "moral treatment," the Retreat's founders meant a form of psychological therapy mixed with rigorous expectations about how a "rational" person ought to think and behave.

As Quakers, the Retreat's backers had firm theories about what constituted upstanding, Christian behavior. They believed that kindness and gentle persuasion, not coercion or physical punishment, would best help patients recover their senses. "Tenderness is better than torture," observed one medical writer of the time.[22] The key to moral treatment, unlike later twentieth-century psychological therapies such as Freudian psychoanalysis, was hospitalization: proponents of moral treatment insisted that it would never work unless an individual was promptly placed in an asylum, away from the stress that allegedly caused the condition in the first place and under the benevolent yet firm guidance of caretakers. Inside the asylum, the patient's schedule would be rigidly divided into times for eating, working, sleeping, and socialization. Moral treatment's supporters emphasized that the sooner patients were admitted to an asylum, the better the chances of curing them.

William Tuke and his son Henry and grandson Samuel, however, did not abolish chains, manacles, and whips at the Retreat solely for kindness's sake. The aim of the Retreat's moral treatment was to ensure that human beings followed strict moral codes without the need for harsh methods. "The natural tendency" of corporal methods, wrote William Tuke, was to "degrade the mind of the patient, and to make him indifferent to those moral feelings, which, under judicious direction and encouragement, are found capable, in no small degree, to strengthen the power of self-restraint." Whatever increased the happiness of the patient "increase[d] his desire to restrain himself."[23] In other words, the aim of moral treatment was to compel patients to internalize the moral attitudes Tuke and others wished all of society would embrace. The asylum, in effect, was a large educational institution designed to help free the deranged from their delusions, hallucinations, fears, and fixed ideas so they could take their places in the community as sober, self-disciplined, and law-abiding individuals. The goal of restoring mental patients to their senses was hardly new. What was new was that asylum officials banned whips and chains as a means of achieving this goal.

Varieties of moral therapy had been around before, notably in England's eighteenth-century "trade in lunacy." English "mad-doctors" of that century experimented with recognizably "moral" methods of treatment that targeted the mind rather than relying on chains and beatings.[24] But the growing international perception in the early nineteenth century was that the coming of the Retreat had changed the course of mental health care history forever. Visitors could hardly contain their enthusiasm; one exclaimed after touring the Retreat in 1812 that it was "at this moment the best-regulated establishment in Europe, either for the recovery of the insane, or for their comfort."[25] In 1813 Samuel Tuke published *Description of the Retreat*, and as word spread about the Retreat's virtues, people increasingly concluded that almost all existing mental hospitals were now obsolete. The reality was never quite that stark, but the practical impact of the York Retreat was that future asylums would be judged according to how they measured up to its standards.

Events in the United States followed much the same script. There, too, the Quakers were active in revolutionizing mental health care. Philadelphia's Quakers, using the York Retreat and moral treatment as their models, raised the funds to pay for the Friends' Asylum in Frankford (opened in 1817), and in New York City Thomas Eddy, a leading Quaker and admirer of the Tukes, proved to be the driving force behind the establishment of the Bloomingdale Asylum in 1821. Even where Quakers were not directly involved in the founding of new asylums, the influence of the Tukes proved to be far reaching. When prominent Bostonians were planning the erection of an asylum physically and administratively distinct from the Massachusetts General Hospital, they consulted Thomas Eddy and learned from him about the York Retreat. The result was the McLean Hospital, founded in 1818 in Somerville, Massachusetts, and later a world-leading psychiatric hospital and center for neuro-scientific research.

Joining the Quakers in the cause of U.S. mental health care reform were the Unitarians, another radical religious group. Unitarians rejected the doctrine of the Trinity, claiming a single God was more consistent with the Scriptures. Unitarianism gathered momentum in the Thirteen Colonies during the eighteenth century. Unitarian preachers emphasized free will and the dignity rather than depravity of human nature. Many Unitarians, impatient with doctrine, embraced the social gospel, the belief that the Christian's first purpose in life was to work to improve the living conditions of the disadvantaged rather than to save individual souls. The Unitarians were never numerous and tended to come from the upper echelons of society, but they like the Quakers exerted a sizable influence over nineteenth-century social reform.

GOOD ORDER AND DISCIPLINE

A cluster of Unitarians, including Horace Mann, Samuel Gridley Howe, and Dorothea Dix, spearheaded the broad-based movement to radically upgrade U.S. prisons, schools, and asylums. As was the case with schooling, Massachusetts was a hotbed of mental health care reform. This was hardly surprising, since reformers envisaged schools, prisons, and asylums as components of the same essential project: correcting the minds of people who allegedly needed special instruction.

Dorothea Dix (1802–87), who grew up in Worcester, was a follower of William Emery Channing, the age's pre-eminent American Unitarian and an anti-poverty activist. While convalescing in England with Quaker friends after a protracted illness, Dix became convinced that government should play an active role in social welfare. She later returned to the United States and became a mental health care advocate after observing people with mental disabilities housed in jails next to hardened criminals. She gradually evolved into the most passionate and determined mental health care reformer of her day; indeed, she may well have been the age's most renowned and effective crusader for social causes. Besides demanding better schools and prisons, she tirelessly visited state legislature after state legislature, including the assemblies of the British colonies to the north, and crossed oceans to urge the building of new asylums for the homeless insane. To Dix, "all experience shows that insanity reasonably treated is as certainly curable as a cold or fever."[26] Throughout her years of campaigning for the homeless, Dix struggled mightily to convince people that those with mental disabilities deserved compassion, not fear, suspicion, or contempt. Her comparison of mental disability and the common cold and her pleas for more humane treatment of the mentally ill proved difficult to resist. Her message of hope and compassion, a contemporary wrote, was like "red-hot shot [fired] into the very hearts of the people."[27] She told the Massachusetts legislature, "I come to present the strong claims of suffering humanity ... as the advocate of helpless, forgotten, insane, idiotic men and women."[28] Dix's heart went out to the many unfortunate individuals living with mental disabilities who ended up on the streets or in society's jails.

As was the case with the Quakers, Dix's Unitarian approach to reform, though based on the use of benign methods of treatment, had decidedly utilitarian ends. Like the Quakers, Unitarians believed that coercion and physical restraint were wrong, for two reasons: they made patients suffer, and they were less effective in shaping the conduct of human beings than gentle persuasion. If reformers were radical in their tactics, they nonetheless hoped for conventional outcomes. As even Dix's sympathetic biographer admits:

> [U]nder the seals of her own conscience, she valued discipline above freedom. Her context for freedom was duty, responsibility, and moral order, not spontaneity. Her struggle was a struggle to suppress her own impulses and subject her whole life to a cast-iron self-control. Thus, the order, the apparent civilization within the madhouse effected by moral treatment, appealed to Dix because, in large measure, it mirrored her struggles with her own demons.[29]

An admirer remarked that she was "in herself alone a whole Prison Discipline Society."[30]

To Quakers and Unitarians (as well as other social commentators), the early nineteenth century demanded renewed "discipline" because it was an age of tremendous change, especially in the United States, where Americans were often separated along pronounced sectional, economic, religious, and ethnic lines.[31] Forging a stable, cohesive society out of this raucous diversity troubled many Americans, some of whom, like the Unitarian reformers, looked to the "common school" as the ideal crucible for the moral instruction they deemed critical to national unity and the prevention of crime. As one Massachusetts educator wrote in 1837, the failure to properly instruct the nation's youth "account[ed] for half the crime and more than half the unhappiness in society."[32]

Many reformers in the field of mental health, including Benjamin Rush (1745–1813), a signer of the Declaration of Independence, felt the same way. A physician, Rush was a crusader against slavery, alcohol, and the death penalty and an advocate of public schools and free clinics for the poverty-stricken. Alongside the local Quaker community, he lobbied for prison reform, believing fervently that his efforts in medicine were "labors in the cause of humanity." As early as 1786 Rush predicted that schools would "render the mass of the people more homogeneous and thereby fit them more easily for uniform and peaceable government." His overall goal was to "convert men into republican machines."[33]

Rush was also a pioneer in mental health care. He treated the mentally ill at the Pennsylvania Hospital in Philadelphia, offered the first U.S. lecture course in psychiatry, and in 1812 published the first text on psychiatry written by an American born in the United States. Indeed, in 1965 the American Psychiatric Association dubbed Rush the "father of American psychiatry." As one early-nineteenth-century French psychiatrist exclaimed: "What an analogy there is between the art of directing lunatics and that of raising young people! Both require great firmness, but not harsh and forbidding manners; rational and affectionate condescension, but not a soft complaisance that bends to all whims."[34] The hope was that revolutionizing methods in the fields of schooling and mental health care would go a long way toward molding minds, so that law and order would prevail in the young French and American republics.

Like her counterparts in the reform movement, Dix argued that the pace and stress of life in nineteenth-century society bred mental disorders. In asylums people with mental disabilities received the "good order and discipline" that society seemed to lack.[35] The Rousseauian overtones of this link between civilization and insanity led Dix and others to insist that society therefore had the duty to "make the compensation which alone can be made for these disastrous fruits of its social organization."[36] Again and again, she praised the virtues of publicly funded hospitalization. Like advocates of the common school who rejected any other form of formal education, Dix denounced home care for the mentally ill. To Dix, relatives were ignorant of mental illness, and routinely behaved cruelly and inhumanely when confronted with family members living with mental disabilities, often by locking them in cellars, attics, or out-buildings.

Dorothea Dix helped to change the course of mental health care policy on both sides of the Atlantic Ocean. Her pleas for the erection of large-scale, state-supported mental hospitals were responsible for the founding or enlarging of more than thirty such institutions in the United States and abroad. Her remarkable success in convincing stingy legislators to loosen their purse strings and pay to build asylums testified to her formidable powers of persuasion. Some questioned her single-minded pursuit of justice, notably when it took her into filthy and noisy jails. Despite being a woman with no clinical or professional training, however, she gained the confidence of many male psychiatrists. Above all, as a figure of international standing, she persuaded governing elites that mental disease was curable and that the proper place to treat people with mental disabilities was in a modern hospital, not within the community. Even when her powers of persuasion faltered, her stature and passion made her impossible to ignore.

Yet Dix was very much a product of her own time and place. Her sympathies toward people with mental disabilities stopped at Ireland's borders. Like many of her background, she harbored a virulent anti-Catholicism that cast the Irish as "squalid, ignorant, with only one wish stimulating their dull lives; viz. the hope of emigrating to America," a prospect that made her and other U.S. nativists shudder.[37] Dix was so intent on achieving her goal of improving the conditions of people with mental disabilities that she regularly exaggerated and embellished facts. Her overwrought descriptions of some almshouses, jails, and workhouses prompted opponents and friends alike to accuse her of misrepresenting reality.[38] In fact, in her day people with mental disabilities lived under a wide diversity of conditions, not all of which were inhumane. England's notorious Bethlem Hospital – popularly known as Bedlam – compared favorably with the best continental European locales. In the many hospitals on both sides of the Atlantic Ocean where people with mental disabilities were cared for by Catholic religious healers, patients were treated with a mode of consolation that stressed kindness and compassion. In any case, before the early nineteenth century most people with mental disabilities were cared for at home and not in jails or similar penal institutions. If mental health care reform is viewed within the context of similar endeavors in the fields of criminology and education, it becomes evident that Dix believed asylum treatment would both benefit the welfare of individual patients and address society's concerns about deviance in an era when urbanization and industrialization were unfolding at a dizzying speed.

By the end of her eventful life, Dix had succeeded beyond the dreams of many reformers anytime, anywhere. She had played a key role in giving birth to three ideas – that mental illness was a curable condition, that it was best treated in a hospital setting, and that the modern state had a compelling interest in the expansion of publicly funded mental health care to include those social groups that were the biggest source of crime and political disunity. The embodiment of these dreams was the asylum, her chief legacy to history.

THE BIRTH OF PSYCHIATRY

The advent of the publicly funded modern asylum providing moral treatment proved to be a catalyst for the birth of psychiatry, one of the first branches of medicine to constitute itself as a distinct specialty. Until the late twentieth century, no interest group played a bigger role in the modern quest for mental health and no professional specialty labored harder to establish its claims to expertise than psychiatry. The rise of psychiatry was a critical chapter in the history of state involvement in the care of people with mental disabilities.

What made the emergence of psychiatry such a noteworthy occurrence was that prior to the nineteenth century, with few exceptions, the only specialists were the itinerant, unlicensed healers who swarmed over towns and countryside. Some were herbalists, some astrologers, while others – dentists, oculists, midwives, bonesetters, and hernia surgeons – performed operations on specific parts of the body. The professional medical groups of the time – physicians, surgeons, and apothecaries – treated specialists with ill-concealed loathing and dismissed them as quacks. Regular physicians preferred to think of themselves as generalists who practiced medicine as a kind of gentlemanly pursuit of broad knowledge that encompassed the patient as a whole, not specific parts of the body, such as the ear, nose, throat, heart, skin, or uterus. They also worried that specialization might lead to professional conflict and divisiveness. As a result, specialization in medicine was often bitterly contested, and a stigma surrounding specialists endured well into the nineteenth century.[39]

In France and Germany, specialization in medicine moved at a brisker pace than anywhere else. But specialization before the twentieth century was anything but inevitable. For every eager specialist there was a skeptical generalist who believed that physicians focusing on localized parts of the body ran the distinct risk of losing sight of the patient as an integrated whole.

At the beginning of the nineteenth century no branch of medicine was a more unlikely candidate for specialization than psychiatry. Indeed, at that date there was no such thing as psychiatry. Fifty years later it was one of medicine's greatest professional success stories. At the turn of the nineteenth century the nature of the mind and its exact connections to the brain and nervous system were as much a mystery as ever, and few licensed physicians outside England's "trade in lunacy" appeared to be interested in treating mentally ill patients. Yet within a matter of decades, physicians had organized themselves in various countries, claiming expert knowledge about the diagnosis and treatment of mental illnesses and forming their own journals and occupational groups. Initially dubbed "alienists" (for their work with those afflicted with "mental alienation"), these physicians later became known as "psychiatrists," a term coined in 1808 by the German physician Johann Christian Reil (1759–1813) from the word meaning "healing the soul" in Greek. Yet no matter what they were called, psychiatrists quickly constituted a pivotal group of stakeholders with a distinctive professional agenda in the modern struggle for mental health.

The standard explanation for the growth of medical specialization is the rapid expansion of scientific knowledge about human physiology and anatomy in the nineteenth century. Over the course of the century researchers such as François Magendie, Claude Bernard, Louis Pasteur, Hermann von Helmholtz, and Rudolf Virchow made remarkable discoveries in their respective fields. For psychiatry, the most important discovery occurred in 1822. Through the postmortem dissection of patients' brains, researchers found the anatomical lesions responsible for tertiary syphilis, or general paralysis of the insane (GPI), a disease that produced pronounced psychiatric symptoms such as speech impairment, progressive weakening of the arms and legs, and eventual descent into mental deterioration, or dementia. Within two decades of this discovery it was reported that as many as one in six patients admitted to a Paris asylum suffered from GPI. For the first time in history, a cluster of physical and psychological symptoms could be traced to a verifiable injury of brain matter, an immense boost for physicians who wished to carve out a new specialty on the basis of their expert scientific knowledge of the organ of the mind.

However, between the early nineteenth century and the mid–twentieth century, major breakthroughs for psychiatry were few and far between, and even then they were limited to clinical, not scientific, medicine. In the short term, a more powerful impetus for the birth of psychiatry was the wave of revolutions that shook the foundations of long-standing dynasties in the late eighteenth century, notably the French Revolution, which abolished all universities, academies, and other traditional institutions, including the Royal Society of Medicine. The French Revolution in particular sparked a tremendous sense of excitement in France, a tsunami of innovative thinking that radically challenged conventional theories and practices. The field of medicine was no exception: out of this maelstrom of experimentation emerged the first recognizably modern psychiatrists.

Disputes over therapy and theory wracked the new field, breeding bitter hatreds and feuds, but two over-arching beliefs united psychiatrists
in France and elsewhere: that, first and foremost, mental disorders were
medical conditions involving certifiable bodily disturbances – not the
result of sin, malingering, or moral failure – and that physicians were the
sole experts when it came to treating people with mental disabilities and
determining the difference between normal and abnormal psychology.

CHIARUGI

Most of these early psychiatrists shared the enthusiasm for moral
treatment of Tuke, Dix, and the other lay pioneers. However, the first
asylum physician to dabble in moral treatment had no association with
the Quakers or Unitarians. In 1785 Tuscany-born Vincenzo Chiarugi
(1759–1820) was a bright, ambitious twenty-six-year-old physician
working at an overcrowded hospice in Florence when the Austrian grand
duke, Peter Leopoldo, appointed him the head of a new hospital exclusively for people with mental disabilities. As absolute ruler of Tuscany,
Peter Leopoldo was busy enacting a broad program of educational, judi-
cial, economic, and political reforms. Like Catherine the Great of Russia
and Prussia's Frederick the Great, Peter Leopoldo was willing to dispense
with custom and tradition if it meant improving the prosperity, power,
and security of his lands. He abolished torture and the death penalty,
cutting-edge reforms advocated by eighteenth-century thinkers. In health
care, he introduced the widespread use of vaccination for smallpox. The
world-class reputations of the medical schools at Pisa and Florence within
his own domains showed that health care was one of his key priorities.

What was truly pioneering was the grand duke's interest in the care
of people with mental disabilities. In 1774 he approved a law – the first
of its kind in Europe – that paved the way for the hospitalization of such
people and supported the erection of a new mental hospital in 1788 dedicated entirely to the actual cure of mental disease, with Chiarugi as head
physician. Chiarugi went straight to work, and in 1793 and 1794 published a three-volume work on mental disabilities. He eloquently made
the case for moral treatment in asylums. As he wrote, patients did best
when placed in a hospital where a detailed personal history was recorded,
hygienic and dietary standards were high, the sexes were separated, and
the use of straitjackets was seriously curtailed. Chiarugi's view of mental
illness was the usual mix of physicalism and psychology that has marked
psychiatry throughout its history: he believed the condition was due to an

"impairment of the physical structure of the brain," but he also believed that extreme passions or psychological events in one's life could cause mental disorders. This theory of mental illness emphasizing the impact of the environment and education on patients aptly dovetailed with the view that hospitalization was key to curing people with mental disabilities.

Some historians have insisted that Chiarugi deserves the title of *the* first modern psychiatrist, while others have argued that the origins of the modern asylum and modern psychiatry date back further into the eighteenth century, notably to England's "trade in lunacy." What is more important than the debate over who preceded whom is that breakthroughs in mental health care tended to occur wherever leisure time and affluence were on the rise and where a political climate conducive to innovation and unconventional theorizing existed. The pre-condition for the modern search for sanity was some kind of decisive break with the past.

THE PARIS SCHOOL

Nowhere was this truer than in France. In 1789 France was the most powerful nation in the world, but it had reached a political crisis. King Louis XVI, hoping to achieve consensus about which reforms might ease the crisis over his realm's massive debt, convoked the Estates-General, but the king's move unleashed events that ultimately led to his downfall and execution. Soon Paris was gripped by the belief that the status quo was unacceptable and a willingness to experiment with new policies. Absolute monarchy was toppled, a republic was declared in 1792, and the social power of France's elite classes abruptly declined.

By calling into question centuries of tradition, the French Revolution forced organized medicine to undergo a major upheaval. Researchers urged the adoption of clinical methods that overturned medical theories and practices dating back to classical antiquity. The hotbed for these changes was Paris and its cultural toleration for scientific novelty. First and foremost, the Revolution cleared away many of the social obstacles that prevented poor country boys from studying medicine, and some of the most illustrious of those who dominated Paris medicine for the next half-century were gifted fellows from underprivileged social ranks.

Second, the Revolution created a new sort of hospital – publicly funded and state run – which played a major role in the transformation of Paris medicine. In earlier days hospitals, normally staffed by Catholic nuns and monks, had served primarily as charity institutions, places where the destitute could go to convalesce, but more often to die. These hospitals were ideal major research centers for the new, inquisitive, and fiercely ambitious generation of Paris doctors. Within gloomy, dingy, and damp hospital walls, and with this sort of captive clientele, physicians eager for knowledge could begin to sort patients according to their common symptoms and study them over time. The high death rate meant physicians also had at their disposal a plentiful supply of cadavers, which they could probe with their scalpels in search of the bodily causes of diseases. It was not the first time in history doctors had argued that hospitals were superb places for clinical teaching, but at no other time or place prior to the French Revolution did so many in the field believe it so fervently.

Third, physicians of the "Paris school," instead of relying on textbooks, spent more time actually observing their patients and honing their manual skills by doing dissections, operations, and bandaging. "Little reading, much seeing, and much doing" was the Paris school's unofficial slogan.[40]

Fourth, the new schools of medicine taught doctors to correlate patients' symptoms during life with anatomical lesions in organic tissue discovered during autopsy (e.g., the postmortem detection of lesions in the lungs of patients with pulmonary tuberculosis). When this conviction that symptoms were always matched by specific physical injuries sunk in, the practice dating back to the second century A.D. physician Galen (131–201) of using vague names (e.g., "fever," "flux") to designate broad disturbances in bodily humors began to be replaced by the view that there were distinct diseases, each a natural entity and linked to an underlying organic cause. If injuries to different organs accounted for different diseases, the thinking went, then the study of separate organ systems made sense – hence the origins of specialties such as dermatology, obstetrics, urology, and orthopedics. In general, interest shifted away from the study of individual patients with unique clusters of symptoms to the study of discrete illnesses with specific and consistent symptoms. "You should paint diseases rather than diseased people," one Paris physician lectured his colleagues and students.[41]

All these changes resulted in valuable gains in diagnostic precision, hastened the rise of medical specialism, and centered health care in hospitals. Overall, in the words of one historian, "something quite extraordinary and innovative" happened within post-revolutionary Paris medicine.[42]

SCHOOLING THE PASSIONS

This new approach to medicine left an indelible stamp on the emerging specialty of psychiatry. The revolutionary figure who most famously straddled the worlds of general medicine and psychiatry was Philippe Pinel (1745–1826). For years Pinel's memory was encrusted with myths and legends, including the story (later immortalized in paintings) that he unshackled the inmates of the Bicêtre hospital from their chains, seemingly inaugurating a radically new era in the treatment of the mentally ill. This event, it turns out, never actually happened. Nonetheless, Pinel's career in medicine was pathbreaking. He benefited from the revolutionary government's Law of March 1790, which called for the creation of special hospitals dedicated to the mentally ill as a way of ending the arbitrary detention of such people in prisons and jails. At a time when it was easy to run afoul of the Revolution and suffer imprisonment or death at the guillotine, Pinel's career actually took off during the most radical stage of the Revolution. In 1793 he was named head doctor of Bicêtre, an institution housing about two hundred insane men. Two years later, Pinel moved to the Salpêtrière, a hospital with several hundred female inmates. In 1801 he published a landmark textbook on mental illness. The political environment of France during the 1790s may have been a minefield for countless Frenchmen and -women, but for Pinel it was positively invigorating.

Pinel's treatise on insanity was based on the notion, shared by many interested in mental health, that certain forms of madness were curable. He divided mental diseases into four categories: mania, melancholy, dementia, and idiotism (or mental retardation). His major diagnostic innovation was the addition of a fifth category, called "reasoning mania," a form of mental illness in which patients became obsessively fixated on certain subjects while remaining lucid and perfectly sane with respect to others. One example among many involved a Parisian clock maker who was convinced that he had been guillotined but that after the courts had reversed his conviction he had been given back the wrong head. Pinel's assistant asked a recovered patient to chat with the clock maker and mock his belief that such an event could have happened. Confronted with the other man's open derision, the clock maker ceased speaking of the guillotine episode and, returning to his line of work, gradually recovered his reason and never had a relapse. This was typical therapy for Pinel, who alternatively used distractions, diversions, or jolting experiences (he called it "shaking up the imagination"). The notion of "reasoning mania" stuck and pushed the borders of mental illness into territory that had never before been defined as insanity. Pinel's reasoning mania represented the first stage in the imperialistic historical process that gave the world hundreds of different mental disorders by the early twenty-first century.[43]

Pinel's writings on psychiatry were saturated with Rousseau's theories. One story has Pinel and a friend traveling on foot for five days to visit Rousseau's tomb in 1778. Pinel particularly agreed with Rousseau that through its capacity to produce artificial passions, society "alienated" individuals from their real selves – hence the term "mental alienation" used by nineteenth-century psychiatrists as a synonym for insanity. Moral treatment was a means of counteracting this alienation through the "schooling of the passions," restoring individuals to their true nature. Managing the passions became the aim of moral treatment; as one contemporary noted, Pinel proved that "the art of curing madmen is the same as that of governing the passions of ordinary men." Through the prism of Rousseauian theory, it becomes evident how Pinel, like countless other nineteenth-century psychiatrists, thought moral treatment was as much about controlling human emotions as it was about freeing patients from mental disabilities. Akin to mesmerism, moral treatment was a populist medical therapy that thrived in revolutionary times.[44]

Benjamin Rush, Pinel's counterpart in the United States, was similarly dedicated to moral treatment and reforming the conditions of mental hospitals. Like Pinel, Rush associated political values with the breakthroughs in medicine around the turn of the nineteenth century, stressing that political reform went hand in hand with revolution in medicine. Rush shared with Rousseau the view that commercial and urban civilization corrupted basic agrarian virtues (which he associated with the republican form of government) and caused people to lose touch with their natural selves, a pre-condition for the psychological alienation underlying mental illness.[45] Advances in psychiatry – such as moral treatment – were possible only in an era when careers were thrown open to merit and established classes no longer enjoyed monopolies on professional opportunities, whether in the army, law, civil service, or medicine itself. Together Pinel and Rush firmly stamped modern psychiatry with a robust form of populism and egalitarianism that reflected the momentous political changes that had occurred in France and the former American colonies.

PAWING HEADS

The striking emergence of psychiatry in early-nineteenth-century France coincided with the arrival of phrenology, another groundbreaking scientific theory that, like mesmerism, promised to revolutionize medicine, society, morals, and government. Phrenology and mesmerism had several things in common: each originated in Vienna, blossomed within France's revolutionary climate, and proved to be popular in politically radical circles. Phrenology was best known as the theory that personality could be deduced by studying the bumps on a person's head. That aspect of phrenology's appeal faded after the mid–nineteenth century. Meanwhile, however, it stimulated scientists' experimental research on the brain and nervous system and strengthened the belief that the mind and its functions were biological phenomena.

To the fledgling profession of psychiatry, phrenology was a boon. By emphasizing that the brain was the organ of the mind, not only did phrenology appear to explain the mysteries surrounding talent, intelligence, crime, personality, and mental illness, it also seemed to confirm that underlying disorders of the mind were biological conditions that physicians were best trained to treat. Little wonder that phrenologists found a sympathetic audience in psychiatric circles.

Phrenology was the creation of the Viennese physician Franz Joseph Gall (1758–1828), who argued that the mental powers of human beings were divided into different moral and intellectual faculties, including judgment, affection, and memory. Each faculty in turn had its own seat in a separate region of the brain; the size of each region of the brain was a measure of the degree to which its faculty had developed. Gall maintained that the contours on the outer surface of the skull revealed the relative extent of each faculty, giving rise to the popular perception that phrenologists were obsessed with feeling people's skulls for telltale bumps. An Englishman who attended a phrenologist's salon in 1852 came away unimpressed: "I could hardly restrain myself from expressing my contempt and disgust while he [the phrenologist] was pawing my head."[46]

Yet despite the ridicule heaped on phrenology over the years, it was taken seriously by a wide range of respectable thinkers, including Herbert Spencer, Harriet Martineau, Robert Owen, and George Eliot. Auguste Comte, who popularized the term "sociology," celebrated the coming of phrenology as a key chapter in the progress of the human race. Comte's endorsement of phrenology as a theory that could be used to radically reshape society strengthened its reputation as a politically subversive doctrine. On continental Europe, most of the traditional dynasties had been restored to power after Napoleon I's fall in 1815, and although much had changed politically since the Old Regime, people on both sides of the political divide still perceived an attack on society as a blow against the old alliance of church and throne. Hapsburg emperor Francis I proscribed Gall's teaching in Vienna "due to the peril it represented for religion and good morals."[47] Shortly thereafter, Gall's writings were placed on the Vatican's Index of Prohibited Books. In 1822 the Restoration government of France closed down Paris's Faculty of Medicine for a year, in part to stop the teaching of phrenology to medical students, who, by most accounts, could not get enough of it. Gall himself denied that phrenology disproved the existence of the soul, but his admirers were not nearly so cautious. As one phrenologically oriented doctor wrote in 1839, "The soul is a functioning brain and nothing else."[48]

Many psychiatrists, convinced that phrenology held the key to mental health, time and again leapt to its defense. French psychiatrists were well represented in the ranks of Paris's Société phrénologique. Phrenology was attractive to the fledgling profession for the way it justified the existence and value of the field. As one phrenologist asserted, the theory "has awakened us to the connection betwixt a clean skin and a clear conscience – foul linen and foul thought – the indispensability of a sound body to the production and preservation of a sound mind."[49] Phrenology bolstered the theory that mental illness essentially was a derangement of the brain, not a disturbance of the soul or pure mind. The derangement could leave anatomical damage, or it could be purely functional, that is, leaving no lesion observable at autopsy. Either way, phrenology said that mental illness always involved an alteration of the material brain. For a specialty hard pressed to prove that, as in tertiary syphilis, each form of insanity could be correlated to a postmortem lesion in some region of the brain, such an explanation was a godsend. If mental illness was essentially a brain disease, then presumably licensed, highly trained physicians were most adept at caring for people so afflicted. Their intimate knowledge of the brain, thanks to their reading of phrenological doctrine, supposedly left them best equipped to administer the kind of medicine patients most needed. Phrenology, in other words, helped to bolster the claims of early psychiatrists that members of their specialty possessed the expertise to diagnose and treat people with mental disabilities.

Phrenology also came in handy by explaining how moral treatment worked. Phrenology stripped moral treatment of its anti-medical dimensions by showing that it was effective only insofar as it affected the organs of the brain. Moral treatment was not a therapy for the mind alone, but a therapy for the mind in its complex relationship to the substratum of thought, the brain. Undeveloped faculties could be exercised with the right kind of therapy, such as moral treatment within a hospital. The brain, if sick, could be cured using proper treatment, whether psychological or physical (drugs). Mental patients, like criminals, could be rehabilitated through the re-education facilities only a properly regulated institution could provide. A healthy environment with carefully designed amusements and occupations would "divert the attention of the patient from the object of his insanity, by fixing it upon other objects," in Gall's words.[50]

Research in later years confirmed phrenologists' hunches about the structure of the cerebral cortex. One neurologist exclaimed in 1924 that "the phrenologists were right.... We are all phrenologists today."[51] Nonetheless, by the mid–nineteenth century, phrenology was falling into disrepute, suffering the same fate as mesmerism. As the ranks of its popularizers grew, so did the number of phrenology's vulgarizers, and accusations that the theory was "humbug" multiplied. Phrenologists were increasingly shunned by the psychiatrists, physicians, and scientists who previously had flocked to the theory's standard. In 1861 French scientist Paul Broca demonstrated that the center for articulate speech could be localized in the posterior part of the third frontal convolution of the brain, just where Gall had said the faculty of language was, but phrenology's reputation did not benefit. Neuro-scientists drew from the well of phrenology, but they were the last to admit it.

The crucial point is that the rise and fall of phrenology marked a decisive shift in scientific and public thinking about human behavior and nature. Even in the teeth of fierce opposition, phrenology convinced countless people that the brain was the organ of the mind and that problems such as crime, addiction, and mental illness could be traced to physical alterations in brain function and structure. Phrenologists argued that their science represented a medical solution to such intractable social problems.

More broadly, phrenology stated that the mind was a product of natural, biological laws. Phrenology also nurtured the vibrant populist belief, dating back to the French Revolution, that science was not an elitist occupation and that natural, useful knowledge was accessible to the masses. Indeed, phrenology proved to be wildly popular among skilled and semi-skilled workers, especially in England, where they flocked to the more than seven hundred Mechanics' Institutes that dotted the urban landscape of the kingdom. Mechanics' Institutes housed lecture halls and reading rooms, frequently adorned with a likeness of a phrenological skull. Public lectures on phrenology drew large crowds, which found them to be both fascinating and good fun, in contrast to lectures on pure science, which struck audiences as dry and boring.[52] At a stroke, phrenology helped to dismantle long-standing social barriers by empowering everyone with the right kind of learning to become a scientist. Phrenology explained why people were so mentally, physically, and behaviorally different, and suggested methods for achieving social harmony amid all this diversity. Phrenology was an egalitarian science.

Despite its many critics who insisted it was a pseudo-science, phrenology proved to be the right idea at the right time in history. A raucous, democratic age was dawning, and thanks to Rousseau, mesmerism, and moral treatment, interest in mental health at the personal and societal levels had never been higher. A view had crystallized according to which human beings had the rudimentary knowledge necessary to understand and alter the natural laws governing the mind. Such a viewpoint was not restricted to the elite, educated social classes; it had also begun percolating down to the popular classes, who, like their social betters, increasingly believed that the attainment of mental health was tantalizingly within reach. At the same time, within the ranks of medicine, a group of practitioners called psychiatrists was starting to flex its professional muscles. Psychiatrists espoused the doctrine that their medical training uniquely equipped them with the expert knowledge to diagnose and treat people with mental disabilities. Nothing about these trends was inevitable, nor went unchallenged, but by the second half of the nineteenth century their roots had been firmly planted in the cultural and social soil of most industrializing countries.

2

Bricks and Mortar Humanity

If during the first half of the nineteenth century the quest for mental health took some pathbreaking strides, the pace of change during the second half of the nineteenth century and in the years leading up to World War I was even more impressive, as mental health became a pivotal and contested concern for a wide variety of interest groups. Western governments scrambled to build publicly funded asylums to house the victims of mental illness, an enterprise one nineteenth-century critic called "bricks and mortar humanity."[1] In this era the asylum emerged as an institution that evoked fear, loathing, and horror. Yet it also offered hope for thousands of families whose relatives succumbed to the anxieties, suspicions, isolation, addictions, infirmities, and unhappiness that nineteenth-century existence remorselessly and virulently bred, as well as the many mental disorders found in aging societies with falling death rates and longer life expectancies. As the asylum steadily became a presence on the social landscape, families of people with mental disabilities increasingly viewed it as a form of public welfare that served a useful, if doleful purpose. The asylum also embodied governments' willingness to assume responsibility for the mental health needs of their populations. Its longevity as a form of public welfare helped to engender a popular appetite for mental health services and overall respect for professional expertise, paving the way for the emergence of the therapeutic state in the twentieth century.

GOVERNMENT OF MINDS

Observers of the nineteenth-century industrializing world could not help but notice that a major turning point in the history of mental health care

37

had been reached. Up to the mid–nineteenth century, public welfare had been a local issue, and that applied to the care of the mentally deranged. What the parish, community, or home did not offer, private charity (most often in the form of church-run institutions) was expected to provide. If all else failed, people with mental disabilities were housed in local jails. Then, over the middle third of the nineteenth century, against the backdrop of nation-building campaigns, one government after another erected asylums at taxpayers' expense, typically locating these institutions outside city limits and in bucolic settings, staffing them with licensed physicians and other caregivers. In North America, where vast distances delayed national unification on a European scale, central governments remained relatively weak and mental health care was largely under provincial or state jurisdiction. But even in Canada and the United States, mental health care by the early twentieth century had ceased being a local charity responsibility and was instead a key component of public welfare policy made largely by elected officials and civil servants in state or provincial capitals.

Mounting governmental involvement in mental health care in the nineteenth century took place during a momentous spurt of nation building throughout Western civilization. Wars in the 1850s and 1860s produced the newly unified nations of Germany and Italy, while between 1861 and 1865 the United States of America fought its own version of a war of national unification, ending the threat of southern secession. France, Russia, and England also took steps in the late nineteenth century to modernize and centralize. These and other, smaller Western countries introduced political, military, educational, and legal reforms that sought to assimilate more and more of their populations into national life. Whether it was broadening the franchise, introducing military conscription, or enacting social security and health insurance measures, national governments steadily broke down long-standing regional, religious, linguistic, economic, and ethnic divisions. Turning peasants into citizens was a civilizing mission that nation after nation pursued after mid-century.[2]

Perhaps the best example of a national integration project was the building of common schools, a development that dovetailed with the interest in asylum building. Before the 1860s, schooling was primarily a class, not mass, experience. However, Hungary in 1868, Austria in 1869, England in 1870, Switzerland in 1874, the Netherlands in 1876, Italy in 1877, Belgium in 1879, and France between 1881 and 1886 established systems of state-supported and state-directed elementary schools. Normally governments compelled pupils under the age of twelve to attend elementary schools, where they were expected to study a common curriculum that preached the virtues of patriotism, science, self-help, and self-discipline. To François Guizot (1787–1874), minister of public instruction and later premier during France's July Monarchy (1830–48), the "great problem of modern societies is the government of minds." He told the teachers of France that "universal elementary education will become henceforward a guarantee for order and social stability."³ "The opening of every school-house," he affirmed, "closes a jail."⁴

The emphasis of educators on unifying youth from disparate back-grounds coincided with the effort to build institutions for people with mental disabilities, but the similarities did not stop there. As we saw in the preceding chapter, many of the reformers advocating the modern asylum also strongly urged penal reform and mass education at the pri-mary level, notably Guizot, Horace Mann, and Dorothea Dix. Reformers in these different enterprises shared the belief that institutions – schools, asylums, and prisons – should be non-sectarian environments that bred values such as temperance, altruism, deferral of gratification, and moral virtue. There would be no place in these institutions for the doctrinaire religious beliefs that allegedly spawned conflict and disunity, anathema in countries like France and Germany where historically confessional strife had led to bloodshed. Whether it was the Unitarianism of Horace Mann, the positivism of French republicans after 1871, or the pietistic traditions of Prussia, creed was to give way to a kind of "civic religion." As the French republican Paul Bert said, "The supreme task of the school" is to create "elevated sentiments, a single thought, a common faith."⁵

PHILANTHROPY AND GENERAL POLICE

To many nineteenth-century mental health care reformers, the asylum was similarly meant to penetrate hearts and minds. Some believed that the march of civilization, though otherwise welcome, increasingly frayed human nerves, while others argued that civilization, far from progress-ing, was actually degenerating and thereby harming overall mental health. Most concerned individuals agreed both that the stresses and strains of modern life bred mental illness as never before and that the asylum would be an enlightened antidote. Intemperance, an unhappy love life, excessive study, financial setbacks, mass politics, religious enthusiasm, poor physical health: psychiatrists cited these factors and more as the reasons so many people suffered breakdowns. To French observers, the nation's "all-consuming" revolutionary upheavals (1789,

1830, 1834, 1871) created a roller-coaster-like "condition of fever and over-stimulation" in its citizenry.[6]

The problem of "over-stimulated" minds also appeared to be acute in the young American republic, especially during the raucous presidency of Andrew Jackson (1829–37). "In this country," an American psychiatrist remarked, "where all the offices of government are open to every man, and where the facilities for accumulating wealth are so numerous, persons even in humble life cherish hopes which can never be realized." A Rhode Island psychiatrist complained in 1853 that "the public agitation which is never at rest around the citizen of a republic is constantly placing before him great questions of public policy, which may be decided with little knowledge of the subject." Such persons became "nervous, querulous, and despondent, and sometimes insane," another U.S. psychiatrist concluded.[7]

For psychiatrists, the asylum was the best remedy for the jangled nerves of modern human beings. According to this theory, the asylum was everything that society lacked. Borrowing from the rhetoric of Dorothea Dix and others, physicians argued that with the proper location, architecture, discipline, diet, hygiene, and values, the asylum could both counteract the inroads of mental illness and serve as a model institution that the rest of society would do well to emulate. It would not be the last time in history that experts argued that mental health care was capable of solving vast social problems, from war and crime to the breakdown of marriages and families.

Undoubtedly many of the asylum's defenders suspected in their heart of hearts that the institution could never bear the ponderous weight of such expectations. Whatever their private doubts, however, virtually all pre-twentieth-century psychiatrists agreed that patients in the early stages of their diseases would benefit from asylum institutionalization. The message that the asylum would shine as a kind of beacon for the rest of society was enough to persuade normally parsimonious lawmakers to loosen the purse strings and begin building these new institutions. As reformers catalogued the many ways asylum medicine could solve the problems facing emerging nation-states, governments listened attentively.

No one preached that the asylum was the cure for civilization's ills quite like the internationally renowned dean of post-Pinel French psychiatry, J. E. D. Esquirol (1772–1840). He and the French psychiatric community were eager to advertise the virtues of hospitalization for people with mental disabilities and argued that "isolation" in an asylum was the best thing for someone afflicted with severe delusions, obsessions, anxiety, mood swings, or personality changes. Isolation, in Esquirol's words, involved "removing the lunatic from all his habitual pastimes, distancing himself from his place of residence, separating him from his family, his friends, his servants, surrounding him with strangers, changing his whole way of life." Esquirol believed that "lunatics are rarely cured in the bosom of their family," but lest anyone view Esquirol's prescription as an attack on the family, he denied that the family itself was to blame. Instead, he argued, the sick of mind inveterately mistrusted family members and stubbornly resisted their efforts to help. Relations within the household rapidly deteriorated, family life became emotionally painful for everyone, and abuse was often the result. Better that the patient defer to the "guidance" that came from the asylum physician and his absolute supremacy within the hospital's walls.[8]

Esquirol's theory that the mentally ill should be removed from the community and family care appeared to be a felicitous combination of "philanthropy and general police," in the words of France's minister of the interior. Asylum treatment enabled the government to "come to the aid of misfortune, to assuage the most distressing of human infirmities," but also to "preserve society from the disorders which these sick persons can perpetrate."[9]

In fact, Esquirol's vision was an excellent example of "political medicine," what governments in the name of "civilization" do to try to "repair ... the damage it has itself inflicted," a Paris newspaper editorialized in 1837.[10] Like Pinel, Esquirol harked back to Rousseau and his pointed criticism of civilization, to J. P. Frank's theory of "medical police," and to the Tukes' advocacy of asylum moral treatment. But in doing so Esquirol bore witness to the uneasy tension between humane purposes and the practical interests of modern states. The repeated failure of governments in later years to simultaneously meet the goals of both philanthropy and police aroused wave after wave of public indignation. Governments and their populations seemingly could not make up their minds about mental health policy. Should people with mental disabilities be institutionalized for compassionate or custodial reasons? Were people with mental disabilities more to be feared than pitied? The inability to disentangle these two very different motivations behind mental health care policy meant that since the eighteenth century people with mental disabilities rarely have been viewed as fully deserving recipients of health and welfare benefits. The unresolved conflict between compassion and public security was still plaguing the quest for mental health in the early twenty-first century.

GROWTH SPURT

The belief that the asylum was most needed in localities where demo-cratic civilization had progressed the furthest suggested that the first state asylum system would be built in modern countries like Britain, France, and the United States. The exception was Ireland, governed by Britain's Parliament from 1801 to 1922. Ireland was the site of the first attempts to build such a system, well before similar initiatives were undertaken in England. Between 1824 and the end of the century, the number of beds in Irish public asylums rose from roughly 1,000 to more than 16,000.[11]

Yet if Europe's first modern public asylums were erected in Ireland, it was the French state that took the earliest steps toward enacting a nation-wide policy on mental health care. France's own 1838 asylum law, besides permitting the country's eighty-eight departments to construct new asy-lums, regulated the administration of and admission to mental hospitals. Initially, asylum building in France was slow. Between 1838 and 1852 only seven new asylums opened, and by 1874 only forty out of eighty-eight departments had erected special hospitals for the mentally ill.

Nonetheless, a statement had been made. For the next one hundred years government's favorite form of public welfare for people with men-tal disabilities would be the asylum.

In rapid succession, England's Parliament followed suit with its own law in 1845, having already legalized the use of public funds for asylums back in 1808. After 1845 it was mandatory for each of England's coun-ties to provide asylum care at public expense (in Wales there were no asylums at all). The act also established a permanent national Lunacy Commission with the power to inspect all asylums, whether public, pri-vate, or charity foundations. The steep costs of building and maintaining these institutions delayed full compliance with the law until the 1860s, but to reformers the act appeared to be a major victory for science and humanity.

In Germany the shift to publicly funded asylums fittingly took place after national unification in 1871. In the first half of the nineteenth cen-tury numerous church properties all across central Europe were secular-ized and empty cloisters and castles were converted to asylums, while several new mental hospitals were erected. By mid-century there were more than seventy-five public institutions for the mentally ill in German lands, including Austria-Hungary. Private asylums flourished too. When space was not available in public hospitals, the state paid for many patients to stay in private institutions.

Then, between 1877 and 1904, the number of German institutions for psychiatric patients almost doubled, from 93 to 180, and the number of asylum patients almost tripled (33,000 to 112,000). By 1911 Germany boasted 187 public asylums and 225 private asylums, and those data do not include similar German-speaking institutions in Switzerland and Austria.

National legislation on mental health care never materialized in Imperial Germany, due largely to Germany's dizzying variety of institutions for people with mental disabilities. Some asylums were for curable patients; others were not. Some were entirely run by lay staff; others were clerical institutions. Still, the nineteenth-century evolution of state involvement in mental health care in central Europe constituted a remarkable change in policy that mirrored the simultaneous political upheaval created by German unification. Just as Germany was shortly to become one of the world's greatest powers, so almost overnight it displaced France as the foremost nation in psychiatric science. After the mid–nineteenth century, Germany's growing reputation as the world leader in science and medicine ensured that young psychiatrists eager for the best training in their field flocked to central Europe's outstanding universities.

In North America, as in Germany, asylum policy making was more decentralized than in France or England, but the campaign of asylum building was no less robust. In the United States, by 1840 three states had their own public mental hospitals. By 1880 Americans could boast of almost 140 public and private mental hospitals caring for nearly 41,000 patients. Sixty years later there were nearly 450,000 patients in public mental hospitals.

North of the U.S. border the same trend toward asylum building was evident, though events in Canada unfolded more slowly due to its smaller and more scattered population. There, too, families for years had been the main caregivers for the mentally ill. Public and private charity had been limited to the efforts of the churches, as in predominantly Roman Catholic Quebec. Yet to reformers like Dorothea Dix, who in 1843 called on Canadian colonial governments to build new asylums, this situation was no more tolerable than the conditions she found in American states. Following Dix's advice, and particularly after Canada became self-governing in 1867, governments erected public asylums stretching from tiny Prince Edward Island on the Atlantic coast (1847) to Manitoba (1891) on the prairies. Ontario, where industrialization and urbanization had made the deepest inroads, boasted seven public asylums by the end of the nineteenth century, with the Toronto Lunatic Asylum (founded in

1850) as the flagship of the provincial system. At the turn of the twentieth century no state institution loomed larger on the Canadian social landscape than the asylum.

Russia's first asylums, which the peasantry dubbed "yellow houses" because of the color of their inexpensive paint, had been erected during the reign of Catherine the Great (1762–96). These yellow houses, often staffed by serfs or former soldiers sent to work there as punishment, were few in number, normally small scale, usually half-empty, and notorious for their deplorable conditions. With such an option, the vast majority of peasants preferred to take care of their relatives at home.

The era of great reforms under Alexander II (1855–81) witnessed the biggest expansion in asylum building in the country's history. As late as the 1861 emancipation of Russia's serfs, there were still only forty-three "yellow house" asylums, containing a total population of barely 2,000, a tiny fraction of Russia's overall population of 60 million. Yet as Alexander II introduced other sweeping reforms in the 1860s and 1870s that transformed the legal system and armed forces, St. Petersburg simultaneously unloaded political responsibility for health and education onto newly created local government bodies, or "zemstvos." A boom in asylum construction followed. By the eve of World War I, the number of asylums had quadrupled and almost 43,000 Russians were confined within their walls.

As Russian data indicate, with asylums being opened all across Europe the number of hospitalized patients skyrocketed. In 1852 there was 1 psychiatric inpatient in Germany for every 5,300 in overall population; in 1911 the number was 1 for every 500. In neighboring Holland, between 1850 and 1899 the number of patients in asylums rose from 5.16 per 10,000 to 14.12. Across the Channel, by 1900 the asylum patient population in England had shot up tenfold from 10,000 in 1800. In France the total leapt from 10,000 in 1834 to 42,000 forty years later. In Italy the change came later in the nineteenth century, but when it did the shift was similarly pronounced, with its asylum population growing from about 12,000 in 1874 to 40,000 in 1907.

It is worth noting that this wave of asylum building and hospitalization was launched well before the modern, general hospital attained its own respectability. Until the late nineteenth century "the very idea of a hospital," one Massachusetts official noted, evoked "scenes of anguish and terror."[12] Most society doctors shunned hospitals, as they were charitable rather than medical institutions. By contrast, asylums were designed to cure patients, not just house them, and their defenders insisted that public asylums were meant for all social classes, much like the common school. Public asylums tended to be headed by licensed physicians and were perceived to be places where bona fide medicine was practiced.

By the end of the nineteenth century the prestige of the general hospital, with its bright, clean wards, its white-robed staff, its antiseptic surgical theaters, and its bustling, austere-looking laboratories, was fast outstripping the reputation of the asylum. Many asylum psychiatrists tried desperately to update their institutions so they more closely resembled regular hospitals, but it was a losing battle. The modern hospital got all the good press and most of the investment. All but forgotten in the hoopla over the advent of the modern, scientific hospital was that scant decades earlier the asylum had enjoyed higher status, testimony to the importance governments placed on mental health and the role psychiatrists played in the rise of medical prestige during the nineteenth century.

MORAL ENTREPRENEURS

As governments increasingly intervened in the field of mental health care, psychiatry took its first steps toward professional status. Ideally, professionalization depended on four factors: on the specialty's ability to convince governments and the public that it possessed a body of scientific knowledge that no other group could claim, that no other occupational groups should compete with it over the delivery of services, that it should have the freedom to regulate itself without outside interference, and that it was motivated chiefly by a commitment to public welfare rather than self-interest. By the dawn of the twentieth century, psychiatry had made impressive strides toward the goal of professionalization, but the process had been far from smooth. No matter how often psychiatrists lauded themselves for their "scientific curiosity," "professional seriousness," and "respect and pity for the unfortunate," there was no shortage of critics who delighted in pointing out how far psychiatrists fell short of these standards.[13]

The professionalization of psychiatry is often and unaccountably left out of standard histories of medical specialization. Initially asylum psychiatry was a much bigger success story than general medicine. Over the course of the nineteenth century, asylum physicians or "alienists" (the term "psychiatrist" was scarcely used before the twentieth century) assiduously formed their own organizations, founded their own journals, opened their own clinics, fought to have their specialty taught in medical schools, and lobbied to relegate their non-medical competitors to second-class status. By contrast, for much of the nineteenth century the profession of general medicine suffered from low status, divisiveness, competition from unlicensed healers, and poor-quality education and training. Other than digitalis for heart disease, vaccination for smallpox, and quinine for malaria, regular physicians had no scientifically valid therapies before the turn of the twentieth century. U.S. physician Oliver Wendell Holmes famously quipped in 1860 that if all the drugs typically used by doctors could be dumped into the sea, "it would be all the better for mankind, and all the worse for the fishes."[14]

Until the introduction of antisepsis and anesthesia after mid-century, surgical operations were hair-raising events in which patients frequently died of shock, infection, or loss of blood. In a day and age before either private or publicly funded medical insurance, physicians found it very difficult to make a living in private practice. Newspapers, novels, and broadsheets time and again depicted physicians as mired in grinding, embarrassing poverty. Their pauperism fostered the unflattering image of physicians perpetually on the make, a reputation that was popular in the first half of the nineteenth century, especially in the United States, where lax licensing laws made it difficult for regular physicians to distinguish themselves from herbalists, folk healers, patent medicine peddlers, and itinerant quacks.

By contrast, psychiatry's claims to expertise looked more convincing. Moral treatment was ideally suited to medicine's evolving therapeutic ethos around mid-century. Holmes, Frenchman Pierre Louis, Canadian William Osler, and the so-called Viennese school of medicine urged physicians to cease aggressively treating patients with physicalist methods of dubious value, such as bloodletting. Holmes praised what Hippocrates centuries earlier had called the healing power of nature. By placing patients in an orderly, clean, well-ventilated institution where they would gradually come to their senses thanks to the salutary effects of the asylum environment, asylum psychiatrists would be seen as working with nature's benign healing powers in order to effect cures, a distinct departure from the way regular physicians usually appeared to be working *against* nature with their reliance on debilitating drugs.

Buoyed by their initially favorable reputations, psychiatrists were among the very first specialists to found their own journals and organize into interest groups. In 1841 public and private asylum doctors in England formed the Association of Medical Officers of Asylums and Hospitals for the Insane. Two journals with a specifically psychiatric orientation were soon being published: the *Journal of Psychological Medicine and*

Mental Pathology in 1848 and the *Asylum Journal* in 1848. In France, the works of psychiatrists appeared in several medical journals, notably the *Annales d'hygiène publique et de médecine légale*, but in 1843 the *Annales médico-psychologiques* was founded, followed in 1852 by the Société médico-psychologique. (By contrast, a national association of French doctors was not formed until 1858.) In 1844, three years before the founding of the American Medical Association, U.S. asylum physicians formed the Association of Medical Superintendents of American Institutions for the Insane (AMSAII), the forerunner of the American Psychiatric Association, and shortly thereafter the first issues of the *American Journal of Insanity* (later the *American Journal of Psychiatry*) began to appear. In Germany the most influential psychiatric journal, the *Allgemeine Zeitschrift für Psychiatrie und psychisch-gerichtliche Medicin*, was launched in 1844, followed in 1854 by the formation of the *Deutsche Gesellschaft für Psychiatrie und gerichtliche Psychologie*. The first Italian journal of psychiatry appeared in 1852, taking the name of *Archivio Italiano peule malattie nervose e più particolarmente per le alienazioni mentali* in 1864. In 1873 the Società Italiana di Freniatria was formed, that nation's first psychiatric association.

What these and other events in the history of psychiatry indicate is that in most jurisdictions and in this time period, psychiatry was more effective than the rest of medicine at mobilizing to advance its interests, a sure sign of psychiatrists' comparative solidarity, self-confidence, and public support. This brief, heady moment in psychiatry's past stands in stark contrast to its later trials and tribulations as a much-maligned specialty with low status within organized medicine, but in the short term psychiatrists basked in the broad perception that their services were philanthropic, scientific, and socially useful.

These impressive steps toward professional authority emboldened psychiatrists to make forthright claims. In 1868 a prominent Prussian psychiatrist asserted that within the asylum "the doctor must comprise the pinnacle of the institution, the head of the household, ... so that at all times the patient is more or less conscious that only *one* authority governs the healthy and the sick and that the trustworthy authority of the doctor protects him."[15] Where psychiatrists worked side by side with nursing sisters and priests, religious were expected to defer to the psychiatrist, whose authority derived from his patriarchal stature as well as his expertise in both medicine and the art of psychological consolation. Such relations between clergy and physicians over the care of people with mental disabilities were symptomatic of the professionalization under way in France and other nations where the churches had once been deeply involved in caregiving, and led gradually to psychiatry's virtual monopoly over institutional mental health care by the twentieth century.

THAT NOBLE ORGAN

The core belief behind these assertions of professional authority was that no one knew better than psychiatrists how to treat people with mental disabilities. Indeed, nineteenth-century psychiatrists made great advances in their clinical understanding of mental diseases. German psychiatrist Emil Kraepelin (1856–1926) is normally given credit for establishing the view that mental diseases were as natural as any other type of illness and for discovering the conditions that would later be called schizophrenia and bipolar disorder, but in the 1850s a cluster of French psychiatrists had already concluded that a class of patients began to show signs of severe psychosis in their late adolescence and never got better, while other patients suffered from mood swings between intense euphoria (mania) and melancholy (depression).

If psychiatrists' clinical skills appeared to be getting better as the century unfolded, however, their knowledge of how physical changes in the brain caused the symptoms of mental disease lagged behind. This was a crucial consideration, for their efforts to eliminate their competitors depended on society accepting that there was nothing religious or spiritual about mental illness, that it was as organic a disease as cancer or tuberculosis. So long as there was no convincing evidence that mental diseases were caused by somatic changes in the brain, it followed that asylum physicians were not required to bring about a cure. What good was the advantage of a medical education and license if insanity more closely resembled a psychological or metaphysical condition than a brain disease?

When psychiatrists turned to pathological anatomy in an effort to detect signs of brain function, they typically came up short. At the nub of psychiatry's problems was the nature of mental illness itself. For centuries both the educated and uneducated had accepted that physical injuries could trigger an onset of madness. After the landmark 1822 discovery that patients suffering from general paralysis were always afflicted with the same kind of inflammation of brain tissue (general paralysis of the insane), many psychiatrists expected similar discoveries to soon follow. They believed that for every mental abnormality there was a corresponding physiological or anatomical lesion of the central nervous system.

Yet several years later, Esquirol confessed that he was no longer confident that autopsy would reveal the organic cause of mental illness. German psychiatrist Wilhelm Griesinger was no less a believer that it was a disease of the brain, but to him psychiatrists' achievements compared poorly with the kind of results achieved by anatomists such as René Laennec, who had discovered the lesions of tuberculosis in patients' lungs. In 1858 a leading English medical textbook stated that when it came to the "noble organ which lords it over the rest of the body," its "*modus operandi* is, and probably always will be, utterly unknown to us."[16]

In 1906 German neuro-histologist Aloys Alzheimer discovered the well-known disease named after him. Yet despite this advance and some exciting research in neuro-chemistry in the late twentieth century, for years and years it remained true that patients with bizarre emotions, behavior, and mental states could die with seemingly normal brains. All in all, psychiatrists' futile struggles to unlock the secrets of the brain and its functions underlined a chronic problem facing mental health care policy making then and now: mental illness is a riddle both similar and dissimilar to other diseases, no matter how often reformers insist that a psychiatric disorder is as natural as diabetes or heart disease. Each mental disorder involves brain functioning, but what causes it and what specific treatments are most effective against it are still open to debate. Psychiatrists have always known family history is important, but that commonsense observation simply triggers a series of further perplexing questions. These fundamental complexities surrounding mental disease have plagued virtually all approaches to mental health care throughout its long history.

The professionalization of psychiatry, then, helped medicine stake out a role within ever-expanding national systems of mental health care. Many psychiatrists were genuinely humane and sincerely convinced that what they did for their patients was in their best interests. But years of listening to the pleas of patients and their families to do something often left psychiatrists over-eager to experiment with therapies that would shock later generations. This experience forged in many psychiatrists a mindset in which the dividing lines between patients' needs and the specialty's own interests were not always clear. Thus, for years psychiatrists clung tenaciously to the medical model of insanity and the asylum model as the best means of treating the mentally ill. The overall history of mental health care suggests that the proposition that psychiatrists knew how best to diagnose, prevent, and cure mental disorders has enjoyed broad public assent, but it has not gone unchallenged by critics who have questioned the wisdom of relying on state-certified experts to solve the emotional challenges of everyday life.

BREAKDOWN

The cardinal faith that, as a Russian psychiatrist declared in 1889, "the sooner an individual is hospitalized the greater are his chances of being cured," united psychiatrists from one continent to another, but it clashed sharply with reality.[17] "Our whole scheme for the cure of lunatics has utterly broken down," an English physician baldly announced in 1870.[18] Few statements better typified the difficulties asylum psychiatrists faced trying to steer their patients toward recovery as the century ground to a close. Wherever public asylums were erected, the complaints were not slow in coming and were tinged with a dreary sameness. No matter how many asylums were opened, there never seemed to be enough beds. As time wore on, institutional patient populations tended to get older and sicker. The number of patients discharged as cured never seemed to meet the earlier, optimistic expectations of reformers such as Dix, Mann, and Tuke.

Compounding these problems, cost-conscious governments began cutting back original capital plans for asylum construction once the initial enthusiasm for asylum building started to fade. Asylums, quite simply, cost a lot of money. By the late 1880s, for example, roughly 20 percent of the entire budget for the Canadian province of Ontario was consumed by expenditures on its six public asylums, and Ontario was hardly unique.[19] Almost everywhere rising expenditures on mental health care bred taxpayers' resistance to investment in state mental hospitals. This tendency of governments to nickel and dime mental health care programs constituted one of the most powerful factors affecting the search for sanity.

Blame for asylum over-crowding was usually laid at the feet of psychiatrists, whose therapeutic competence never ceased to be a topic of debate, and the asylum itself as a curative institution was often caught in critics' crosshairs. But in one important sense, these circumstances actually were a sign of the asylum's success. Demand for access to asylums mounted in the late nineteenth century because public officials, largely convinced of the arguments of reformers, readily transferred people with mental disabilities from jails and local workhouses to nearby asylums, where the hospital staff was expected to mitigate their suffering. The "silting up" of asylums with aged, chronically ill patients, rather than being a symptom of failure, was instead the result of societies attempting to rectify a perceived injustice through augmented access to welfare services. In turn, public demand for these services escalated as families increasingly petitioned authorities for the hospitalization of their elderly relatives.

The crowding within asylums became apparent almost as soon as they opened. The first complaints surfaced as a million and half Irish immigrants reached the United States in the 1840s. Driven from their homeland by poverty and famine, Irish (and mostly Roman Catholic) newcomers flooded the wards of newly built asylums, horrifying nativists. Asylum doctors – typically Protestant – showed little patience for these immigrants' customs and habits, especially their seeming intemperance. To psychiatrists the behavior of Irish-born patients was a malign influence on their wards and made the practice of moral treatment exceedingly difficult, if not downright impossible. Psychiatrists tended to blame the immigrants' misfortunes on their bad heredity, their apparently biological predisposition to descend into mental illness. The tide of Irish newcomers abated in the 1850s, but many of the same concerns surfaced in the early twentieth century with the arrival on America's shores of 18 million immigrants – this time mainly from eastern and southern Europe. Then, too, psychiatrists in both the United States and Canada cited defective heredity as a major reason for immigrants' propensity to land on the doorsteps of the nation's public asylums. Meanwhile, psychiatry's first brush with immigrants in the form of Irish Catholic mental patients signaled that the brief heyday of the asylum was swiftly drawing to a close.

FAST COACH TO THE MADHOUSE

The medical backlash against Irish immigration also helped to raise awareness of the link between alcoholism and mental illness. Within a few years numerous observers, including French novelist Émile Zola, were highlighting the impact of drink on mental health. The asylum soon became society's most reliable line of defense against the disorder, crime, and family breakdown spawned by addiction, whether in the form of drink or drugs.

Alcoholism and other forms of addiction deeply shaped the quest for mental health in the modern era. For centuries farmers had been distilling their own spirits, but the nineteenth century – what one historian called the "golden age of inebriation" – marked an abrupt shift.[20] The consumption of distilled alcohol (gin, vodka, whiskey) vied with that of the more familiar beverages of wine and beer, and the incidence of drinking soared.

The French were widely recognized as the world leaders when it came to drinking. When children under the age of fourteen (30 percent of the population in 1900) are excluded from France's national average, the data show that every French adult had to have consumed 325 bottles of wine per year.[21] Beer consumption in Bavaria doubled during the middle decades of the nineteenth century.[22] William Booth, founder of the Salvation Army, declared the British people to be "sodden with drink." At the turn of the twentieth century, per capita rates of pure alcohol consumption ranged from 17 liters in France to 11.5 in Switzerland.[23] A study of urban workers in Russia in the same time period found that they spent 25 percent of their total income on alcoholic beverages.

Despite the exertions of temperance activists in the nineteenth century, heavy drinking remained socially acceptable. It was not uncommon for a politician to address Britain's Parliament visibly under the influence of alcohol. Grinding poverty and wretched living conditions were additional reasons for drunkenness. Millions of urban dwellers spent long hours in bars and beer halls seeking solace through the abuse of alcohol. In France, where a thriving wine industry was viewed with patriotic pride, denial helped to mask the magnitude of the problem. Distillers and bar owners did everything they could to downplay the threat of alcoholism. In 1853 a Frenchman said, "France has many drunkards, but happily, no alcoholics."[24]

Physicians, however, were highly vocal about the escalating toll of beer, wine, and spirits on the health of the masses. In 1849 the Swedish medical researcher Magnus Huss coined the term "alcoholism" to describe a range of symptoms associated with drunkenness, including hallucinations, delusions, memory loss, mental confusion, and tremors. Huss's theory that abuse of alcohol was a disease medicalized heavy drinking, which for centuries had been viewed as a sin or personal vice. In a hugely significant development in the history of mental health, psychiatrists began applying the disease model to intemperance and documenting the impact of drunkenness on the nervous system. Perhaps the worst culprit was the highly alcoholic, green-colored absinthe, a liquor distilled from the medicinal plant grand wormwood. Valentin Magnan, the head psychiatrist at Paris's Sainte-Anne asylum, went so far as to coin the word "absinthism" to designate a disease that reportedly caused hallucinations, convulsions, and ultimately severe psychosis. Its high alcoholic content (55 to 75 percent) and the fact that it was often drunk on an empty stomach led its opponents to dub it *la correspondance*, a reference to *la correspondance à Charenton*, or the fast coach to the madhouse.[25]

Thanks to beverages such as absinthe, alcoholics were processed on a daily basis at the special infirmary at the Paris Prefecture of Police and then sent to the city's public asylums, notably Sainte-Anne, the jewel of France's burgeoning public asylum system. At the Prefecture of Police, alcoholism was the leading diagnosis among men. Between 1872 and 1885 almost 30 percent of all men admitted to Paris asylums were alcoholics. The Scottish asylum doctor David Yellowlees believed that "half the existing cases of insanity are due, directly or indirectly, to this social curse" of intemperance. One German psychiatrist remembered that while he was a psychiatry resident in the city of Breslau in the 1890s, "the admission room was dominated by the numbers of alcoholic patients wandering about in delirium."[26]

As the century wore on, politicians began to take notice too. In 1896 the future French statesman Georges Clemenceau remarked that alcoholism was "the whole social problem." Some of the rhetoric of public figures surrounding alcoholism was inflated for political purposes, but such language nonetheless mirrored the very real rise in alcoholic consumption across the industrialized world.[27]

Drug addiction too exacted a fearsome toll on human health in the nineteenth century. Opium, used medicinally for millennia, was widely consumed as a basic medication in the form of lozenges, syrups, and pills throughout much of the nineteenth century. When late in the century concern mounted over opium's addictive properties, its distribution was finally restricted in countries like Britain, but by then numerous literary figures, including John Keats, Samuel Coleridge, and Walter Scott, had consumed it habitually, often writing poems and novels while under its influence. Once opium became less socially acceptable in the 1880s and 1890s, cocaine's popularity soared, winning commercial acceptance in patent medicines, soft drinks, and fortified wines. In 1886 an Atlanta-based inventor added cocaine to his popular French wine cola and renamed it Coca-Cola. Physicians prescribed cocaine for complaints ranging from tuberculosis to indigestion. The French actress Sarah Bernhardt and the Norwegian playwright Henrik Ibsen were cocaine users, as was the up-and-coming neurologist (and later inventor of psychoanalysis) Sigmund Freud.

Yet Freud soon learned that heavy cocaine use can lead directly to severe symptoms, including seizures, cardiac arrest, the sensation of insects crawling over and under the skin, and delusions of persecution and jealousy. It is impossible to tell how drug abuse affected the incidence of mental diseases in the late nineteenth century, but it is striking how often asylum psychiatrists of the time reported large numbers of patients suffering from paranoid delusional states.[28] Widespread drug taking, like intemperance, dramatically affected mental health care in the nineteenth and twentieth centuries.

Next to alcoholism, however, the epidemic that troubled psychiatrists most by the end of the nineteenth century was neuro-syphilis. Syphilis had been around for centuries, but its effects on the central nervous system began to draw attention only in the late eighteenth century when doctors started noticing middle-aged patients with insidious paralysis and dementia. The condition affected men more than women but did not discriminate between rich and poor. After venereal infection, a latency period ensued, which could last years, but if untreated the disease often followed a fatal course. The 1822 discovery that such patients were suffering from a chronic inflammation of the brain's lining taught psychiatrists that they were dealing with a brain disease, but its cause eluded scientists until the early twentieth century when researchers discovered the corkscrew-shaped micro-organism responsible for GPI and traced it to brain tissue. At that moment GPI's nature as a sexually transmitted disease was confirmed.

Commentators in the nineteenth century, alarmed at how encroaching urbanization appeared to spread prostitution and loosen sexual morals, called neuro-syphilis the "disease of the century." GPI was the AIDS of its day. Both GPI and acquired immune deficiency syndrome were linked to sexual transmission and if untreated often resulted in a lingering, painful, and undignified death. At the end of the nineteenth century, 13 to 15 percent of all Parisian males were said to be infected, 1 million people nationwide.[29] According to other estimates, 5 to 20 percent of the population in Europe and North America was infected with syphilis, with roughly 6 percent developing the disease. In the 1860s a private clinic near Breslau reported that 32 percent of its male patients had the disease.[30] For medicine and society alike, penicillin's arrival in the 1930s as a cure for syphilis was none too soon. By then, syphilis's horrific impact on mental and physical health was a matter of grim historical record, another doleful indication of how lifestyle affected the quest for sanity in the modern era by throwing up challenges of an unprecedented magnitude to mental health caregivers.

A SWEEPING EMERGENCY

As if nineteenth-century asylum physicians did not have their hands full already with alcohol-soaked, syphilitic, or drug-addled patients, by the end of the century a pattern familiar to twentieth-century observers was becoming increasingly noticeable: many public mental hospitals were also becoming old-age, senior citizens' residences. In the United States, New York State, home of the nation's flagship state asylum system, led the way. Legislation there in 1890 abruptly ended county care of the mentally ill and officially abolished the distinction between curable and incurable patients. New York State psychiatrists and asylum physicians all around the country were appalled by the effects of the 1890 act and similar legislation in other states, including Massachusetts, which essentially shifted the burden of care from one level of government to another. In the Empire State, 1,500 patients were immediately transferred from county asylums to state hospitals, and in the eyes of state psychiatrists that meant an influx of

> old people, some of them very old, who are simply suffering from the mental decay incident to extreme old age. A little mental confusion, forgetfulness, and garrulity are sometimes the only symptoms exhibited, but the patient is duly certified to us as insane and has no one at home capable or possessed of means to care for him.

North of the border, the results were the same. In 1897 the Canadian psychiatrist C. K. Clarke looked around his asylum in Kingston, Ontario, at the mounting number of incurable patients and blamed "the old story of careless relatives, who take advantage of the warrant system, to get rid of the feeble dements who need a little care and nursing, not detention in a hospital for the insane."[31] To many, these practices turned psychiatrists into little more than gatekeepers for elderly people suffering from various degrees of dementia. Asylums were in danger of becoming glorified nursing homes. The graying of asylums was, in the words of a German psychiatrist, a "sweeping emergency."[32]

The decline in the asylum's status overshadowed the fact that mental hospitals were doing something right. Custodialism was not their only purpose. The quality of treatment varied from one asylum to another, but some patients actually benefited from asylum incarceration.[33] Many patients spent less than a year in the hospital and were discharged as "improved" or "recovered." At the Toronto asylum, for example, over the second half of the nineteenth century, 50 percent of men and 60 percent of women admitted stayed for twelve months or less, data that compare with the lengths of stay at many British and European asylums.[34] The quality of care had little to do with the ethnicity or wealth of patients. More crucial was the personality of individual doctors. When the physician in question was Alice Bennett at Norristown Hospital or Margaret

Cleaves at Harrisburg Asylum in Pennsylvania, among the first women to serve as asylum physicians, care was frequently individualized and compassionate. Countless women patients, some abused and beaten, obtained much-needed relief in asylums from the stresses and strains of trying to maintain hearth and home in dire, poverty-stricken environments. Those women suffering from gynecological problems, including prolapsed uteruses and severe uterine bleeding, received welcome rest and relaxation, often returning to their homes in much better health than when they left. Yet ordinarily this good news about recovered asylum patients was buried beneath the avalanche of bad press surrounding mental hospitals by the end of the nineteenth century.

Thus, by the late nineteenth century the asylum had become the centerpiece of the struggle for mental health, but the swirl of events had left its imprint on the institution's history. Gone were the great hopes for moral treatment as asylum doctors gradually reconciled themselves to their evolving duties as caretakers of increasingly older and sicker patients. Clearly, asylums were meeting needs as the demands for custodial mental health care kept rising in nation after nation, but the changing nature of patient populations compelled psychiatrists to alter their interpretations of mental disabilities. Once viewed as eminently curable, by the end of the nineteenth century people with mental disabilities were depicted less as patients worthy of compassionate treatment than as pressing social problems seeking urgent policy solutions.

DEGENERACY

The malaise that gripped asylum medicine in the late nineteenth century overlapped the mounting interest in biological interpretations of human nature, notably the various theories accounting for the modification of species over time. Physicians often contended that the more the public viewed mental illness as a biological condition, the more medicalized it became and the less people with mental disabilities would be held accountable for their symptoms. However, biological interpretations of mental disease also fostered the belief that people with mental disabilities were a threat to seemingly sane people and that governments concerned about mounting crime and declining birthrates required the expertise of psychiatrists.

The best-known theory of biology was Charles Darwin's theory of evolution according to natural selection. Darwin argued that throughout natural history species were modified because the fittest individuals survived the fierce struggle for existence over nature's limited food supply. Those that survived tended to transmit their most advantageous traits through heredity more often than did supposedly "unfit" individuals, thus accounting for the changes species underwent over time. Darwin called the whole process "natural selection," claiming it dispensed with the need to invoke the creation of species by God.

Darwin, it turns out, took a keen interest in mental illness. After consulting with English asylum psychiatrist James Crichton Browne, Darwin became convinced that the facial expressions of many mentally ill persons were echoes of more primitive forms of human expression from the distant mists of time.[35] He agreed with Henry Maudsley, a pre-eminent English psychiatrist, that people who were developmentally delayed – the mentally retarded or, as they were called in those days, "idiots" – were throwbacks to earlier stages of species development. Darwin's overall message in works such as *The Descent of Man* (1871) and *The Expression of the Emotions in Man and Animals* (1872) was that the human mind and all its powers – intelligence, reason, artistic creativity, moral instincts – were products of natural evolution. Darwin's countless followers and admirers interpreted his theory in various fashions, but there was no escaping the conclusion that after Darwin social scientists increasingly viewed human thought and behavior through a biological prism. Like Darwin, many learned figures perceived people with mental disabilities as human relics of evolution.

Reinforcing the Darwinist way of viewing people with mental disabilities was the theory of degeneration, the brainchild of the Vienna-born French psychiatrist Bénédict-Augustin Morel (1809–73), who over the course of his brilliant career served as head physician in several French asylums. Between the 1850s and the outbreak of World War I in 1914, degeneration actually rivaled Darwinism as the most popular theory of biological science. Morel, a devout Roman Catholic, believed that a new, all-encompassing approach to mental and physical health was necessary to relieve the massive suffering of Europe's laboring classes. Morel looked to government and organized medicine for leadership in the endeavor to reduce the disturbing incidence of mental disease.

Morel arguably was the psychiatrist who had the biggest impact on his own day and age. A keen clinician, Morel defied psychiatric custom by classifying mental illnesses according to their course over time rather than the symptoms a patient displayed at the moment of admission. He was the first in history to record that some people suffered from bizarre delusions in adolescence and then over time underwent severe mental deterioration. Morel called the condition *démence précoce*, or "premature dementia," what later generations called schizophrenia. Emil Kraepelin received the headlines for "discovering" dementia praecox later in the century, but Morel really deserves the credit.

In the shorter term it was Morel's introduction of the concept of degeneration that helped to change the very vocabulary the world used for the next sixty years to discuss mental illness in its protean forms. Like evolutionary theory, degeneracy theory was subject to a wide variety of interpretations, but that only seemed to facilitate its acceptance among fin-de-siècle scientists, doctors, intellectuals, artists, politicians, and journalists. Degeneration theory said that the human race was in severe danger of becoming less biologically robust as time went on. After studying how Europe's teeming millions of poor people lived, Morel and others argued that the laws of heredity ensured that pathological conditions such as alcoholism and mental illness, once acquired, could be inherited by later generations and lead to the steady deterioration or extinction of racial stock. If Darwin's theory of evolution according to natural selection accounted for the progressive development of species, degeneracy theory had a much gloomier message: evolution could end with degenerate misfits just as easily as it could produce a genius like Darwin.

Darwin himself was haunted by the specter of degeneration. In his *Descent of Man* he openly worried about how hospitals, asylums, and medicines protected society's "unfit" from the blind ruthlessness of natural selection, thus enabling the weak, sick, and improvident to survive and beget their own kind. To Darwin, the fertility gap between the fit and the "reckless, degraded, and vicious" members of society was widening as time went on, leaving civilization in deep trouble. These dark thoughts did not lead the mild-mannered Darwin to advocate stringent policies to reverse this alarming differential birthrate, but his brilliant cousin Francis Galton (1822–1911), whose studies of inheritance Darwin frequently cited, had no such compunctions. Galton would later (1883) coin the term "eugenics," helping to launch a movement that in the twentieth century would advocate measures that either encouraged the fit to have bigger families or prevented the breeding of the unfit. In the eyes of most social scientists, the unfit included people with mental, physical, and nervous disabilities. In the twentieth century, eugenic theory would be translated into practice in various jurisdictions around the globe, affecting the lives of thousands upon thousands of people with mental disabilities and their families.

In the meantime, Morel's ideas spread from country to country, finding a receptive audience among psychiatrists. Cesare Lombroso, an Italian criminologist and asylum director, was one of Morel's most fervent followers. Lombroso maintained that people with mental disabilities and their degenerate cousins were regressions in time to prehistoric ancestors. In no time at all, references to Lombroso were cropping up in the novels of Joseph Conrad and Leo Tolstoy and in Bram Stoker's *Dracula*. In the newly unified Italian state, Lombroso's studies of social deviants ranging from street thieves to bomb-throwing anarchists also appealed to many worried about the new nation's ability to assimilate so many different social groups, as well as its overall fitness in the international "struggle for survival."[36]

The highpoint for degenerationism was the 1892 publication of *Degeneration*, a book by journalist and Zionist Max Nordau and the most controversial international best seller of the 1890s. *Degeneration*, translated from German into English, French, Spanish, Italian, and Russian, was the talk of Europe. Nordau, a former medical student, borrowed freely from the works of psychiatrists of his day, including England's Maudsley, Italy's Lombroso, France's Morel, and Germany's Richard Krafft-Ebing. "We stand now in the midst of a severe mental epidemic," he darkly announced, "a sort of black death of degeneration and hysteria." Critics accused him of being "soaked up to his neck in Darwinism."[37] Nordau's success as a popularizer of medical knowledge about emotional states was an eminent example of the dawning trend in public consciousness toward reliance on medical experts to interpret age-old feelings as symptoms of illness.

Degeneracy theory resembled phrenology in that both viewed the functions of the human mind as products of biological laws. Yet one crucial difference between phrenology and degeneracy theory was the overall tenor of phrenology, which optimistically stressed the improvability of human nature. By contrast, degenerationism captured the mood of a world wracked by terrorism, militarism, and class conflict and uneasy about future peace, progress, and prosperity.

Around the turn of the century, as fears about public security mounted in capitals such as Paris and London, some psychiatrists explicitly defended their social usefulness in the face of the "morally perverse" degenerates who roamed city and square. As one Russian psychiatrist declared in 1884, "One lone mad individual is capable of terrorizing an entire city."[38] An 1892 petition signed by German psychiatrists warned about the "horrendous murders" and the "butchery of entire families" committed by the mentally ill "in an incredibly large number of cases."[39] In 1903 a French psychiatrist cited the "massacres of innocents, victims of delirious individuals that indifference, fear, and ignorance permit to wander without care or surveillance in our towns and countryside." At no time in history had mental illness been so closely aligned with criminality as it was in the years leading up to World War I.[40] By the end of the nineteenth century, mental illness was widely viewed as a scourge that threatened the personal security of countless citizens and respectable families; it (and by extension its sufferers) were a distinct threat to life and limb. The earlier optimism surrounding the quest for mental health had evaporated amid serial concerns about dangerous persons with mental disabilities haunting the streets of the fin de siècle.

One reason for the appeal of degeneracy theory to psychiatrists was its capacity to rationalize the occupational troubles of asylum medicine as the nineteenth century drew to a close. Nothing explained away their growing custodial function like the theory that mental patients were beyond hope of recovery because of their ancestry. Psychiatrists from Russia to North America found it expedient to stress a theory that essentially blamed factors other than their inability to cure their patients. It helped psychiatrists, reeling from attacks on their scientific credibility, that degeneracy theory fit in well with the rising reputation of biological science. By employing the language of degeneracy theory to describe people with mental disabilities, psychiatrists increasingly forged an alliance with the state at a time when governments' involvement in mental health care policy continued to grow and when worries about law and order and national fitness were rife.

A RIGHT TO BE SICK

In the early twentieth century the alacrity with which degeneracy theory was received faded among mental health caregivers. Family studies on the inheritability of psychiatric illness continued throughout the twentieth century, confirming the hunches of physicians like Morel, Maudsley, and Lombroso, but the belief in a large class of patients united on the basis of their "degeneracy" rapidly fell out of favor in the years before World War I.

Meanwhile, the expanding – if uneasy – alliance between psychiatry and the state in the nineteenth century coincided with the rise of another medical specialty that quickly began playing a crucial role in the history of mental health care. Before the nineteenth century, neurology, the branch of medicine that studies the diseases of the nervous system, had been a sub-field of internal medicine, but after 1800 it impressively took off as outstanding researchers, including Paul Broca, Theodor Meynert, John Hughlings Jackson, and Carl Wernicke, made discovery after discovery about how disturbances in motor functioning could be traced to specific regions of the brain. For example, in 1874 the German Wernicke discovered the sensory speech center in the temporal lobe.

The main impetus behind the ascent of neurology, however, came from events outside the laboratory or dissection room. In the wake of the U.S. Civil War (1861–65) American physicians who treated soldiers with nervous tissue wounds began calling themselves neurologists. Similarly, many of the most illustrious German neurologists served as field doctors in the 1870–71 Franco-Prussian War, during which they encountered soldiers who exhibited nervous symptoms without any physical injuries. At the same time, a growing number of people were traveling at unprecedented speeds, routinely visiting far-flung parts of the world, and living in huge metropolises with a dizzying array of sensory stimuli. In 1879 Thomas Edison invented the electric lightbulb. Telephones and telegraphs rapidly became everyday modes of communication. The arrival of the cinema in the early decades of the twentieth century exposed countless viewers to a rapid succession of often intense images.

The series of innovations in military weaponry also heightened concerns about the impact of technology on human nervous health. As national armies and navies tested the latest products of arms manufacturers Krupp, Vickers, and Schneider-Creusot, some wondered how the human nervous system would be affected by such devices. The stage was set for the discovery of "shell shock" in the European war that many were expecting to break out at any time.

As the twentieth century approached, people increasingly viewed the nervous system as under attack from the grating sights, sounds, pace, and pounding of modern life. One German blamed "over-civilization" for his nervous breakdown in 1902.[41] The Rousseauian, late-eighteenth-century viewpoint that human health was incompatible with modern civilization was gaining impressive strength one hundred years later.

An early sign that modern civilization was taking a heavy toll on human nerves was the rising incidence of "railway spine," a condition first reported in 1866 by the English doctor John Erichsen. Railway spine, according to Erichsen, was produced by the shocks on the central nervous system from jarring accidents or simply the prolonged, jerking motion of railway travel, which began to climb in popularity as the century unfolded. Yet even before Erichsen's announcement about railway spine, Britain's Parliament in 1864 had made railway companies legally liable for the health and safety of their passengers. A series of court decisions in the United States as well as the advent of workmen's compensation laws in England and America established that railroads were responsible for injuries to railway passengers and industrial accidents.

In 1889 German chancellor Otto von Bismarck's *Reich* recognized "traumatic neuroses" when it included them as bona fide medical conditions covered by his government's landmark 1884 workmen's compensation legislation covering sickness, accidents, and disability. Within a few short years German workers were flooding hospitals, insisting that their job-related nervousness warranted compensation, sick leave, or pensions if they were disabled. Nervousness in turn-of-the-century Germany was fast becoming a mass condition. A sign of things to come in the twentieth century, the introduction of state or private insurance stimulated the reporting of emotional and nervous sickness. Democracy in the form of the welfare state extended benefits to the deserving poor, teaching the masses that they had a right to compensation for their disabilities.[42] What initially was a trickle of nervous patients soon became a comparative flood.

Modern society's assault on human nerves was nowhere more evident than in the bustling and rapidly growing German city of Berlin, capital of the new Wilhelmine *Reich*. Dubbed "Electropolis," Berlin to many observers was the nerve center of the Bismarckian Empire, a pulsating, urban goliath whose lights, power lines, machines, and popular press day and night played on the nervous systems of the entire population, notably workers such as railroad switchmen and telephone operators. As a burgeoning world city, Berlin was the archetypal hotbed of nervous collapse, the crossroads between medical specialists eager to recruit patients and a public feeling increasingly irritable, listless, excitable, or anxious due to a seemingly incessant barrage of stimuli.

Physicians calling themselves neurologists were quick to claim that they knew how civilization affected the nerves, and what to do about it. For their part patients readily accepted these claims and flocked to neurologists to complain of "nervous exhaustion," sleeplessness, ephemeral pains, headaches, mood swings, and digestive problems. Central Europe became the center for nerve doctors and clinics.

The trend toward treatment for nervous complaints benefited immensely from U.S. neurologist George Beard's 1869 coining of the term "neurasthenia," "*the* fatigue neurosis," as one physician called it at the turn of the century.[43] Patients told Beard and other neurologists that they had no energy, their stomachs hurt, their heads ached, they could not sleep, they were depressed, or they could not move their arms or legs. Patients worried about being labeled hysterics, hypochondriacs, or degenerates discovered that finally there was a diagnosis that exonerated them of blame for their illness. Thanks to neurasthenia, they could insist that their complaints were real (i.e., bodily in nature) and not just in their heads. Once again in modern history – though this time affecting more people – it became fashionable to suffer from "nerves." Neurasthenics claimed a "right to be sick."[44] After 1881, when Beard's treatise was translated into German, neurasthenia soon became a badge of honor for countless European patients who liked the idea that their busy, productive lives sapped their nervous energy. The research of nineteenth-century physiologists Hermann von Helmholtz and Paul Du Bois-Reymond had popularized both the electrical nature of the nervous impulse and the theory of the conservation of energy, which implied that each human being had a finite supply of energy. The idea caught on that one's nervous system was just a battery that could be either run down or boosted. Doctors turned to electro-therapy to rejuvenate their patients' nerves. They administered electrical currents to their patients by applying electrodes to heads, chests, backs, hands, feet, and genitalia. Electricity was viewed as both a treatment mode and a frame of reference for understanding how social existence weakened one's ability to function as a productive, modern citizen.

Some physicians declared that "neurasthenia" was just a fancy word for malingering or laziness, while others complained that it was a "dustbin" diagnosis that masked medicine's ignorance of what was really wrong. Despite this opposition, neurasthenia's fame (and that of its French close cousin "psychasthenia") spread far and wide. The long list of eminent neurasthenics included Florence Nightingale, Virginia Woolf, Theodore Reiser, Mark Twain, Emma Goldman, Marcel Proust, and Theodore Roosevelt (when he was young).

The U.S. neurologist S. Weir Mitchell (1829–1914), a onetime Union army surgeon in the Civil War, introduced the much ballyhooed "rest cure" for neurasthenia. The rest cure involved isolating (mostly female) patients in a home or sanatorium – without visitors, reading, or writing – and sending them to bed for a month or longer. A nurse would spoon-feed patients a steady diet of milk. Among the luminaries who underwent the rest cure were novelists Virginia Woolf and Edith Wharton. Charlotte

Perkins Gilman, the noted women's rights advocate, recounted with horror her own brush with the rest cure, in *The Yellow Wallpaper* (1892). Gilman described her treatment at Mitchell's hands in 1887 as symptomatic of the male profession's ignorance of women's mental health, but in the short term her allegations did little to discredit Mitchell's rest cure and the theory of neurasthenia.

In 1909 a French psychiatrist noted that "neurasthenia was on everyone's lips." At about the same time, a Berlin doctor claimed doctors' offices were being overrun by an "army of neurasthenic city dwellers." In the 1890s it appeared, as a German psychologist observed, that "the future belonged to the nerve doctor, that the twentieth century would be one of neurasthenia and its conquest, that as nerve doctor one was a made man."[45] Such predictions failed to materialize. By the 1960s the term "neurasthenia" had fallen out of fashion. By then, however, it had left a substantial mark. It paved the way for other diagnoses, notably post-traumatic stress disorder and the various anxiety-related disorders. The emergence at the end of the twentieth century of chronic fatigue syndrome – with its many similarities to neurasthenia – struck many as a case of old wine in new bottles, a reminder of how scientific metaphors help to rationalize a rapidly changing and stress-filled world for an anxious populace.[46] The fate of neurasthenia as a diagnosis was less important than its role in the widening definition of mental and nervous illness to encompass more and more everyday complaints humanity had lived with for millennia.

Were these kinds of nervous diseases the product of physicians' efforts to convince people they were sick when they were not? No one can deny that some doctors fueled the epidemic of nervous illnesses in the late nineteenth century with their propensity to label commonplace complaints with fancy words that suggested a bodily –and hence medical – condition. There are "medically correct" symptoms that mental and nervous patients often learn to exhibit because they anticipate that this is what their doctors expect to see in their patients on the basis of prevailing medical theories.[47] As the historian Edward Shorter has argued, the history of such illnesses involves a sort of "*pas de deux* between doctor and patient," a joint enterprise in which both parties play a crucial clinical role.[48] The medical profession may have been keen to expand its cultural authority and stimulate popular demand for its services, but the public was patently receptive to its messages about the links between nerves, fatigue, unhappiness, and sickness. To men and women who fell short of their own and society's standards of success, there was something flattering about a diagnosis that acknowledged that their fatigue-like symptoms were due to the fast pace of life. Women, who disproportionately suffered from neurasthenia, tended to find the neurasthenia label to their liking. American author Catherine Beecher (1800–78) confessed that "I am not able to recall, in my immense circle of friends and acquaintances all over the Union, so many as ten married ladies born in this country and century, who are perfectly sound, healthy, and vigorous." To women who were told their troubles were all in their heads or a "slight hysterical tendency," it was gratifying that medicine decreed them sick after all.[49]

In its promotion of neurasthenia and other nervous disorders, the medical profession was not simply imposing its will on a passive and innocent public. Organized medicine was just another player – though a powerful one – in the evolution of the democratic state, which, by steadily satisfying the "most urgent wants of the body" (in Alexis de Tocqueville's words) through the provision of "worldly welfare," escalated emotional longings among the millions of its citizens and subjects. By the end of the twentieth century such longings appeared to be insatiable.

ANTI-PSYCHIATRY

The advent of neurology signaled that asylum medicine's overall status was shaky in the late nineteenth century. The enormous scientific and popular interest in nervous illness took place largely beyond the field of asylum psychiatry. Asylum physicians could only look on in envy as neurologists tapped a more affluent and socially respectable patient market. Neurologists' patients tended to display more refined manners and tastes. While neurologists ran rest homes, the public perception was that psychiatrists managed madhouses, a contrast that deeply irked asylum physicians.

For their part, neurologists looked down their noses at psychiatrists. They prided themselves on their medical knowledge and derided that of psychiatrists'. In 1879 a U.S. neurologist attacked the very raison d'être of asylum psychiatry when he alleged that "sequestration" in a mental hospital was "not only unnecessary but positively injurious."[50] He asserted that "a general practitioner of good common sense, well-grounded in the principles of medicine, with such a knowledge of the human mind and of cerebral physiology and pathology as can be obtained by study, and familiar with all the clinical factors in his patient's history, is more capable of treating successfully a case of insanity than the average asylum physician."[51] In Germany physicians intent on doing research decided that their stints in asylum service were "scientifically barren." They spent so much time performing clinical and administrative tasks that they could not get to the lab. By the end of the nineteenth century, neurologists claimed that German asylums were scientific backwaters.[52]

The tensions between psychiatry and neurology were especially acute in the United States. Attacks on asylum psychiatry spawned the 1880 formation of the National Association for the Protection of the Insane and the Prevention of Insanity (NAPIPI). The organization, made up of a cross-section of medical and non-medical people, folded after only a few years of operation. Yet in defending the rights of people with mental disabilities, NAPIPI anticipated the twentieth-century democratization of the quest for mental health through the proliferation of grassroots groups involved in mental health care policy.[53]

The status of asylum psychiatry also suffered from the trend toward governments' assuming more and more responsibility for administering and funding public assistance to the socially and economically disadvantaged. In the United States, state governments created boards of charities that quickly began treating the asylum as simply one institution in a much larger network of public welfare facilities that included prisons, almshouses, and orphanages. In the 1880s future president of the United States Theodore Roosevelt, then a New York state assemblyman, was an avid sponsor of civil service reform that increased government oversight over the state's asylums, a move that predictably sparked howls of protests from Empire State psychiatrists.[54] Elsewhere, on the national level, governments assumed the responsibility for social welfare programs once entrusted to municipalities. Public asylum psychiatrists were caught in the middle of this sweeping international trend toward centralized regulation and control at the hands of state officials. Critics heaped abuse on asylum psychiatrists, who, it was routinely said, were indistinguishable from prison wardens. Many opinion makers believed that asylum medicine posed a threat to the rights of ordinary citizens.

Fanning the flames of anti-psychiatric sentiment was the growth of the press and the rise of high-circulation newspapers in the late nineteenth century, the first time the mass media played a major role in the quest for mental health. Up to the 1880s most of Europe's six thousand newspapers had no mass circulation. But the expansion of public schooling stimulated an increase in literacy, and magazines for the family and women readers thrived. European newspapers doubled in number between 1880 and 1900. Newspapers such as London's *Evening News* (1881) and *Daily Mail* (1896) sold millions of copies a day. Alongside the venerable

London *Times*, Paris's *Temps*, Berlin's *Kreuzzeitung*, and Vienna's *Neue Freie Presse*, and thanks to better printing technology as well as liberal press laws in many nations, new, inexpensive newspapers sprung up, including London's *Daily Telegraph*, the *New York World*, and Rome's *Messaggiero*. These new papers sought to appeal to the masses and often ran sensationalist headlines. In the United States, such papers were called the "yellow press" and, like the tabloids of a later age, published lurid articles about crime, sports, gossip, and human interest stories of love and adventure. The slogan of the new journalism was "what the people want."[55]

Among the stories that seemed to appeal to readers were exposés of life in mental hospitals. Over the course of the second half of the nineteenth century, such stories became commonplace. The *New York Tribune* described asylum wards as "holes not fit for a dog." In 1887 *New York World* reporter Nellie Bly went undercover as an asylum patient and told her story in a series for her paper, titled "Ten-Days in a Mad House."[56] A favorite human interest story of "yellow journalism" involved wrongful confinement in public asylums. In most countries there were two basic ways for someone to be committed to an insane asylum: either patients and/or their families could request admission, or the state could incarcerate mentally disturbed individuals for their own safety and society's. In either case, there was wide scope for abuse, and sometimes communities held public hearings to determine if any injustice had been done. When the asylum in question was a private establishment, suspicions were rife that its head doctor – eager to add another paying customer – was in cahoots with callous family members. In the case of public asylums, nineteenth-century libertarians argued that innocent people were being thrown into them because psychiatrists routinely defined strange behavior, political dissent, or counter-cultural opinions as symptoms of mental illness.

As the nineteenth century unfolded, press coverage of stories alleging wrongful confinement in asylums snowballed, aided and abetted by popular novels such as Henry Cockton's *Valentine Vox* (1840) and Charles Reade's *Hard Cash* (1863). In Victorian Britain anger over asylum psychiatry and commitment laws led to the appointment of parliamentary committees to look into the matter of confinement. In France opponents of the nation's 1838 law predicted that it merely gave the state a new means of imprisoning political enemies. Critics were fond of calling the asylum a latter-day Bastille and characterizing warrants for admission to asylums as a modern version of *lettres de cachet*, the notorious documents used by French kings prior to the 1789 revolution to throw political enemies into prison without trial. Amid the frequent regime changes in France between 1830 and 1871, the political opposition often found it expedient to attack psychiatry and the asylum system as a vicarious way of discrediting the sitting government. The ephemeral nature of such attacks became evident once psychiatry's critics entered government and proved to be just as supportive of asylum medicine as their predecessors. Standard complaints about asylum psychiatry reflected the overall reality that the specialty and the state had become close partners by the end of the nineteenth century.

ELIZABETH PACKARD

If any single group was vulnerable to unfair confinement, it was women – especially wives. Worries about men disposing of unwanted wives in asylums dated as far back as the writings of *Robinson Crusoe* author Daniel Defoe, who demanded that Parliament inspect private madhouses to prevent such abuses.[57] The first case of unfair confinement of a woman to draw extensive press coverage was that of Elizabeth Packard (1816–97). Packard, born in Ware, Massachusetts, was the wife of Congregationalist minister Theophilus Packard. Their marriage proved to be unhappy, chiefly because of Theophilus's impatience with Elizabeth's unorthodox beliefs, which included a deep interest in spiritualism. In 1860, as their marital relations deteriorated, Reverend Packard had Elizabeth committed to the Jacksonville Asylum in central Illinois, claiming that she was a danger to herself and their children.

In Illinois, as in many other localities and American states, a person could not be admitted to an asylum without a public hearing, but it was legal for a husband to admit his wife without the evidence required in other cases. Once behind the asylum's walls, Elizabeth began writing about her confinement, and in 1863 her husband removed her from the asylum and boarded her with a relative. When that did not work out, Elizabeth returned home, where Reverend Packard locked her in her room. Elizabeth then sued her husband, and after a five-day trial a jury declared her sane.

After her release Packard refused to retire quietly into private life. She became a pioneering advocate for the rights of people accused of mental illness – notably women. She founded the Anti-Insane Asylum Society and, marshaling all her persuasive skills, convinced the Illinois legislature to guarantee jury trials for all people admitted to the state asylum. Her outspokenness helped to spark an investigation of her former asylum physician, Andrew McFarland, whose later suicide was popularly blamed on Packard's campaign of vilification.

Packard was similar to other, spirited women activists of the time who campaigned for causes ranging from temperance to women's suffrage, and she also blazed a trail for later generations who were eager to demystify psychiatry and discredit mental hospitals. Yet Packard, unlike later anti-psychiatry activists, never denied the reality of mental illness, the scientific status of psychiatry, or the need for asylums.[58] Though a role model for later reformers, Elizabeth Packard was a product of her own time and place. She urged more – not less – government regulation of mental health care policy. She articulated the slowly emerging consensus that mental health care was too important to be left in the hands of asylum physicians alone and required thorough government oversight.

Thus, by the end of the nineteenth century the struggle to improve mental health was well under way. The century had witnessed momentous events, including the growing involvement of governments in mental health care policy. Throughout the industrialized world hundreds of either privately owned or taxpayer-funded asylums had been built to house people with mental disabilities. Two medical specialties dedicated to the study and treatment of mental and nervous diseases had been organized as professions and achieved breakthroughs in clinical and experimental medicine. Both elite and popular interest in mental health, as well as faith in psychiatric expertise, had never been higher in history. At the same time, the public – especially the poor – appeared to harbor a deep ambivalence about mental health policy: in Michael Ignatieff's words, the popular classes "were suspicious of institutions, but nevertheless supported them."[59] The public increasingly relied on state-run mental health and welfare programs – chiefly the asylum – and pressured governments to correct abuses that time to time cropped up in mental health care. Many underprivileged families gratefully discovered that the asylum was a place where relatives with disabilities could be cared for at state expense. Yet the burgeoning popular press tended to express a deep undercurrent of distrust of the state's motives as governments took mounting responsibility for the mental health of its citizens.

For their part, governments had trouble allaying these suspicions. Lawmakers repeatedly sent out conflicting signals about the aims of their policies, captured in the concept of "political medicine." As the nineteenth century ended, these cross-purposes characterizing the goals of mental health policy were becoming increasingly evident, but by that point the asylum's shortcomings were overshadowed by a deeper consensus that the asylum was one institution that mass society could no longer do without. The public had grave concerns about the power of psychiatry, but that did not translate into any groundswell in favor of returning to the pre-asylum era. Instead, whipped up by the media of the day, the public demanded more and more governmental involvement in and accountability for asylum medicine. The arrival of the asylum had not gone unopposed, but at the dawn of the twentieth century it had become such a familiar part of the social landscape that people found it difficult to imagine modern existence without it.

3

Mental Hygiene

In the twentieth century the search for mental health took people down both old and new avenues. As nation after nation mobilized to fight mental illness in the nineteenth century, the asylum grabbed most of the headlines as society's first line of defense. But while asylum populations may have been growing by leaps and bounds in the nineteenth century, the family and local community continued to serve on the front lines of care into the twentieth century. In most regions, by World War I more people with mental disabilities still lived outside the asylum than inside.

In the meantime, amid the overall cultural ferment of the early twentieth century, interest in both normal and abnormal psychology spread briskly throughout society. A burgeoning popular press fanned renewed scientific interest in old ailments like hysteria, as well as new psychological disorders such as neurasthenia. At the same time, an increasingly affluent and literate public, intent on unlocking the mysteries of the mind, dabbled in self-help approaches to mental wellness, including Christian Science, New Thought, and the Emmanuel movement. The idea of preventing mental illness also caught on widely, notably in the eugenics and mental hygiene movements, enabling medical specialists to investigate other opportunities beyond the walls of the asylum. By the outbreak of World War II, the asylum had tenaciously survived as an all-purpose site for treating people with mental disabilities, but the stage was set for both its swift demise and a major expansion in the egalitarian quest for mental well-being.

FAMILY MATTERS

Throughout history mental disabilities have struck down the wealthy and powerful as well as the poor and disenfranchised. For example, George Coles, a three-term premier of Prince Edward Island off Canada's east coast, suffered a nervous breakdown in 1866 and never truly recovered. By the time Coles's unhappy battle with mental illness ended at home in 1875, he had followed a well-worn path for people with mental disabilities throughout modern history. First hospitalized at the Saint John Asylum in New Brunswick and later at the Charlottetown asylum, Coles ended up being cared for at home by his family. His fate underlined how, despite the emergence of the modern asylum, family members continued to be key mental health caregivers.[1]

Not so long ago the striking burst of asylum building in the nineteenth century led historians to conclude that, over the same time period, the mental hospital steadily replaced the family and community as the center of care for people with mental disabilities. The asylum was certainly the most publicized option available to society, but it never came close to eliminating the centuries-old custom of caring for people with mental disabilities at home or in the community. In other words, the history of mental health care is not synonymous with the history of psychiatry.

Some historians, awed by the nineteenth century's "discovery of the asylum," have argued that the supremacy of the asylum introduced a new system of surveillance and discipline targeting the mentally ill, spearheaded by psychiatrists who in their role as "medical police" locked up the mad and the bad. The power of psychiatrists, so the argument goes, reached into the private precincts of the family and undermined its customary tolerance for kin with inconvenient mental and behavioral symptoms. Yet whatever social power psychiatrists enjoyed seldom went uncontested and co-existed with the heavy influence exerted by families and the public on mental health care practices. On close examination, the theory that psychiatrists were the new wardens of industrialized society, dictating who was or was not committed to the asylum, is not supported by the evidence. Normally, the committal process involved not just asylum physicians, but also family, friends, and local authorities, as well as general practitioners. Family decision making along the "road to the asylum" was often the pivotal factor in determining who ended up in a mental hospital – as well as why and when. The practice of mental health care at the grassroots level was never a purely top-down process imposed on a passive public.

Community involvement in mental health care included the practice of inquests before a civil court into the mental capacity of individuals to manage their own affairs. An originally English legal proceeding, especially popular in Scotland, the lunacy trial or commission in lunacy was adopted by various U.S. colonial jurisdictions such as New York and New Jersey.[2] Wherever they were held, lunacy trials – especially those of affluent individuals – were public events that ordinarily drew big crowds of curious and concerned onlookers. The lunacy trial, a civil and public process, involved judges, juries, and the calling of witnesses from the community, including neighbors, clergymen, policemen, and the like. It was designed chiefly to determine an individual's mental state, as well as the fate of the defendant's property and mode of treatment. What normally emerged from the lunacy investigation was a consensus about the welfare of persons whose behavior and emotional states raised questions about their ability to function as members of the community. By involving a host of non-medical figures, lunacy trials underscored the power that families, neighbors, and local officials exerted over methods of care that nineteenth-century psychiatrists dearly wished to dominate but ultimately could not.[3]

Even in Paris, where for much of the nineteenth century official asylum admissions (*placements d'office*) tended to be explicitly police matters, families had an important say in the treatment of people with mental disabilities. Parisian families were active users of asylum services. Up to the Franco-Prussian War (1870–71), most inmates were processed at the Paris Prefecture of Police. Patients, according to psychiatrist Valentin Magnan, often arrived "feeling that they have been imprisoned," upsetting status-sensitive relatives and making patients themselves more difficult to treat.

In 1876 a new form of "voluntary" committal was introduced which permitted families and patients to bypass the Prefecture of Police entirely and go straight to the asylum. (The fact that committal was "voluntary," however, did not mean that the consent of the patient was required.) Voluntary admissions proved to be popular, accounting for roughly half of all admissions to the Sainte-Anne asylum by the 1890s. Families ordinarily felt that by using the voluntary rather than the official process, their insane relatives were going to "a true hospital and not a prison," a comforting thought for fretful families. Under voluntary committal, families had the power to reclaim their relatives without the consent of the asylum doctor.[4]

The involvement of families in the decision to "knock on the door" of the asylum, as it was called in nineteenth-century France, can be traced to the continuing practice of caring for the mentally ill in extramural settings. A quarter century after the first public asylums for the poor insane were erected, the 1871 census of England and Wales found that the total of all people labeled "lunatics," "idiots," or "imbeciles" was close to 70,000, of whom almost 40,000 were in public institutions. Given the likely under-reporting of people with mental disabilities, it is safe to say that at least as many could be found outside as inside the asylum.[5] In Scotland the boarding-out of insane people in households with non-relatives had been going on long before it became official policy in 1857. In France in 1872 there were more registered insane people living at home than in the nation's mental hospitals. Even after the Montréal Lunatic Asylum, the Saint-Jean-de-Dieu asylum, and the Protestant Hospital for the Insane were founded in 1839, 1873, and 1881 respectively, the family continued to serve as a locus of care for the mentally ill in the greater Montréal area.[6]

In other parts of the world, family care of people with mental disabilities was even more pronounced. In Japan only 3,000 were confined in state mental hospitals as late as World War I, and on the eve of World War II that figure reached only 22,000 out of a population of more than 70 million. There, too, the family in its interaction with neighbors, local government, and asylum doctors played a key role in the institutionalization process.[7] Where industrialization and urbanization unfolded more slowly, as in overwhelmingly rural and peasant Russia, hearth and home continued to be far and away the main site of care for the mentally ill. As late as the reign of Nicholas II (1896–1917), the number of confined mentally ill persons was a drop in the bucket in contrast to the country's huge population. No matter where one traveled in the modern era, mental ill health was first and foremost a family experience.

The prevalence of home care for people with mental disabilities dictated that women bore the brunt of primary caregiving. For centuries women had been more likely than men to undertake the care of the sick and dying as a customary part of their nurturing role within the family, and that included the mentally disabled. When widows or widowers succumbed to depression, female neighbors often pitched in to provide elementary nursing, as well as cleaning and cooking. Additionally, when the mental health of husbands and fathers broke down, economic ruin stared families squarely in the face, and wives frequently became the main source of emotional and financial support.

Caring for people with mental disabilities within the household was never easy. In the 1830s, a New Jersey woman's thirty-three-year-old daughter kept the rest of the family up at night with her "loud and boisterous talk," violent mood swings, and hostility toward visiting friends and relatives. While everyone in the household was affected by the daughter's behavior, it was her mother whose physical and emotional resources were most seriously taxed. Abused women, threatened by their alcoholic husbands, sometimes used committal as a temporary means of defense against domestic violence. One Parisian woman had her drunken husband "voluntarily" committed to Sainte-Anne after he broke furniture, threatened to strangle her, and provoked complaints from neighbors.[8] The daily care of people with mental disabilities supplied by female kin helps to account for families' deep and enduring interest in coping strategies since the nineteenth century and their increasing reliance on the state to provide services to ease their burdens.

ORDINARY LIVING

To psychiatrists, the home was "generally the worst place that can possibly be found for the sufferer from mental disease," in the words of a British physician in 1862, but everyday life dictated that they work closely with families.[9] When institutional over-crowding forced asylum psychiatrists to be creative, they sometimes relied on families to care for convalescent patients through trial leaves or temporary release. In turn, families periodically consulted asylum doctors about how to treat relatives at home. Like it or not, in the discharge of their duties asylum psychiatrists repeatedly discovered that they had to co-operate with families.

Even as the rage among psychiatrists for "bricks and mortar" solutions was at its height, discussion of alternatives to the asylum never died out. One prominent option was the Gheel Lunatic Colony in Belgium, nowadays the site of a world-famous sanatorium. The origins of the Gheel Colony date back to the late sixth century and the tale of a beautiful Irish woman named Dymphna, the patron saint of dementia victims. Legend has it that Dymphna fled her incestuous father to Belgium, where he later found her and had her beheaded when she refused to surrender her celibacy. The story of her dramatic life spread far and wide, and by the fourteenth century pilgrims in search of a cure for mental afflictions were flocking to the Flemish shrine where she supposedly met her fate. The treatment regimen was heavily religious, featuring ceremonial offerings, processions, penances, and copious prayers. Over the years more and more accommodations were built for pilgrims, who were also boarded out with inhabitants of the village. Gheel earned a reputation as a place where people with mental disabilities could be either cured or boarded indefinitely with few restraints on their movements, and though secularized in the early nineteenth century, it continued to attract pilgrims who believed that a visit to the shrine could miraculously cure neurological and mental disorders. The Gheel model inspired efforts to find community-based alternatives to housing people with mental disabilities in large, public asylums.[10]

Interest in the Gheel model persisted for much of the nineteenth century, as visitors from around the world continued to flock to the Flemish village. Word of Gheel spread as far as British India, where colonial officials saw its potential in the absence of a public asylum system.[11] In the 1860s, as the first misgivings about asylums began to crop up, the topic of Gheel sparked lively debates across Germany and France. At the 1867 Paris World Exhibition, a Gheel proponent from Austria exhibited a model for family care patterned after the Belgian village.

Still, professional resistance to the Gheel model remained stiff. "Perfectly utopian and absurd" was the verdict of a British psychiatrist in 1862. At the end of the century France and Germany launched several family care initiatives, but the chief reason was to relieve asylum overcrowding, not any faith in the inherent merit of the Gheel program. Where such family care provisions existed, psychiatrists considered them little more than appendages to nearby, overcrowded asylums. As one Berlin psychiatrist argued in the 1920s, the Gheel model was at best a regrettable necessity in emergency circumstances.[12]

Further east in late-nineteenth-century Russia, a handful of psychiatrists proposed their own version of deinstitutionalization, introducing community care programs in which non-threatening patients would be boarded out in foster homes. However, Russian psychiatrists were no different than their counterparts elsewhere. They remained emotionally and intellectually wedded to the asylum; boarding-out and other alternative methods were only release valves for asylums congested with incurable patients.[13]

Psychiatrists had reasons to be skeptical about community care. Much household care was substandard and some even cruel. Locking away people with mental disabilities was not uncommon, nor was physical and sexual abuse. Yet privacy was not tantamount to cruelty. In Scotland, where boarding-out was official policy, the aim was to make the insane boarder an accepted member of the family, anticipating the twentieth-century theory of "normalization," which advocated the inclusion of people with disabilities in mainstream settings of "ordinary living," rather than confining them to special institutions.

By the end of the nineteenth century people were growing increasingly uneasy about the family as a primary care provider. Was this due to psychiatrists browbeating the public into believing that home care was no care at all? Was it because the various outbursts of fin-de-siècle moral panic over "degenerates" roaming the streets led people to prefer custodial approaches to mental illness? Or was it due to society itself gradually coming to the conclusion that the welfare of the mentally ill was better served when they were in the hands of psychiatrists? The likelihood is that as the nineteenth century unfolded, psychiatrists became more and more sensitive to the family's burdens and more skilled at winning relatives' confidence in their healing powers and moral probity. A kind of alliance between the family and psychiatry had materialized by the dawn of the twentieth century due to propagandizing on medicine's part, but also because relatives and friends continued to play a role in shaping modes of mental health practice at a time when the family still found itself on the front lines of care. As much as families and asylum doctors might eye each other warily in everyday matters, they shared a common belief in the virtues of medical approaches to mental health care.[14]

CHURCH AND PSYCHOTHERAPY

As the family and the medical profession struggled to care for the seemingly inexhaustible pool of people with mental disabilities at the turn of the twentieth century, a wave of populist movements stressing spiritualism, supernaturalism, parapsychology, telepathy, hypnotism, the paranormal, and the occult swept across polite society in Europe and North America. The headquarters for most of these currents was the United States, with its powerful streak of egalitarianism and its vibrant cultural climate of self-improvement. These cultural trends reflected a mass craving for emotional wellness among the educated classes that steadily filtered down to other classes of society as the twentieth century wore on. What united all these trends was the optimism that everything from unhappiness and anxiety to physical handicaps could be cured through the power of the human mind. Popular demand for mental health services took one of its biggest leaps in modern history.

Physicians, trained to believe in material causes of illness, considered these myriad theories of mental healing to be little more than superstitions.

To the Viennese neurologist Sigmund Freud, they were a peculiar mix of "church and psychotherapy," a tempting combination for a public that "has always had a certain weakness for everything that savors of mysteries and the mysterious." That literacy and levels of schooling were climbing, and official support for science and technology was never higher, made the trend all the more baffling to Freud, who liked to think of himself as a hard scientist. In his opinion, there was "absolutely nothing mysterious" about the theories behind the mind cure movement, but to his profound dismay many outside – and some inside – the scientific community did not share his views.[15]

The social foundations of this wide-ranging interest in mental healing can be traced to both improving physical health and spreading affluence throughout Western society as the nineteenth century drew to a close. Over the course of the century the diets of all social classes had improved markedly, if unevenly. Average nineteenth-century citizens were better fed than any of their ancestors. Technologies such as vacuum canning, steam-ships, and refrigeration drove down food prices, and the introduction of the potato alone stimulated food consumption.

Alongside the dietary revolution of the nineteenth century, the incidence of infectious and contagious diseases was falling fast. In the waning years of the century governments responded to the advice of public health advocates by building new housing, cleaning streets, draining cesspools, quarantining communities, regulating water supplies, and inspecting food and drugs. These and other measures were designed to prevent disease, and by the early twentieth century mortality related to tuberculosis, cholera, typhoid, diphtheria, and similar killer diseases was falling impressively while life expectancy was on the rise. The incidence of cancer was inching upward, too, but jubilation over the results of the war on contagious illnesses drowned out the sporadic concerns voiced over the incidence of chronic diseases.

As fears about malnutrition and infectious diseases began to recede in the last decades of the nineteenth century, people grew more and more attuned to their emotions. Expanding prosperity meant more time for education and leisure activities rather than routine physical labor and the dreary day-to-day toil to survive, and more time to dwell on personal feelings and one's innermost thoughts. As essayist Agnes Repplier noted in 1914, a "repeal of reticence" was sweeping much of English-speaking society as educated men and women grew increasingly willing to talk openly about formerly intimate, taboo topics – notably sex, reproduction, and death.[16] Some argued that the repeal of reticence merely coarsened and degraded emotional experience, but women activists such as America's Margaret Sanger, Germany's Agnes Bluhm, and England's Marie Stopes and Annie Besant advocated a new frankness about sex and reproduction that flouted nations' obscenity laws and moral codes. Mental health experts urged the same candor about dreams, hallucinations, multiple personality, and other involuntary mental acts long viewed as inferior to the operations of the rational mind. The repeal of reticence was fiercely contested in numerous quarters and never quite reached revolutionary levels in the early twentieth century. Until the 1960s public opinion in all countries remained solidly traditional on a wide range of private matters. Yet as the twentieth century wore on, the reticence surrounding these matters receded, including discussion of the topic of mental health itself. The stigma surrounding mental disabilities remained strong, but with the introduction of the term "neurasthenia" to describe depression and overall malaise, it was no longer so embarrassing for individuals to admit openly that they suffered emotionally.

The readiness to discuss unconventional forms of psychological experience coincided with a striking social trend whose origins stretched back to the days of Mesmer's theory of "animal magnetism." In the late eighteenth century the mesmerist Marquis de Puységur had discovered "somnambulism," the waking sleeplike state that seemingly rendered certain individuals susceptible to both spoken and unspoken commands, as well as an astonishing ability – dubbed "clairvoyance" – to read others' thoughts, find hidden objects, and predict the future. Puységur argued that an induced form of somnambulism was a cure for nervous disorders.[17] Somnambulism appeared to open up enormous new vistas in psychology and proved to be a prime factor in the rise of "dynamic psychiatry," the study of the immaterial operations of the mind in the hope of unlocking the key to curing mental diseases.[18] Thanks to Puységur and likeminded nineteenth-century therapists, the belief gradually took hold in the social and medical sciences that the mind had slipped its moorings in the organic brain and was now open for the first time to in-depth study. At the dawn of the twentieth century the possibilities for psychological healing appeared to be endless.

ESCAPE FROM MATERIALISM

Once it was accepted that altered states of consciousness empowered certain individuals, there seemed to be little standing in the way of people communicating with the unseen world of spirits and souls. Thus, over the course of the nineteenth century an ever-growing number of well-heeled and well-educated people consulted mediums, patronized astrologers and palmists, attended séances, and avidly followed research into mysterious phenomena such as hypnotism, dreams, sleepwalking, multiple personality, materialization, levitation, and automatic writing. The spiritualist movement was so well entrenched by 1900 that Théodore Flournoy's *From India to the Planet Mars*, an account of the celebrated nineteenth-century medium Hélène Smith and her interplanetary psychic visions, far outsold Sigmund Freud's *The Interpretation of Dreams*, published that same year.[19]

A series of events that did more than anything else to launch the modern spiritualist movement featured the celebrated 1848 antics of the two teenage Fox sisters from Hydesville, New York. In séance after séance the Fox sisters enthralled hundreds of onlookers with their supposed ability to communicate with the dead. By 1853, amid a stunning proliferation of journals and books on spiritualism, there were already 30,000 mediums in America alone. The rage for spiritualism even invaded the White House. Presidential first lady Mary Todd Lincoln organized séances so she could communicate with her son Willie, who died in 1862. Overseas, spiritualism also flourished. During his exile on the Island of Jersey in the 1850s, Victor Hugo, author of *Les misérables*, repeatedly tried to communicate with a daughter who had drowned ten years earlier and in a series of séances claimed to communicate with Moses, Socrates, Plato, Jesus, Voltaire, and other notables from history. In 1869 estimates pegged the total number of spiritualists in America at 4 million, with 1 million in Europe (including 600,000 in France).[20] The 1889 Congrès spirite et spiritualiste international drew 40,000 participants to Paris from all over the world.

Such trends spilled over from the parlor into the laboratory when in 1882 a group of Cambridge philosophers and scientists founded England's Society for Psychical Research. Eminent scientists such as Cesare Lombroso, Oliver Lodge, Pierre Janet, Nobel Prize winner Charles Richet, and Alfred Russel Wallace (co-discoverer of the theory of evolution according to natural selection) advocated the rigorous study of the full range of psychical phenomena. The movement continued into the interwar period as a series of international conferences brought together researchers and practitioners from a variety of European, American, and Asian countries. The scientific credibility of spiritualism plunged after World War II, but its status as a kind of religion remained strong into the early twenty-first century in countries such as Vietnam and Brazil.

The vigor of the spiritualist movement in America and France, the world's two oldest republics, derived from its appeal to people who valued transparency and inclusiveness. There was a strong egalitarian element to the movement, empowering people from all walks of life to believe they did not need licensed doctors to explain their heartfelt longings. Yet unquestionably a major cause of these fads and fashions was the mass death toll due to modern warfare. Beginning with the U.S. Civil War (1861–65) an enormous outpouring of grief, surpassing anything witnessed in hundreds of years, swept across the industrialized world. The Civil War's horrendous death toll (620,000) launched the republic into a "new relationship with death," according to historian Drew Gilpin Faust.[21] The war's carnage meant that few households were spared the loss of a loved one, and grief-stricken kin repeatedly speculated about the fate of their departed. Countless families were never able to recover the bodies of their slain men, and many turned to spiritualism in the form of séances and table tapping in a desperate effort to deal with the pain of bereavement.

The equivalent of America's Civil War experience with death was postponed in Europe until 1914, when World War I broke out. When it came to death and dying, Victorians in England had devised alternative rituals of grief and mourning rather than give up a belief in angels, spirits, souls, and the afterlife. Then came the staggering casualties of 1914–18, unleashing mass mourning on an unprecedented scale. More than 700,000 British soldiers lost their lives, including a high percentage of well-educated middle- and upper-class officers. France's suffering was even greater: 1.3 million Frenchmen were killed, the highest per capita rate of all the major powers in World War I, so it is no accident that support for psychical research and spiritualism blossomed in France in the 1920s. Many single families lost more than one son. The emotional pain of surviving family members was acute. One Englishwoman recalled that after her brother's death on the western front:

> I was haunted by the most terrible recurring nightmares that he had not been killed but was lost somewhere, insane and helpless, and that I could never reach him, though often he was near. These nightmares were always accompanied by that unearthly depth of sorrow, horror and freezing terror that one only experiences in dreams.[22]

Numerous individuals, such as Sir Arthur Conan Doyle, the creator of the literary character Sherlock Holmes, refused to accept the finality of their own losses and by way of reassurance affirmed the reality of an afterlife

where their loved ones resided, able and presumably eager to communicate with their kin through the spiritual world. By the end of the war the
number of societies affiliated with the spiritualist movement had doubled
since 1913. Membership in the English branch of the movement kept
growing until the 1930s, when it peaked at about a quarter of a million.
By then it was obvious that war-related grief had unleashed a mammoth
wave of unhappiness that crashed over Europe after 1914, fostering an
intense longing for a different reality behind the pain and sorrow of the
mundane, physical world.

Mediumism was a truly mass movement. To many observers in the late
nineteenth century, this interest in and longing for a mysterious realm
beyond the accepted precincts of science – what one historian called
the desire to "escape from materialism" – was a defining aspect of the
age.[23] It succeeded in spreading the idea that a sphere beyond the senses
and material world contained secrets that could ultimately satisfy deep
emotional needs.

Thanks to this widespread "lure of the invisible," mesmerism made a
comeback in the late nineteenth century, stimulating fashionable interest in hypnosis. At the center of this fad was the Paris-based neurologist
Jean-Martin Charcot, whose own interest in hypnosis spiked in the late
1870s, thanks to the research of future Nobel Prize–winning physiologist Charles Richet. As the *Times* reported in 1892, "Some of the most
advanced practitioners in Paris are being led back to processes and theories strangely like Mesmer's own, but even more transcendental."[24]

To Charcot and most of his colleagues in medicine, Mesmer's old theory about magnetic fluids pervading the natural world was nonsense, but
hypnosis – which produced many of the same effects as mesmerism –
could be explained by the latest advances in physiology and physics.
Hypnosis was also viewed as a means for exploring that strange affliction
called hysteria. By that point in his career Charcot – a born showman –
was a medical and social celebrity whose lectures on hysteria drew over-
flow crowds at the Salpêtrière hospital in Paris. Physicians and the public
were fascinated by hysteria's many dramatic symptoms – blindness, fits,
seizures, paralysis, an inability to speak. Despite Charcot's claim that
men could be hysterical too, hysteria's links to women's health added to
its theatrical attraction. The age-old theory that hysteria originated in the
uterus was in steep decline, but specialists in gynecology still argued that
its causes lay in women's sexual and reproductive organs.

In the 1880s, with the help of hypnosis, Charcot put hysteria squarely
on the medical and cultural map, its notoriety soon rivaling that of

neurasthenia. Before the assembled throngs of deferential students and curious onlookers in his crowded, brightly lit lecture amphitheaters, Charcot hypnotized patient after patient and dramatically produced the colorful symptoms of hysteria by merely suggesting them. Later it was revealed that Charcot's assistants had coached his patients, but in the short term, Charcot's scientific prominence helped to make hypnosis a respectable topic of research while also articulating a kind of diffuse disenchantment with impersonal naturalism and secularism. His studies raised the fascinating question, Could psychological and physical disorders be actually mental in origin? The crucial lesson many drew from Charcot's teachings was that if it was easy enough to manufacture the symptoms of hysteria through hypnosis, then it ought to be just as easy to get rid of them using similar, mentalist means. And if it was so easy to make such symptoms come and go, logic dictated that a medical degree was not necessary to heal a broken mind.

A FEELING OF SELF

The populist applications of this message were most evident on the other side of the Atlantic, where faith in the ordinary person's inner light burned brightly and the healing power of grassroots religion was a belief shared by millions. There the American penchant for mind cures, keenest in New England, spread far and wide in the second half of the nineteenth century. The chief currents within the mind cure movement included Christian Science, New Thought, and the Emmanuel movement. Though they differed to one extent or another, they all shared the conviction that thoughts and feelings had a huge impact on the body. As most everyone knew, love altered one's heartbeat and fear affected one's breathing. Surely, then, mental processes could be harnessed to fight disease. In the words of the Boston Metaphysical Club, founded in 1895, the mind cure movement was designed to

> promote interest in and the practice of a true philosophy of life and happiness; to show that through right-thinking, one's loftiest ideals may be brought into present realization; and to advance intelligent and systematic treatment of disease by spiritual and mental methods.[25]

The mind cure movement drew inspiration from the writings of eighteenth-century Swedish mystic Emanuel Swedenborg (1688–1772). A scientist for most of his adult life, Swedenborg became disenchanted with the study of the physical universe when, in his fifties, his eyes were "opened to the spiritual world." From then on he claimed to pass back and forth between the material and spiritual worlds, communing with angels and visiting both heaven and hell. Some of Swedenborg's devotees in the nineteenth and twentieth centuries felt uneasy about his claims to have conversed with angels, but because his teachings seemed to prove that mental healing was a respectable exercise of mind over matter they were happy to invoke his memory.[26]

Shortly thereafter, the U.S. mental healing fad began with a New Hampshire clock maker's apprentice named Phineas P. Quimby (1802–66). As a young man, Quimby came down with tuberculosis and took calomel prescribed by a physician but soon came to the conclusion that people were cured of illness not by drugs but by their faith in their healers. Wrong belief and false reasoning caused disease, according to Quimby, and he started to dabble in mesmerism, hypnosis, and mental suggestion. Quimby began attracting followers drawn to his message that the visible world – what he called "the shadow of Wisdom's amusements" – was merely the outward manifestation of a more enduring, non-material reality. With Quimby's revelation the New Thought movement was born and, though poorly organized, claimed almost 100,000 adherents by the onset of the twentieth century. The International New Thought Alliance, consisting of groups from around the world, was founded in 1915 in London.

Almost as many adherents belonged to the Church of Christ, Scientist, founded by Quimby disciple Mary Baker Eddy, who, though she later bitterly broke with her mentor, concurred that right thinking could banish illness. Eddy was strongly bound to biblical Christianity, unlike Quimby, and looked to Jesus Christ, the ultimate healer, as the source of her curative power. Eddy was convinced that since the world was a product of God's thought, the millennium was not some event in distant time but already existed. Using thought, human beings could create reality just as God did. Deliverance in the form of health was at hand, Eddy and her disciples preached. Together Christian Science and New Thought drew a mostly white, Protestant, native-born following of white-collar men and educated women, but their opinions were anything but conventional. Many women attracted to New Thought demanded equal access to positions of spiritual leadership, freedom from the male medical elite, and the right to sexual pleasure.[27]

The burgeoning number of mass circulation newspapers and magazines in the early twentieth century conveyed to hundreds of thousands of Americans on a regular basis the message of mental healing. Highbrow

Harvard University philosopher William James wrote approvingly about "American religious therapy" in mainstream publications. Women's magazines such as *Good Housekeeping* and *Ladies' Home Journal* carried story after story about mental healing. In 1907 *Good Housekeeping* featured advice by a British spiritualist and psychic researcher on how "to Become Beautiful by Thought."[28]

Dismissed by acerbic journalist H. L. Mencken as "optimistic taffy" for "women with vague pains and inattentive husbands," mental healing nonetheless captured the avid imagination of people in the United States and beyond.[29] Mencken was only one of many skeptics who scoffed at the movement, but the belief in the power of positive thinking to radically change personal lives persisted for the rest of the century. In the 1950s clergyman Norman Vincent Peale's *The Power of Positive Thinking* was a runaway best seller, testimony that a century after Quimby's death his spirit was alive and well.

VIRTUOUS HEALTH

Organized medicine tended to take a patronizing attitude toward New Thought and Christian Science, which, it believed, were outright quackery, but the medical profession was more conflicted about the Emmanuel movement. Its founder was the Reverend Elwood Worcester, rector of Boston's Emmanuel Episcopal Church from 1904 to 1929. Worcester's interests took him to Europe, where he was exposed to Charcot's ideas and the work of noted Leipzig experimenter Gustav Fechner, whose cutting-edge research focused on the energy relationship between nerve stimulation and bodily reaction. Worcester returned to the United States armed with a Ph.D. and the belief in the "soul as a living organism" and proceeded to open a clinic dedicated to treating "unhappy, unstable men and women" in the Boston area. Like Mary Baker Eddy he imagined he was continuing the "healing ministry of Jesus," but unlike Eddy he collaborated with a variety of reputable doctors, including his close friend S. Weir Mitchell.[30]

The Emmanuel movement sprung to life on November 11, 1906, when to Worcester's amazement 198 people showed up on his church's doorsteps looking for mental healing. For the next few years Worcester and his colleagues assiduously worked to provide therapeutic services to a patient pool that only seemed to grow as the press avidly publicized the goings-on at his pastoral clinic. So great was media interest in the Emmanuel movement that *Ladies' Home Journal* offered Worcester

$8,000 – a sizable sum in those days – to write a series of articles on his approach to psychotherapy.

Despite early encouragement from physicians, Worcester's Emmanuel movement rapidly lost its medical support amid rumors that, among other things, cancer was being treated with mental suggestion. The differences between clergyman and doctor were often fuzzy in the Emmanuel movement, leading one erstwhile medical defender to admonish clergymen to stick to comforting patients and leave the business of curing them to physicians. A grave concern of physicians – whose social status was still somewhat shaky – was that patients would flee the doctor's waiting room for the minister's study. Worcester's brand of psychotherapy was just "one more gospel from New England, once the land of witchcraft," a Baltimore psychiatrist sardonically reminded his readers. In 1909, with press coverage flagging, the Emmanuel clinic closed.[31]

Yet Worcester was undaunted and continued his work through an independent foundation. Meanwhile, the Emmanuel movement spread far and wide. Versions of Worcester's therapy were reported in operation in Brooklyn, Buffalo, Detroit, Chicago, Seattle, and San Francisco, as well as England, Ireland, Australia, South Africa, and Japan. Protestants from various churches joined, as did Jews and Roman Catholics. Worcester's teachings had an enormous impact on the twentieth-century history of psychotherapy. His views challenged medical resistance to lay treatment, triggered interest in group therapy, and addressed the vast emotional needs that the medical profession at the time seemed unable to meet. In the midst of rising addiction rates, the Emmanuel movement spawned the Jacoby Club, whose programs to combat drunkenness ultimately became Alcoholics Anonymous (AA) in 1935. In its early years AA, a society that offered fraternal support to problem drinkers, eschewed medical approaches to alcoholism and promised a 50 to 60 percent recovery rate, far more than the medical profession could claim with its various therapies. Seventy years later, AA had 2.2 million members worldwide.

Thus, in the early twentieth century, when the presence of organized medicine in Western society was still generally thin, the Emmanuel movement and its spinoff organizations helped to fill a gaping void created by the mounting thirst for emotional and physical wellness in various communities around the world. The medicalization theory of history, according to which organized medicine steadily quashed grassroots self-healing, does not apply to an age that witnessed a resurgence of un-churched religious yearning for spiritual ease. As S. Weir Mitchell admitted in the late nineteenth century, the physician who treated people with nervous complaints was more priest than medical scientist and medicine was akin to a religious calling. "So great is my reverence for supreme wholesomeness," he announced, "that I should almost be tempted to assert that perfect health is a virtue."[32]

As the twentieth century began to unfold, for the first time in history a broad-based public hunger for psychological healing was forming, making the rage for "animal magnetism" in Mesmer's day seem puny by comparison. The evolution of this trend in favor of mental healing sharply varied from one country to another, but its progress was unmistakable. A nerve doctor like S. Weir Mitchell, who suspected he was more priest-confessor than hard scientist, never lacked converts to the new and growing faith in mental healing.

TALKING CURES

Despite his caustic opinions about popular mind cures, no psychologist benefited more from the notoriety of Christian Science and New Thought than Sigmund Freud. And few public figures did more to bolster these movements than Freud himself, though he hardly intended it that way. In the early twentieth century any American reading a newspaper, or subscribing to a popular magazine, or worshipping at a mainstream Protestant church would be aware that everyday respectable people around the country were being cured of their emotional troubles without drugs. By the time Freud visited the United States on a 1909 lecture tour, the country was poised to welcome the Viennese physician who claimed to have discovered how to make patients less nervous by harnessing the power of the mind.

Until his 1909 arrival on America's shores, the most important stop in Freud's journey to twentieth-century celebrity status was his stay in Paris in 1885–86. At the time, Freud was a young, aspiring neurologist whose burgeoning interest in psychological trauma took him to France's capital to study under the flamboyant Jean-Martin Charcot. Neurologists like Charcot tended to emphasize hysteria's roots in the curious process by which emotional conflicts were converted into bodily disorders. Other French researchers, including psychiatrist Pierre Janet, shared Charcot's interest in hypnosis, hysteria, and suggestion. Indeed, Janet too visited America and lectured at Harvard University, Columbia University, and Johns Hopkins University, setting the stage for Freud's stateside travels. To observers like Freud the exciting lesson of Charcot's teachings was that hysterical symptoms could come and go with the right kind of psychological persuasion. Freud concluded, based on hints from Charcot himself, that the core cause of hysteria lay in some traumatic event earlier in life – in all likelihood sexual in nature.

Freud's admiration for Charcot's theories coincided with a wave of rich, medical writings about the concept of trauma. Before the watershed decade of the 1870s, researchers had used the term "trauma" mainly to describe the physical effects of violent blows to the body. By the 1880s physicians had extended the meaning of trauma to include the psychological effects of shocks to the nervous system, such as "railway spine." New studies reported that patients sometimes concealed the memories of trauma because of embarrassment or shame. For women such hurtful memories often hid secrets involving seduction, rape, or incest. To Charcot's rival Pierre Janet, digging out these memories from a patient's resistant mind opened up a vast world of emotional pain that threatened to overturn comfortable medical assumptions about mental functioning.

When Freud returned to Vienna after his stay in Paris, he opened a private practice and in the 1890s experimented with hypnosis as a means of uncovering the memories of such unpleasant events. Yet he claimed that he soon discovered two things: that memories of sexual traumas frequently led back to childhood events and that not all patients were hypnotizable. At that stage he began using the free-association method, asking patients to say whatever came into their minds. One of Freud's patients dubbed psychoanalytic therapy "the talking cure."

Freud also started to suspect that dreams might be the key to the subconscious mind, and so he asked his patients to recount theirs. At the same time, Freud underwent a self-analysis, systematically examining and decoding his own dreams in an emotion-laden attempt to uncover his personal history as a child. His studies of dreaming culminated in his landmark *The Interpretation of Dreams* (1900), the cornerstone of what he called psychoanalysis, his distinct theory of psychology.

After the publication of *The Interpretation of Dreams*, Freud's notoriety as an unorthodox therapist spread. People suffered from hysteria, Freud daringly argued, because their minds had suppressed memories of childhood sexual seduction at the hands of parents. To uncover these reminiscences, Freud advocated, therapists needed to be schooled in the science of dream interpretation.

Saying childhood seduction lay at the roots of hysteria was disturbing enough to his audiences, but Freud went even further: he insisted that in most cases his patients' confessions of traumatic seductions were not historically true. They were, in his own words, "emotionally-charged fiction." Freud maintained that children were not the sexual innocents that society imagined but libidinous creatures who were prone to their own perverse fantasies about their parents and other kin.[33]

Freud's preference for a psychological interpretation of mental health sparked opposition from the medical community, notably German-speaking neurologists who insisted that the path to understanding the mind always led back to brain anatomy and physiology. Freud's emphasis on sexuality triggered other instances of backlash, such as the accusation by an English doctor in 1914 that Freud was disseminating a "new pornography." Yet resistance to Freud's theories was never as concerted as he later alleged, and beginning in central Europe, psychoanalysis in the interwar era spread to one country after another. "We are all psychoanalysts now," England's *New Statesman* declared in 1923.[34]

In France Freud's popularity was delayed until the post–World War II years. Elsewhere, however, Freudianism made deeper inroads. Membership in the British Psycho-analytic Society jumped from 92 in 1939 to 175 in 1954. The American Psychoanalytic Association grew in membership from 92 in 1932 to about 1,300 in 1968. By that date in America, there was one psychoanalyst for every thirteen psychiatrists. In American universities, by the 1950s more than half of the chairmen of psychiatry departments belonged to psychoanalytic societies. It was virtually impossible to get a U.S. academic post in psychiatry without being psychoanalyzed. By the 1960s psychoanalysis had captured U.S. psychiatry, so much so that the two were well nigh indistinguishable: when the public thought of psychiatrists they imagined healers who, resembling Freud himself, had German accents, pointy beards, and therapists' couches.[35]

In introducing the world to psychoanalysis, Freud had imagined he was a scientific revolutionary, no less important than Copernicus, Newton, and Darwin. Yet he was not as pioneering as he and his disciples maintained. In addition to the widespread public interest in spiritualism, mind cures, and religious healing, Freud was part of a sizable wave of scientific research into sleep, dreams, sexuality, and the unconscious that swept the Western world around the turn of the twentieth century. Freud, like many other researchers in these fields, was heavily indebted to Darwinist biology. Freud liked to propagate the view that he was a lonely genius marooned in a hyper-traditionalist culture that rejected his ideas out of hand, but the reality was nowhere near that stark.[36]

In fact, psychoanalysis deeply penetrated twentieth-century thought. Freud lived long enough to see psychoanalysis twisted and tweaked in the service of diverse agendas. Franz Alexander, who after moving from

Berlin founded the Chicago Institute for Psychoanalysis in 1932, applied
Freudianism to internal medicine and founded the theory of psychosomatic medicine, according to which mental conflicts were able to manifest
themselves in such physical ailments as hypertension, asthma, dermatitis,
and irritable bowel syndrome. Follower Wilhelm Reich reduced all of
Freudianism to the notion that guilt-free, pleasurable sex culminating in
the orgasm was the cure for all psychic conflicts, an idea that appalled
the straitlaced Freud. Swiss-born Carl Jung, the man Freud once wanted
to succeed him as head of the psychoanalytic movement, rejected Freud's
theory that psychological disorders could be traced back to infantile
sexuality. Freud later ran him out of the psychoanalytic movement amid
veiled accusations that Jung was an anti-Semite, but Jung went on to
become at least as well known and influential as Freud. By the end of
the twentieth century, Jungian psychology counted millions of adherents
around the world.

Nowhere was the deviation of psychoanalysis from Freud's own
beliefs more evident than in the United States, yet nowhere else did psychoanalysis enjoy so much success. Initially, in Germany, France, Spain,
and other countries, psychoanalysis caught on mainly in educated circles
due to its usual association with the cultural avant-garde and political
radicalism, including feminism and socialism, two political causes for
which Freud himself had no sympathy. But the popularization of Freud's
ideas happened faster in the United States, where it seemed to represent a
healthy break with past practices rather than an abrupt revolution in values. By the 1920s the risqué reputation of Freud's theories had seeped into
popular culture. The words of a popular 1925 song warned its audience,
"Don't tell me what you dream'd last night / For I've been reading Freud."
An onstage flapper proclaimed in a 1927 play, "Don't you know, mother,
that everybody's thoughts are obscenely vile? That's psychology." By the
Great Depression, the popular perception of psychoanalysis as a modern,
scientific brand of self-knowledge had taken root in American culture.[37]

Psychoanalysis caught on in the United States because countless
Americans thought it justified their sunny optimism that all problems
could be licked with the right methods, something the more pessimis-
tic Freud clearly did not believe. In later years Freud developed bleak
theories such as the death instinct, the notion that the organism harbored a "force" or "drive" toward its own destruction. Yet American
psychoanalysts reshaped these gloomy ideas to justify a faith that education and social reform could make people happier. Where Freud had
emphasized the conflict between human desire and civilization's mores

and institutions, U.S. psychoanalysts amiably preached how individuals could adapt to social reality with the right dose of information and professional help. The figure of the psychoanalytically inclined psychiatrist showed up in Hollywood movies, such as *The Three Faces of Eve* (1957), Alfred Hitchcock's *Psycho* (1960), and John Huston's *Freud* (1962). In defiance of Freud's own view that laypeople were quite capable of being analysts too, the U.S. medical community – while accepting psychoanalysis – restricted its practice to licensed doctors. If Freud had been alive in 1956, he would most likely have objected strenuously to how U.S. psychoanalysis had evolved, but he could hardly have disagreed with one observer who noted that year that psychoanalysis had become about as "controversial as the American flag."[38]

Scant decades later, however, Freud's legacy was in shambles. Scientists complained that Freud's theories simply could not be verified experimentally. Researchers could find no empirical evidence that Freudian therapy worked. Feminists accused him of misogyny, and therapists tasked with recovering patients' traumatic memories charged him with fudging his clinical evidence. To author Jeffrey Masson, onetime project director of the Sigmund Freud Archives, Freud had denied the painful reality of child sex abuse, thereby committing a colossal disservice to humanity and a whopping scientific mistake. In 1983 Masson quipped that psychoanalysis would, like automobile manufacturer Ford and its ill-fated Pinto model, "have to recall every patient since 1901."[39]

Overall, however, Freud's theories had an immense impact on twentieth-century history. Freud's voluminous writings popularized the Rousseauian idea that human instincts were on a collision course with the demands of civilized morality. Freud also gave credence to the view that the roots of personal unhappiness lie in childhood, helping to unleash a huge professional industry of therapists who in books, on television, and through other media have spread the gospel that adult misfortunes are the result of dysfunctional family relations. Despite Freud's efforts to draw firm distinctions between psychoanalysis and the principles of New Thought and the mind cure movement, Freudianism in twentieth-century America tended to blend in with a more general "psychological mindedness." Psychoanalysis has been consistently conflated with the notion that below the surface of the conscious mind are mental powers that can dramatically improve human health. Few theories in twentieth-century medicine have attracted more believers than this core idea that emotional healing is as close as a therapist's couch, a group workshop, or a personal program of self-actualization.[40]

PROTECTING SANITY

The acceptance of theories of mental functioning like psychoanalysis fostered an optimism – notably in North America – that mental disabilities could be not only cured, but also prevented by mitigating the conditions that supposedly bred emotional disorders in the first place. The notion that mental diseases could be prevented dated back to J. P. Frank's theory of "medical police" and the nineteenth-century Paris school of medicine. Typically psychiatrists had advocated early hospitalization as a means of nipping mental disabilities in the bud. The public apparently did not share this view, however, as families normally postponed institutionalization until their relatives' illnesses were ingrained. It was not until the end of the nineteenth century that the welfare and rehabilitation of the individual patient ceased to be the overriding interest of psychiatrists and the mental health of entire societies became an abiding concern.[41]

Faith in the merits of preventing mental disease would never have enjoyed so much popularity if it had not been for the rise of the public health movement. During the last decades of the nineteenth century, governments spent huge sums of money in an effort to reduce maternal and child mortality, curb the incidence of infectious diseases, and improve nutrition. These trends coincided with the widespread enthusiasm for organized sport and physical fitness as means of developing skills, learning teamwork, and improving overall health. In the late nineteenth century, sport teams multiplied and organizations such as the English Football Association (1863), Rugby Football Union (1871), the National and American baseball leagues (1876 and 1899, respectively), and the National Hockey League (1917) were established. Gymnastics clubs flourished in France and cricket spread throughout the British Empire. In 1896 the indefatigable Frenchman Baron Pierre de Coubertin succeeded in reviving the Olympic Games for the first time since classical antiquity.

Sport as leisure-time entertainment for spectators exploded in popularity, but sports as a pathway to good mental and physical health also caught on. Proponents of athletics urged both men and women to take up swimming, cycling, horseback riding, or Swedish "rational gymnastics" – though always in "moderation" for women. Coubertin talked about the "hygienic" virtues of sport, the "art of virilizing bodies and souls." In 1913 he declared his intent "to establish the correlation between psychology and physical movement and create a social therapeutic that will halt the universal neurosis of modern life."[42] In 1908 Robert Baden-Powell founded the Boy Scouts, and his sister started the Girl Guides in

1910. "One step toward happiness," Baden-Powell told his Scouts, "is to make yourself healthy and strong while you are a boy," and scouting was designed to do just that. To Baden-Powell and many of his contemporaries, an outdoor life was the tonic for melancholy, discontented people.[43]

As the emphasis on sport and physical culture indicated, the quest for mental health on the eve of World War I had expanded to include the community at large and the maintenance of health, not just the cure of illness, an enterprise dubbed "mental hygiene" by the Swiss-born psychiatrist Adolf Meyer. In Germany psychiatrists had blazed paths by opening university clinics designed to treat people in the early stages of their mental and nervous illnesses, when they allegedly were curable. In contrast to asylums, which were normally located on the outskirts of cities, psychiatric clinics in Germany tended to be situated in urban areas, in the vicinity of universities where psychiatrists could also teach their subject, thereby shoe-horning their field of study into medical school curricula. Envious of their German colleagues' professional success, adventuresome physicians elsewhere experimented by setting up similar clinics in the community, hoping the "higher type" of patient with comparatively mild symptoms would seek their services. This trend in favor of community mental health gathered momentum up to and beyond the 1960s, when country after country began closing down public asylums.[44]

If the idea behind mental hygiene was "in the air" by the early twentieth century, it took a former mental patient, Clifford Beers (1876–1943), to launch this new movement. In 1908 Beers, a businessman and Yale graduate born in New Haven, Connecticut, authored *A Mind That Found Itself* and thereby carved for himself a place in the history of the mental health field as towering as that of other laypeople, Dorothea Dix, William Tuke, or Elizabeth Packard. A compelling, eloquent autobiography of genuine literary merit and poignant self-revelation, *A Mind That Found Itself* told the story of how Beers was hospitalized in a private Connecticut asylum in 1900, shortly after a suicide attempt. Beers spent the next few years in a variety of mental hospitals, the worst being the Connecticut Hospital for the Insane. His description of his treatment, appearing at a time when muckraking journalism was exposing scandal after scandal in industry and government, sparked nationwide indignation over hospital conditions for mental patients. Unlike a later generation of critics of psychiatry, Beers never denied that he suffered from real mental illness – he fought depression and paranoia for much of his adult life – nor maintained that mental hospitals should be closed down. His over-arching goal was to write a book that did for people with mental disabilities what *Uncle*

Tom's Cabin did for African American slaves: expose society's ignorance, cruelty, and apathy regarding a grave injustice.[45]

In 1909 Beers was largely responsible for founding the National Committee for Mental Hygiene, renamed the National Mental Health Association in 1979 and Mental Health America in 2006. Beers's ally was Adolf Meyer, who also played a prominent role in the early history of the movement. The choice of the term "mental hygiene" was deliberate: both Meyer and Beers wanted to signal to the world that the top aim of the mental health field was, as Beers put it, "protecting *sanity* [his emphasis]." A major turning point in the quest for mental health had been reached. The goal was to achieve mental health, not just cure mental disease.[46]

The idea of mental hygiene steadily spread beyond U.S. borders. In 1930 the First International Congress on Mental Hygiene met in Washington, D.C. By that time there were twenty-five separate national societies of mental hygiene. In 1948, at the Third International Congress, the World Federation for Mental Health was formed. Since then it has enjoyed increasing contact with various United Nations agencies as well as the World Health Organization, which in 1946 defined health as "a state of complete physical, mental and social well-being and not merely the absence of disease or infirmity." By denying that there were sharp distinctions between illness and health, the WHO supported the basic goal of mental hygiene: the maintenance of emotional health and the prevention of nervous and mental disorders.

No matter how instrumental Clifford Beers was in launching the mental hygiene movement, he quickly discovered it would go nowhere without the active collaboration of psychiatrists and funding from wealthy foundations, including the Rockefellers. So over the years leading to his death in 1943, Beers watched as leading psychiatrists such as Meyer, Thomas Salmon, and Clarence Hincks steered the movement away from reforming public asylum conditions to psychiatric research, the inclusion of psychiatry in medical school curricula, public education about mental illness, and systematic surveys of the incidence of mental disability in prisons, schools, reformatories, and other institutions. Beers's misgivings about these directions for the movement he had created were not eased by the fact that he and Meyer had two decidedly different personalities. The two men also disagreed over who should assume leadership of the new movement: Beers wanted laypeople, Meyer wanted psychiatrists. Meyer won out, another milestone in the steady expansion of medical dominance over the quest for mental health.

Yet there is no discounting the enormity of Beers's accomplishment. When a contemporary said that Beers did for mental health reform what

Thomas Paine's *Common Sense* did for the cause of American independence, he was not far wrong. Mental health care was on the verge of sweeping change, and Clifford Beers could legitimately claim to have personally helped to accelerate the transition – in the United States at least – from an ethos of self-reliance and personal accountability to the attitude that society at large was responsible for emotional wellness.

Beers's life story was ringing testimony to the belief that patients could recover from mental illness and contribute to society, as well as the theory that there were ways to treat mental illness other than hospitalization. Sadly, Beers's death in a mental hospital also suggested that no matter how hopeful people were that severe mental disease could be defeated, its mysterious power to lick the best of intentions and up-to-date science remained intact. All of Beers's five siblings were struck down by mental illness – two brothers committed suicide – reinforcing the impression that psychological disorders ran in families and genetics played a key role in causing mental disabilities. Nonetheless, in both the short and long terms, Beers put the concept of mental hygiene on the map, helping to revolutionize thinking about emotional health.

PENSION WARS

The theory that there was a fine line between psychological normality and abnormality received a huge boost from the sequence of events that began in the sun-kissed summer of 1914, when millions of men from around the world left their homes and marched off to war, ushering in the most violent and destructive century in all of human history. By the time the warring parties agreed to an armistice on November 11, 1918, more than 10 million had died.

The 1914–18 war, involving armies from around the world and the most up-to-date killing technologies, also devastated large swaths of property and toppled huge multi-national empires. The shock waves of World War I continued to ripple over the next two decades, unleashing another, more destructive world war and an uneasy peace between the surviving superpowers, the United States of America and the Soviet Union.

World War I was also a landmark event in the history of mental health. In the aftermath of 1914–18 many accepted that war could exact a deep, wide, and lasting emotional toll on soldiers. Mental health experts in later years drew the conclusion that if healthy young men in uniform could have nervous breakdowns, then no one was safe from the ravages of mental illness. The distinctions between psychological health and psychological illness became more and more blurred.

During the war, nation after nation was forced to confront the enormous challenges of mustering millions of citizen soldiers and sending them off to fight in conditions guaranteed to test even the most emotionally stable individuals. Soldiers crouched in damp, rat-infested trenches as shells rained down on them from distant artillery. Or they went "over the top" and hurled themselves against barbed-wire, flamethrowers, poison gas, and murderous machine gun fire. Stretches of mind-numbing boredom alternated with chaotic periods of sheer terror. Between 1914 and 1918 millions of soldiers were told that sacrificing oneself for God, king, and country was noble, but the grim and dirty reality of war convinced many that these high ideals were mere rhetoric.

Casualty lists were staggering. By Christmas 1914 the entire British regular army was almost wiped out. In June 1916 about 60,000 men were killed, wounded, or missing on only one day of the Battle of the Somme. Two years later, over much the same terrain, the British army sustained a further 300,000 casualties. Seventeen percent of all mobilized soldiers in the French army perished in the war.

The strain on human nerves from all this mud, murder, mayhem, and mutilation was immense. The first reports of soldiers' nervous breakdowns had come from Russian doctors during the Russo-Japanese War of 1904–1905. Much worse occurred in 1914–18 when an epidemic of mental and physical trauma swept through the ranks of all national armies. Reports of uncontrollable shaking, stuttering, excitability, paralysis, and disorders of sight, hearing, sleep, and gait among enlisted men turned up again and again. In the words of one historian, "It was as if a hundred colossal railway smash-ups were taking place every day, for four years."[47] As the conflict wore on, the words of German Kaiser Wilhelm II ("To the nation with the strongest nerves will go the victory") appeared more and more prophetic.[48]

A varied nomenclature quickly sprang up to account for soldiers' breakdowns on the field of battle, but it was "shell shock," a term coined in 1915 by Charles S. Myers, an English psychologist with the British Expeditionary Force in France, that stuck in the collective imagination. Initially, Myers and neurologist Frederick Mott thought the negative atmospheric pressure from artillery explosions or the carbon monoxide poisoning from being buried in a trench caused the amnesia, acute anxiety, and refusal to fight characteristic of shell shock, but later studies showed that many cases did not occur in the presence of exploding shells or carbon monoxide. By 1917 the British army officially disallowed the diagnosis of shell shock, but the term stuck in popular usage as a name for the trauma experienced by soldiers. "Shell shock" proved to be handy as a less stigmatizing word to describe symptoms that closely resembled hysteria. It was a medically sounding term that freed distraught fighting men from the charge of malingering.

By the end of 1918, at least 80,000 British troops had been treated for shell shock in the Royal Army Medical Corps. Eventually German authorities treated almost 600,000 soldiers for neurological disorders. The U.S. Army discharged 72,000 servicemen with neuro-psychiatric disabilities, even though America's participation in the war was much shorter than that of the other Great Powers. Symptoms lingered well into the interwar period. By 1932 fully 36 percent of veterans receiving disability pensions from the British government were still listed as psychologically sick. In Germany so many veterans applied for disability pensions due to nervous causes that a veritable "pension war" broke out in the 1920s, pitting a skeptical government and its doctors against hordes of insistent former soldiers. Doubters claimed that soldiers seeking such war-related pensions were often not as sick as they thought and that instead they suffered from a "pension neurosis," caused by the presence of the social insurance system itself. Whatever veterans' motivations, the mass applications for mental disability pensions in the interwar period highlighted the expanding public acceptance that nervous breakdown was due to stress-related circumstances and reflected the burgeoning popular dependence on third-party benefits for mental ill health.[49]

Morale was a key factor affecting the incidence of shell shock and war neurosis. Doctors for armies that seemed to be losing, for example the Russians in 1904–1905, tended to report shell shock more often than other doctors. British and French soldiers, reeling from German offensives in 1914 and 1915, were the first to succumb to the condition in large numbers, while the German literature on the topic developed later once the prospect of an early victory looked increasingly dim for the kaiser's armies. Nonetheless, by the end of the war the armies of all the Great Powers had acknowledged that modern warfare could breed psychological disorders that were fundamentally different from cowardice or malingering.

Soldiers who broke down under the stress of battle could expect to be sent behind the lines for treatment, which included baths, hypnosis, persuasion, or electro-therapy. All these methods of therapy were designed to restore the soldier's shattered nerves, the ultimate objective being to counteract his "will to sickness" with a "will to health." The use of electro-therapy – passing an electric current through electrodes attached to the patient's body – derived from peacetime treatments of neurasthenics, but within the context of wartime emergency the distinctions between punitive and humane therapy often broke down in practice, as one German soldier with mutism recounted:

> The current was switched on. At first I had a prickly feeling, which suddenly burst into intense pain.... The moment the doctor's suggestions began, I felt like an object with no will of my own, being fought for by two opposing powers. Gradually my own came into play as a result both of my own reasoning and the doctor's means of domination.... I held on to the doctor's scolding as a lifeline, clung to it tightly, and pulled my nerves along with me.

This type of treatment was actually closer to behavior modification than medical therapy, but it would be a mistake to characterize it purely in terms of persecutors and victims. Patients frequently testified that it did them good.[50]

To deal with its long list of psychological casualties, the French army pioneered "forward psychiatry," or "proximity to battle" (PIE), based on advance treatment units that minimized the separation of soldiers from their comrades and were designed to increase rates of return to duty. The Americans and British used PIE in both world wars, and the United States also used it in Korea and Vietnam. Australians and New Zealanders likewise concluded in World War II that nervous disorders were best treated close to the front lines.[51]

Psychoanalysis and psychotherapy in general benefited from the credence given to the theory of shell shock. Indeed, the fighting had barely stopped before the Berlin Psychoanalytic Institutewas founded in 1920, as was the international General Medical Society for Psychotherapy in 1926. The popularity of shell shock rivaled Freud's theories in spreading the idea of mental and nervous disorders that left no permanent physical damage – in other words, the notion of the purely functional psychological disorder that can come and go, even in the minds of intelligent and brave soldiers. The British psychologist Cyril Burt spelled out this message for the twentieth century:

> It was perhaps the First World War that most effectively brought home the artificiality of the distinction between the normal mind on the one hand and its abnormal conditions on the other. In the military hospitals the study of so-called shell-shock revealed that symptoms quite as serious as the well-defined psychoses might arise through simply stress and strain and yet prove quickly curable by psychotherapeutic means. And

thus it gradually became apparent that much of what had been considered abnormal might be discovered in the mind of the average man.[52]

The good news was that mental disorders were curable. The bad news was that virtually everyone was a little bit deranged.

MASTERS OF THE WORLD

The challenges army doctors faced trying to treat soldiers suffering from combat stress convinced many military officials that a better course of action was the prevention of battlefield breakdowns. The steep incidence of war-related mental casualties drew attention to armies' poor screening and monitoring of recruits during the early stages of patriotic mobilization. For example, the German army in World War I discovered to its chagrin that a large number of epileptics had made their way into the ranks. With interest in detecting the mental status of recruits climbing, the stage was set for the introduction of army intelligence testing.

The theory that intelligence, like the physical body, was a measurable, scientifically analyzable, biological reality had been first proposed in the pre-1914 era. Two French psychologists, Théodore Simon and Alfred Binet, devised a measuring scale for determining intelligence in 1908, but it was American psychologists who were most impressed with its potential for identifying gradations of intelligence within and between groups. In 1916 the Stanford psychologist Lewis Terman completed his landmark Stanford Revision of the Binet–Simon Intelligence Scale, effectively "Americanizing" the study of intelligence. For the rest of the century, in professional circles intelligence would readily be equated with IQ. Later in the twentieth century, debates raged over the accuracy of IQ testing, especially testing of minority groups, but by then the notion of intelligence as a biological entity that could sort populations from smart to dumb had staked out a firm foothold in American culture.[53]

Despite Binet's and Simon's nationality, the French army ignored intelligence testing in World War I. When America joined the war in 1917, the U.S. Army, desperate to train and select inductees, mobilized a significant segment of the country's psychological community under the leadership of Harvard psychologist Robert M. Yerkes to administer intelligence examinations to all new recruits. At its height mental testing processed 10,000 examinations a day. Almost 70,000 men (2 percent of those tested) were rejected by army examiners. Testing revealed to everyone's shock and dismay that the mental age of the average American soldier was thirteen.

The sense of alarm over these findings from psychological studies meant that in the 1920s opinion makers, worried about the overall intelligence of American society, began urging "scientific men [to] take the place that is theirs as masters of the world." Soon psychologists and psychiatrists were moving into industry, government, education, advertising, and the like, eager to apply their wartime expertise to the challenges of peacetime. The new discipline of psychiatric social work also emerged in the interwar years.[54]

A key figure in the endeavor to achieve newfound respect for psychiatric expertise was the U.S. physician Thomas Salmon (1876–1927). A noted expert on the public mental health dimensions of immigration policy, Salmon was named the medical director of the National Committee for Mental Hygiene in 1915 and in 1921 was elected to the presidency of the American Psychiatric Association in 1921. His election as the first non-asylum psychiatrist to that post was a clear sign that the nature of professional psychiatry was shifting to include aspects of mental health care other than hospital practice.

Earlier, in 1917, Salmon was appointed director of the U.S. Army's program in neuro-psychiatry. Salmon set up the intensive training programs for psychiatrists who then were dispatched to the front lines to serve alongside regular physicians, treating head wounds one day and combat stress the next. According to Salmon, war experiences "went far toward breaking down the isolation of mental medicine." "The exigencies of the war," another observed, enabled psychiatry to achieve its "proper place in the domain of medicine."[55]

In 1922 the president of the American Psychiatric Association announced, "There was never a time in the world's history when there was such a widespread interest in the mind and its disorders in their relation to human life."[56] The thinly veiled concern was that the average American was too stupid to be left alone for very long without scientific guidance. So began what one historian has called the "romance of American psychology," the discipline's rapid ascent throughout American life. There was nothing inevitable about the trend, which saw psychological ways of thinking penetrating everyday life and a growing number of people depending on scientific expertise to ease personal unhappiness. In fact, the theory of mass, war-related emotional breakdowns fell out of favor after World War I as various governments and psychiatrists reconsidered the wisdom of veterans' pensions for psychiatric injury.[57] Yet the basic theory revived during World War II when a leading U.S. psychiatrist declared, "It would seem to be a more rational question to ask why the soldier does *not* succumb to anxiety rather than why he does."[58] If peace was "simply a period of less violent war," according to one U.S. psychologist, the psychiatric lessons of World War II would have to be applied to all of society. It was not difficult to make this argument when the two nuclear-armed superpowers eyed each other warily. In the post-1945 era the distinctions between peace and war seemed fuzzy to many Americans who increasingly accepted that even healthy men and women could easily fall ill from the stress of everyday life in the nuclear age. By then, many in industry, government, education, medicine, and the media had concluded that life was well nigh impossible without the guidance of experts in mental health, a historical process hastened by the stories of World War I Tommies, Doughboys, and Fritzes "shocked" by the terrors of combat on the killing fields of Europe.[59]

EUGENICS

In 1996 Fred Aslin, a native American who won a Purple Heart in the Korean War, requested his personal file under the state of Michigan's Freedom of Information Act. The file's contents shocked and angered him. The file told of Aslin's stay at the Lapeer State Training School, where in 1936 he and eight of his siblings became wards of the state of Michigan following their father's death. Aslin was so appalled by what he read that he decided to file suit against the state seeking compensation for damages. Unfortunately for Aslin, his claim was turned down in March 2002. The statute of limitations had expired.

Aslin's suit was based on the fact that in 1944, at the age of eighteen, he was forced to undergo a vasectomy, the surgical severing of his vas deferens. Training school officials had diagnosed Aslin as a "feeble-minded moron," grounds for sterilization under state law, and had never explained the nature of the operation to him.

Half a continent away, and at about the same time that Fred Aslin decided to take legal action, Calgary-born waitress Leilani Muir sued the Canadian province of Alberta for sterilizing her under its 1928 law. In 1955, just before her eleventh birthday, at the request of her alcoholic mother, Leilani had been admitted to Alberta's Provincial Training School (PTS) for Mental Defectives. The PTS officials decided to sterilize Leilani after she scored a 68 on an IQ test. Muir was one of 2,822 Albertans who suffered the same fate before the law was repealed in 1972, but she ended up having better luck than Aslin. In 1996 a court awarded her $750,000 (Canadian) in compensation. The ruling opened the door to a class action lawsuit filed on behalf of 700 other victims of Alberta's law, resulting in 1999 in an $82 million settlement that grabbed national headlines in Canada.[60]

The stories of Leilani Muir and Fred Aslin became front-page news as the twentieth century drew to a close, alongside similar shocking press accounts from countries such as Switzerland and Sweden that also had vigorous sterilization programs. Yet the first chapter of Muir's and Aslin's stories had been scripted a century earlier. Their sterilizations had been done in the name of eugenics, a word coined by Charles Darwin's cousin Francis Galton in 1883 and normally defined as the scientific study of measures designed to improve the biological quality of future generations. Galton (1822–1911) wrote copiously about the need to boost the birthrate of society's best and brightest, and hence preferred "positive" eugenics to "negative" eugenics, or efforts to reduce the birthrate of the "unfit." Like Darwin, Galton, a brilliant mathematician and amateur scientist, was worried about the way civilization seemed to shield the weak and infirm from natural selection. Eugenics, Galton argued, was the solution to this perennial dilemma, at once a humane, scientific, and socially beneficial alternative to leaving the unfit to nature's deadly embrace. In return for protection against "nature red in tooth and claw," the unfit forfeited their reproductive freedom. "What nature does blindly, slowly, and ruthlessly, man may do providently, quickly, and kindly," Galton wrote.[61]

The rise to prominence of eugenics, an updated version of J. P. Frank's theory of "medical police," occurred against the backdrop of interest in shell shock, intelligence testing, mental hygiene, and the overall mental fitness of recruits during World War I. State mobilization for total war between 1914 and 1945 created a stark climate of crisis throughout the industrialized world that encouraged governments to enact policies designed to improve the mental and physical quality of their citizens. Not only did elites fret over the mental fitness of their enlisted personnel, they were also concerned about the way modern war seemingly killed off the best and brightest of the nation's youth, while the supposedly less fit stayed behind to produce their own kind. These apparent trends, when studied against the background of falling birthrates in many Western countries and the mass migration of peoples across continents, raised questions about the martial usefulness of future generations and the very survival of nation-states. Lawmakers from Washington to Moscow responded with legislation that addressed the biological quality and quantity of their populations. And when elected officials were slow to act, activists in various non-governmental organizations, including labor and women's groups, agitated for policies that underscored the high stakes for nation-states in a twentieth-century world marked by a grim scramble for land, food, and natural resources – what in the 1890s the German geographer Friedrich Ratzel had dubbed *lebensraum*.[62]

The eugenic mentality led governments to prioritize the spending of scarce resources. During World War I, care for indigent social groups, especially hospitalized people with mental disabilities, suffered severe cutbacks in staffing, housing, and food. Shortages in German mental hospitals during the war meant that more than 70,000 patients died of hunger, disease, or neglect. It was not until 1925 that the death rate in German mental hospitals rebounded to pre-1914 levels, but much the same could be said about English asylums, such as the Buckinghamshire County Pauper Lunatic Asylum, where wartime rationing played havoc with inmates' health.[63] German asylum psychiatry never really recovered from its wartime experience, and once the economic depression of the 1930s set in, government decree after decree underlined the custodial function of asylums. As one official report from Hesse stated in 1930, "The activity of the doctors and nursing staff in mental asylums is entirely different from work in a hospital. Since there is no treatment for mental illness, one can scarcely speak of medical activity." The grimly utilitarian view that from the national standpoint some lives were more valuable than others took root in Germany, where psychiatrists sometimes used the phrase "ballast existences" to describe their chronic patients. The director of the Elfing-Haar asylum told a visitor in 1939 to a children's ward, "These creatures naturally only represent to me a burden upon the healthy body of our nation."[64] These and other sentiments linked to the ability of nations to wage war on a modern scale provided the eugenics movement with a powerful rationale for its existence.

Though in the early years its appeal was limited mainly to elites, eugenics by the 1920s had caught on like few other ideas in history and played a crucial role in the quest for mental health in the modern era. Eugenic organizations were founded in Japan, North America, Latin America, England, and throughout western and central Europe. Colleges, universities, and public schools taught the principles of eugenics, which typically stressed the heritability of traits such as genius, schizophrenia, alcoholism, depression, and low IQ. The Rockefeller and Carnegie Foundations supported eugenic research. Biology textbooks accepted eugenics as scientific truth. Contests were held at U.S. county fairs to determine the "fittest families."

By the 1930s most scientists agreed that psychological characteristics could not be traced to single genes, but the view persisted that preventing the handicapped from breeding relieved them and their offspring of emotional suffering. Eugenic sterilization – by enabling hospital administrators to discharge patients into the community – saved cash-strapped governments money, adding to the movement's appeal, notably during the Depression.

Liberal Protestant pastors, inspired by the social gospel message of reforming earthly conditions as a way of saving the world, preached eugenics from their pulpits.[65] The only concerted opposition to eugenics came from the Roman Catholic Church. In 1930 Pope Pius XI issued *Casti Connubii*, his encyclical on Christian marriage, which declared sterilization and other forms of artificial contraception sinful, yet Catholic physicians tended to agree with other eugenic methods to improve the overall health of families.

Governments from Scandinavia to South America jumped on the eugenics bandwagon, making it one of the most remarkable social reform movements of modern history. Eugenicists, eager to apply science to social issues, branched out into the fields of euthanasia advocacy, birth control, sex education, marriage counseling, population control, and abortion rights.[66] Eugenics became a "dirty word" after World War II when the media reported the medical crimes against humanity committed by Hitler's Third Reich, but Nazi Germany was far from alone in putting Galton's theories into practice.

In the name of eugenics, governments around the world introduced family allowances, pre-marital examinations, and the medical screening of immigrants. To officials in the United States, which took in 18 million newcomers in the quarter-century before 1914, and Canada, where 400,000 newcomers landed in 1913 alone, the arrival of immigrants was a major public health challenge. Study after study found that asylums and other public charity institutions were swamped with disabled immigrants. The escalating costs of caring for burgeoning asylum populations led governments to order the medical inspection of newcomers as they stepped off the boat. The hope was that inspection would prevent those with mental disabilities from entering the country and reproducing. According to Johns Hopkins University neuro-pathologist Stewart Paton, in immigration "we are dealing with one of the great biological problems which fundamentally affect not only the future of this country but the future of the race." In Canada, psychiatrist C. K. Clarke, head of the University of Toronto's medical school, repeatedly warned about "defective immigrants" arriving on ships from the United Kingdom and continental Europe.[67] Eugenicists decried the hereditary weaknesses of immigrants, but interest groups such as big business and ethnic organizations lobbied hard to ensure that laws for screening aliens rarely had teeth. Ultimately, the U.S. Congress passed the 1921 and 1924 acts introducing national quotas for newcomers, measures that pleased nativists but made little sense from a public health standpoint.

STERILIZATION WITHOUT UNSEXING

Those most affected by the eugenics movement were the developmentally delayed, people earlier generations called "morons," "imbeciles," or "idiots." Belying the popular belief that in pre-modern days all people with mental disabilities were lumped together indiscriminately, for centuries society and medicine had distinguished people with permanent mental disability from "lunatics," those who presumably had lost their reason temporarily but enjoyed lucid intervals. Among the developmentally delayed were (and are) people diagnosed with Down syndrome, named after John Langdon Down, the British asylum psychiatrist who in 1866 first described the condition. Since 1959 Down syndrome has been known in many European countries as trisomy 21 because Down syndrome (or "mongolism") is caused by an extra twenty-first chromosome.[68]

Interest in the developmentally delayed (or "mentally retarded") rose just as the great wave of asylum construction was petering out in the late nineteenth century. Having erected at great expense asylums for the mentally ill over the course of the nineteenth century, governments began building similar institutions for the mentally retarded around the turn of the twentieth century. The main reason for building institutions to house the developmentally delayed was the widespread perception that something had to be done about those who appeared to be "mentally deficient" or "feeble-minded." (A "Mr. Feeble-Mind" had appeared in John Bunyan's 1678 *A Pilgrim's Progress*.) The noun "feeble-mindedness" was replaced in the 1920s by "mental defectiveness," and later by "mental retardation," but generally it referred to people of various degrees of sub-normal intelligence.

In earlier times attitudes toward the developmentally delayed ran the gamut from pity to cruel mockery. They were viewed as deserving of Christian charity and sometimes, as in William Wordsworth's poem "The Idiot Boy" (1798), as innocent and closer to nature than saner human beings. By the early twentieth century, sentiments toward the developmentally delayed were more conflicted. H. H. Goddard, research director of the Vineland Training School for Feeble-Minded Children in New Jersey, wrote in 1913 that the task was to "[d]etermine the fact of their defectiveness as early as possible, and place them in colonies under the care and management of intelligent people who understand the problem; train them, and make them happy; make them as useful as possible, but above all, bring them up with good habits and keep them from ever marrying or becoming parents."[69] In 1914 a leading U.S. social welfare journal editorialized: "Among the social tasks that confront state governments today, none is more pressing than the care of the feeble-minded.... It is because they, at least as much as any other class, complicate and involve every social problem, and because they, more than any other class, tend to increase on our hands." In the early twentieth century, eugenicists focused on the so-called high-grade morons who supposedly were not easily detected but abounded in the community. "You can't always tell by appearance," one U.S. eugenicist cautioned in 1936, especially with regard to "defective" girls. "[T]rained sufficiently to pass for normal by those with superficial judgment," these girls "were the greatest menace to the race."[70]

Throughout the nineteenth century, under the influence of reformers such as the French-born Onésime-Édouard Séguin, governments built custodial training schools for those thought to have inborn mental retardation. In 1876 the American Association for the Study of Feeble Mindedness was founded, renamed in 1934 the American Association on Mental Deficiency. In the United States the rate of institutionalized feeble-minded people rose from 17.3 per 100,000 in 1904 to 46.7 in 1923.[71] Feeble-mindedness was thought to run in families alongside tendencies toward crime, prostitution, and indigence. Caregivers hoped that custodialism for these patients would be a humane option and provide inmates with training and rehabilitation. Living in special institutions also shielded the developmentally delayed from the many dangers lurking in the community, chiefly sexual predators. But experts also believed (incorrectly) that persons with these types of mental disabilities were unusually fertile and, if allowed to roam in the community, would breed repeatedly, producing more of their own kind.

These rationales and the high cost of institutions for the developmentally delayed fostered support in professional and political ranks for another, more controversial eugenic measure: sterilization. Over the course of the late nineteenth century, physicians at various asylums had been performing surgery on the reproductive organs of patients with mental disabilities, including the removal of normal ovaries to induce premature menopause. Surgeons sometimes removed diseased ovaries, but the removal of healthy ovaries – called "Battey's operation" after the Georgia (Alabama) surgeon who originated it – was also advocated as a means of improving emotional well-being, reducing sexual desire, preventing reproduction, or deterring anti-social behavior. Battey's operation was based on the theory of reflex irritation, according to which nervous connections running via the spine throughout the whole body regulated its organs, including the brain. It followed that women's uteruses might influence brain functioning. Mortality associated with Battey's operation ran as high as 22 percent, but that did not deter Battey, who himself operated on several hundred women between 1870 and 1890. Auguste Forel, a professor of psychiatry at the University of Zurich, readily admitted to authorizing the castration of female patients, including a fourteen-year-old girl whose mother and grandmother were prostitutes.[72]

However, gender prejudice, while present, ultimately had a small influence on these operations. Often women patients pleaded with their doctors for gynecological operations; one British doctor noted in 1895 that they "much prefer an active and energetic doctor" to one who relied on the healing power of nature.[73] Female physicians in the United States both performed and approved of Battey's operation. Auguste Forel described himself as a "zealous apostle of women's right to vote, of women's rights in general," and echoed the calls of birth control proponents to "separate love and the need for sexual satisfaction from reproduction."[74]

By contrast, vasectomy and tubal ligation were safe operations, thanks to advances in surgical technique in the nineteenth century, notably anesthesia and antisepsis. Because such operations ended fertility without diminishing sexual drive, sterilization proponents emphasized how the procedures differed from castration. "Sterilization without unsexing" was how one eugenicist described them.[75] Psychiatrists tended to believe that both society and mental patients would benefit from sterilization. For example, low-IQ patients would be better off without the worry of pregnancy and the stress of parenting. Some psychiatrists in California even believed – incorrectly, as it turns out – that the absorption of testicular secretions thanks to vasectomy had therapeutic effects.[76]

The most notorious example of eugenic sterilization was Nazi Germany's 1933 law permitting the forcible sterilization of alcoholics, epileptics, the mentally retarded, and others with mental disabilities. By 1945 roughly 400,000 Germans had been sterilized according to the law's provisions. To eugenicists – called "race hygienists" in Germany – eugenic sterilization cleansed the gene pool of pathological traits that were believed to be transmitted as unit factors. Eugenic theory also paved the way in Germany for its so-called euthanasia program, which resulted in the medical murder by poison, gas, starvation, or shooting of roughly 200,000 men, women, and children with disabilities by war's end.[77]

As the Nazis were introducing their 1933 sterilization law, researchers were discovering that mental retardation was in fact a recessive hereditary factor, which meant that both parents would have to carry the trait for it to be expressed in offspring. It was simply not true that "superior people will have superior children and inferior people inferior children," a Johns Hopkins University biologist stated in 1927. As the *New York Times* editorialized in 1932: "The evidence is clear that normal persons also carry defective genes which may manifest themselves in insane progeny.... Even if we discovered the carriers of hidden defective genes by applying the methods of the cattle-breeder to humanity, the process would take about a thousand years."[78]

Such news did not deter advocates of eugenic sterilization, however. They merely altered the rationale for sterilization. In the words of the president of the American Association for Mental Deficiency in 1936, "The most powerful argument for sterilization today is that which urges that no feeble-minded person is fit to be a parent, whether or not his condition is hereditary and therefore likely to be genetically transmitted." In other words, nurture was as good a justification as nature for sterilization.[79]

This shift in the rationale for eugenic sterilization signaled that eugenics appealed not just to those who harbored racial prejudices. Eugenic sterilization laws flourished in Progressive Era America and social democratic Sweden, home of the world's most advanced cradle-to-grave social welfare system. Eugenic sterilization enjoyed robust support from numerous socialists, liberals, conservationists, birth control activists, and women's rights advocates around the world.

Eugenic fortunes also benefited from the growing involvement of governments in public health. To Englishman Karl Pearson, the first holder of the Galton Chair in Eugenics at the University of London, eugenics was a branch of public health par excellence. "I am convinced," Pearson declared in 1912, "that every officer of the public health service who really appreciates the magnitude and importance of his work both for medical progress and with it for social welfare, is, however unconscious he may be of Sir Francis Galton's definition, a true eugenist."[80] Campaigns against venereal disease and the infant welfare movement dovetailed with eugenics as supporters stressed how charitable help for the fit and eugenics for the unfit most effectively improved the human race. The similarities between eugenics and public health were evident in Justice Oliver Wendell Holmes, Jr.'s, reasoning in *Buck v. Bell*, the 1927 U.S. Supreme Court ruling that forcible sterilization was constitutional. "The principle that sustains compulsory vaccination," Holmes wrote, "is broad enough to cover cutting the Fallopian tubes." Holmes's fateful remarks revealed that eugenicists agreed with public health activists and public opinion that prevention was the best approach to health issues, that the well-being of the community trumped the interests of individuals, and that when persuasion failed to correct poor lifestyle choices state coercion was permissible.[81] Just as twentieth-century eugenicists and public health proponents repeatedly joined forces to combat tuberculosis, venereal disease, and infant mortality, so they recognized that eugenics provided them with a formidable array of weapons with which to prevent mental disorders from spreading.

EUGENIC WELFARE

The links between eugenics and public health were particularly firm in Germany. No country in the industrialized world harbored more social scientists convinced that the state had to intervene aggressively in the field of public health to offset society's impact on the natural struggle for existence. Led by medical scientists such as Alfred Ploetz, Ernst Rüdin, Eugen Fischer, Wilhelm Schallmayer, and Fritz Lenz, German racial hygienists mobilized in an effort to reduce the incidence of disease throughout the Second Reich (1871–1918). A major figure in German racial hygiene was the brilliant psychiatrist Emil Kraepelin, who was convinced that the march of civilization placed heavy burdens on human evolution, and more specifically on the health of the German populace. Again and again Kraepelin warned about the effects of syphilis and alcohol on the mental and physical health of Germans. Kraepelin tended to emphasize how mental diseases could be acquired due to lifestyle, but like other German race hygienists he maintained that if governments sought the "recuperation of our race," they had to listen carefully to the advice of experts in psychiatry like himself.[82]

Germany's mammoth national effort in World War I dramatically intensified the sense of urgency around questions of public health. As the number of psychiatric inmates rose from 185,397 to more than 300,000 between 1924 and 1929, debate heated up over how the Weimar Republic could afford care for its dependent population. The belief that from the national perspective some lives were worth more than others and the collective good eclipsed all individual considerations steadily made headway in medical and scientific circles. In 1932 a German psychiatrist stated that doctors would become the "executors of the eugenic will of the nation."[83] The next year, when the Nazis came to power, Adolf Hitler himself asked rhetorically, "What good are [Germany's] struggles if the health of our people is in danger?" Geneticist Fritz Lenz stated in 1933 that "it is the will of the Führer, that the demands of racial hygiene should be put into practice, without delay."[84] By that point in Germany's troubled interwar history, public health was being swiftly politicized as the nation began to mobilize for another world war.

Given the key role played by governments in the eugenics movement, it is tempting to think that eugenic policies were imposed from above on an unwilling public. Eugenics possessed a distinctly paternalistic flavor, some of its variants had racialist overtones, and no groups advocated eugenics more loudly than biologists, journalists, social scientists, university professors, civil servants, and the medical profession. On the other hand, great swaths of society also supported eugenic measures, notably sterilization and institutional segregation. The notion of informed patient consent, whether for medical research or clinical decision making, began to take root after the mid-point of the twentieth century, but in the meantime the consensus was that expert physicians knew what was in a patient's best interests and were not bound to practice full disclosure. Talking patients into specific treatments or conducting experiments with unwitting human subjects was not necessarily considered to be a violation of medical ethics if the aim was to advance scientific knowledge, a goal most people in industrialized countries heartily endorsed.

Surveys in the United States in the late 1930s found that more than two-thirds of Americans polled endorsed the sterilization of people with mental disabilities.[85] Experts argued that eugenics protected the unborn's "right to be well-born."[86] Time and again parents or guardians willingly cooperated with medical superintendents to have their children sterilized, relieved that in a day and age when artificial contraception was widely considered to be immoral there was a routine surgical procedure that could prevent unwanted pregnancy. In North Carolina some women, desperate to stop having children and undeterred by the stigma of mental deficiency, petitioned the state's eugenic board to have their tubes tied. Forel in Zurich refused numerous appeals for sterilization, protesting that the patients in question were healthy.[87] Affluent families arranged privately for their handicapped relatives to undergo the operation. Legal sterilization of mental patients in Scandinavia, Alberta, and numerous American states continued to be performed up to the 1970s, reflecting a diffuse acceptance of contraceptive surgery as a method for dealing with the lifestyle challenges facing people with mental disabilities. Celebrated Swedish social scientist Gunnar Myrdal, a proponent of the modern welfare state, was just one of many defenders of sterilization who advised using government and corporate "propaganda" to convince "borderline" groups to submit to "severe family limitation." Few seemed to mind Myrdal's endorsement of sterilizing "borderline" people.[88]

By the end of the twentieth century revulsion over the coercive nature of eugenic sterilization – notably when it involved poor women and minorities – had sparked a backlash. The pendulum swung in the opposite direction as courts and governments outlawed the sterilization of people with mental disabilities, although countless families and professionals continued to believe the operation to be a solution to the practical, everyday dilemmas of trying to raise developmentally delayed children. Yet experiments with mass sterilization in India and the People's Republic of China in the 1970s, 1980s and 1990s, though performed in the name of population control, were recognizably eugenic because they routinely targeted the poor and people with mental disabilities.[89] The PRC had no qualms about enacting a eugenics law as late as 1995, hastily renamed the Maternal and Infant Health Law under a torrent of foreign criticism. The law required that anyone deemed to be "unsuitable for reproduction" could be compelled to undergo sterilization or abortion.[90] The word "eugenics" may have fallen out of favor by the end of the twentieth century, but meanwhile in the name of eugenics governments had assumed greater responsibilities for the mental health of their populations than ever before.

LESSER OF TWO EVILS

On May 14, 1948, the day after Britain's mandate over Palestine was due to expire, the new state of Israel declared its independence. Over the next three years Israel, carved out of contested Palestinian territory west of the Jordan River, absorbed roughly 700,000 immigrants, half of them from Africa and Asia. Many of Israel's immigrants needed hospitalization for psychiatric disabilities, placing great strains on the country's limited mental health care facilities.

One newcomer to Israel was Margaret K., one of three schizophrenic sisters who in 1945 arrived in Palestine from the Iraqi city of Baghdad. In the words of David Bental, the European-born Israeli psychiatrist who treated them, the sisters came from a traditional, "typically oriental" Sephardic Jewish family ruled by an authoritarian father who insisted that the girls marry only in order of their age. Before reaching Israel the two eldest sisters had been hospitalized in Iraq. Ultimately, all three sisters were hospitalized and submitted to a barrage of psychiatric checkups and therapies. In 1951 Margaret K. underwent a lobotomy, the surgical destruction of nerve tracts to and from the frontal lobe of the brain.

To Bental, the decision to operate was the "lesser of two evils," the choice between the calculated risk of irreversible surgery and a life of acute mental distress. At the time, the growing interest among psychiatrists in prevention kindled optimism among mental health caregivers, but mental hygiene did little to help those who suffered from severe mental disabilities, such as Margaret K. Lobotomy was first proposed in the mid-1930s as a treatment for mental illness by Portuguese neurologist Egas Moniz, who received a Nobel Prize in 1949 for his exploits in brain surgery. Moniz had been impressed by experiments performed by John Fulton and Carlyle Jacobsen, two Yale University researchers who had observed dramatic emotional changes in chimpanzees after they had removed large portions of the primates' frontal lobes. After the operation the chimpanzees, once aggressive, were noticeably more placid. In Jacobsen's words, it was as if one of the primates had joined a "happiness cult." Moniz went on to develop what he called the "prefrontal leucotomy," the surgical cutting of the long fibers that connected the cells of the frontal lobes to other brain centers.[91]

In the United States, thanks mainly to the efforts of neurologists Walter Freeman and James Watts, 40,000 people were lobotomized, 5,000 per year between 1948 and 1952. In the United Kingdom there were about 12,000 leucotomies up to 1954, approximately 17,000 in total, although the final figure will most likely never be known.[92] British physicians exported lobotomy to India. Neuro-surgeons in the three Scandinavian countries performed almost 10,000 lobotomies, with Sweden contributing 4,000 to that total. (The Ford Foundation and the U.S. Department of Defense funded psychosurgical research at the Norwegian hospital where many were performed.)[93] By 1950 about 2,000 operations had been performed in Japan in twenty-eight different hospitals. In Israel between 1946 and 1960 several hundred people underwent the operation, a number that takes on new meaning when it is compared with the small number of hospitalized mentally ill in the nation (3,000 in 1955).[94]

The interest in lobotomy among physicians mirrored psychiatrists' deep concerns about conditions in asylums and the grave obstacles they faced in trying to make their patients better. The heyday of lobotomy spanned the early Cold War, but its roots lay in the crisis of hospital psychiatry that had been festering for decades. By the interwar era U.S. mental hospitals housed roughly a half-million inmates and employed three-quarters of all members of the American Psychiatric Association. In the 1930s the number of hospital beds occupied by mental patients was roughly equal to the total number of hospital beds occupied by all non-psychiatric patients combined. In 1955 a U.S. study of federal medical services called the large number of psychiatric inpatients the "greatest single problem in the nation's health picture."[95] Schizophrenics made up the majority of hospitalized psychiatric patients; many others suffered from severe depression, with little likelihood of remission. Any therapeutic proposal that held out the hope of discharging patients from the hospital was bound to attract keen attention across the entire mental health care field. Psychiatrists were willing to try almost anything if there was some scientific reason – such as Fulton and Jacobsen's research – for believing it might work.

Medical interest in lobotomy also reflected the faith during the interwar era that scientific research could unlock the mysteries of the mind and reveal bona fide breakthrough cures for psychiatric illnesses. This curious blend of urgency, desperation, optimism, and experimentation between the Great Depression and the Korean War laid the foundations for a therapeutic trend in psychiatry that many condemned in later years but at the time seemed an understandable reaction to the ravages of mental illness.

Psychiatrists in the first half of the twentieth century had to live with a glaring contrast that haunted the performance of their professional duties. Those years witnessed a stunning flurry of revolutionary advances in medical treatment. Beginning in the late nineteenth century with an antitoxin for diphtheria, the introduction of Salvarsan for syphilis (1910), insulin for diabetes (1922), and liver extract for anemia (1926) coincided with abrupt improvements in surgical technique and hospital conditions. Then came the discovery of penicillin for bacterial infections in 1928, which in the short term saved the lives of thousands of wounded soldiers in World War II, followed by the hormone cortisone in 1949, also hailed as a wonder drug for its ability to combat ailments from Addison's

disease to rheumatoid arthritis. The introduction of the polio vaccine in
1955 by Jonas Salk capped this wave of scientific innovations, literally
inspiring bell ringing across the United States. For the first time ever, medical research seemed to be making genuine progress in the war against
disease. Medicine's weapons were dubbed "magic bullets" by a public
that seemed ready to confer on physicians such as Salk the mantle of
scientific miracle worker. One American writer described the U.S. population as "completely under the supposedly scientific yoke of modern
medicine as any primitive savage is under the superstitious serfdom of
the tribal witch doctor." In the 1960s, doubts about the ultimate benefits
of scientific medicine began to multiply rapidly, but until then medicine
basked in the glow of its "golden age."[96]

By contrast, the mental health field possessed hopes and bold theories,
but little else. Like their counterparts in other branches of medicine, some
psychiatrists labored in laboratories searching for the causes and cures
of mental diseases. Others reached out to the community in an effort to
prevent illness. But by the 1930s the fruits of all these labors were mea-
ger. Therapeutics had not progressed much since the pre–World War I
years, when some psychiatrists openly admitted their treatments were
"rubbish." Asylum medicine was a "realm of psychiatry where despon-
dency reigns," two U.S. state hospital physicians confessed in 1942.[97]

Thoughtful psychiatrists everywhere were also uneasy about what
they felt was the overuse of diagnostic categories of mental illness such
as schizophrenia that seemed to condemn patients to incurability. "With
every unnecessary diagnosis of schizophrenia," a German psychiatrist
wrote in 1928, psychiatrists "lend support to the old view ... that to be
mentally ill is the same as to be mentally crippled." He added, "When I
have diagnosed schizophrenia I have more than once heard the father
of a patient say, 'I would rather my daughter had died today.'"[98] The
perception that the gap between psychiatry and the rest of medicine was
growing adversely affected psychiatry's prestige. Heinz Lehmann, later an
international leader in psycho-pharmacology, recalled that in the 1930s
psychiatry was considered to be a "rather derelict career. People only
went there if they couldn't do anything else – or were alcoholic."[99]

Nonetheless, after World War I a curious kind of energy gripped the
mental health field. Adolf Meyer, largely responsible for substituting the
term "psychiatry" for the older word "alienism," boldly proclaimed in
1921 that modern psychiatry had "found itself." Meyer introduced the
theory of "psycho-biology," which called for the end of the dualistic distinction between body and mind and a viewpoint that depicted them as

merely two different aspects of the same thing. If someone fell ill, Meyer argued, it was not because of a fundamental defect of brain or psyche but because of "maladjustment," an unsuccessful adaptation to one's social environment. Meyer's vision of mental health care invited contributions from a wide variety of disciplines – psychiatry, neurology, psychology, psychoanalysis, anatomy, physiology, general practice, public health, nursing, experimental medicine, and the social sciences. His paradigm – the "newer psychiatry" – drew enough support within psychiatry's ranks to inject a welcome semblance of unity into a profession whose different factions threatened at any minute to rent it asunder.[100]

SHOCK THERAPY

The eagerness to borrow findings from other fields led to a wave of innovative therapies in the 1920s and 1930s, including the so-called shock therapies. Before their advent, the word "shock" meant the physiological effect of a steep drop in venous blood pressure. Yet that changed in the 1930s when the discovery of insulin inspired Manfred Joshua Sakel (born Menachem Sokol in 1900 in a small town in the Austro-Hungarian Empire) to experiment with insulin-induced hypoglycemia, in the hope that the resulting coma would have a beneficial effect on a patient's brain. Sakel, who coined the term "shock therapy," advocated insulin injections because they plunged his patients into unconsciousness and, after regaining consciousness, they seemed to be less agitated and more coherent. His insulin shock therapy (ICT) was the first of the three shock therapies – Metrazol and electro-convulsive therapy (ECT) being the others – and ever since, "shock therapy" has stuck in common parlance.[101]

Meanwhile, in 1934 Budapest-born László Meduna injected some of his patients with the camphor-style drug Cardiazol (called Metrazol in the United States), preferring it to insulin as a means of producing the convulsions that were thought to be therapeutic in shock treatments. In almost no time at all, both Metrazol and ICT were being applied all over the world. Notable recipients of ICT included Russian ballet star Vaslav Nijinsky and mathematician John Nash, whose life was chronicled in the book and film *A Beautiful Mind*.

Both ICT and Metrazol therapy were short lived. Because ICT was used chiefly to treat schizophrenia, the arrival of the first anti-psychotic drugs in the 1950s – easier and less expensive to administer – ended the practice abruptly by the 1960s. ICT use lingered in Soviet Russia and Communist China, but primarily because political barriers prevented pharmaceutical companies from promoting their drugs for schizophrenia. Metrazol for its part soon proved to be less effective than ECT.

ECT, the passing of electricity through a person's brain through electrodes applied to the head, has had a much longer history. In April 1938 Enrico X., a mechanic from Milan, was picked up by the Rome police trying to board trains without a ticket. Within days he was sent to Ugo Cerletti's psychiatric clinic in Rome. Shortly thereafter Enrico X. became the first patient in history to be treated with electro-shock. Unlike the other shock therapies, ECT was still in use at the outset of the twenty-first century.

Cerletti, born in 1877 in a small town near Venice, was ECT's founder. Cerletti and his team of experimental researchers soon realized that in Metrazol therapy it was the convulsion that cured patients, not the drug, so electricity might actually be an improvement, as its effect was instantaneous on patients, who typically dreaded their impending loss of consciousness. Cerletti's team then visited the Rome slaughterhouse where by observing pigs being electro-shocked they learned the difference between the convulsive dose (120 volts) and a fatal dose (400 volts).

Starting with Enrico X., ECT spread around the world. As psychiatrists added anesthesia and muscle relaxants to the procedure, its adoption spread to India and Latin America. By the First World Congress of Psychiatry in Paris in 1950, ECT was in its heyday and the French led the world in their use of the practice. However, ECT fell out of fashion in the 1960s and 1970s as opponents claimed it led to memory loss. The stigma surrounding ECT made headlines in 1972 when Missouri senator and U.S. Democratic vice presidential nominee Thomas Eagleton had to resign when it was disclosed that he had undergone ECT in the 1960s for depression. The perception that ECT "fried" brains gained ground, and California and Massachusetts were just two of many American states to pass legislation restricting ECT use. By 1980 ECT had disappeared from almost every U.S. mental hospital.

Then, suddenly, a turnaround occurred. Studies in the 1980s showed that ECT actually helped severely depressed people who were resistant to drug therapy. During that decade ECT began to make a comeback. In 1990 an American Psychiatric Association task force helped to rehabilitate ECT. A 2001 editorial in the *Journal of the American Medical Association* declared that it was "time to bring [ECT] out of the shadows." In 2004 the World Psychiatric Association endorsed ECT, and its use was on the upswing in Germany, Austria, and Israel. Like lobotomy, ECT through the years has aroused loud protests, but its longevity suggests that it must have been doing something right.[102]

If time appeared to vindicate ECT, the verdict on Henry Cotton's focal infection therapy was comparatively swift, negative, and irreversible. Cotton was the medical director of the Trenton (New Jersey) State Hospital, founded originally in 1848 by Dorothea Dix, who lived out her last years there as a guest at the institution. Cotton was impressed with research on toxin-producing bacteria and came up with the theory that psychosis was caused by localized infections in various parts of the body, including teeth and tonsils. Cotton decided that patients' symptoms, caused when toxins reached the brain, could be mitigated through surgical removal of infected body parts, and so he ordered hundreds of operations, the majority of which involved removing all or parts of patients' colons.[103]

Though he encountered plenty of skepticism in medical circles, Cotton enjoyed the friendship and support of Adolf Meyer. Cotton's belief that curing mental disease was not a hopeless task impressed a Canadian colleague, who said he was "glad that we have the optimist in medicine." Cotton's eagerness to try new physicalist methods briefly inspired other psychiatrists who longed for ways of discharging patients from their back wards.[104]

However, Cotton's stature in the profession plunged in the 1920s as doubts multiplied about his claims of high cure rates. His death in 1933 at age fifty-seven may have been merciful, if only because he did not live long enough to see his theory consigned to the dustbin of medical history.

LAST RESORT

Often dismissed as desperate stabs in the dark by self-interested psychiatrists obsessed with the goal of proving that their discipline was a legitimate medical specialty, lobotomy, ICT, ECT, and focal infection theory were instead the result of a mix of motives. To many psychiatrists, lobotomy seemed to prove that mental disabilities were indeed rooted in the anatomical structure of the brain, thus confirming that their specialty was not limited to the study of the psyche. The reason usually cited for the rapid falloff in the lobotomy rate in the 1950s was the introduction of the new anti-psychotic drugs, notably chlorpromazine. Undoubtedly, the arrival of medications that made schizophrenic patients in hospitals not only less agitated and troublesome, but also eligible for discharge into the community was a major advance in therapy. However, in some localities such as Israel, lobotomies were still being performed into the 1970s, long after such drugs had been introduced, and by the dawn of the twenty-first century, ECT, far from declining due to increased drug use, was enjoying a revival in many countries.

The dominance of psychoanalysis and similar forms of psychotherapy within psychiatry was another factor contributing to the decline of psychosurgery. Yet even Freud's biggest converts conceded that psychoanalysis was useless for "mental patients in the mass."[105] It would be comforting to imagine that enthusiasm for lobotomy ebbed because of humane revulsion over the operation among psychiatrists, but in the procedure's early stages even its advocates grimly conceded that it involved the destruction of brain matter. No one had any illusions about what the operation did to either brain tissue or a patient's personality.

Early on, media coverage certainly helped to quiet doubts about lobotomy. The press, often relying on what pro-lobotomy physicians told them, normally showered the operation with praise. Some U.S. journalists were critical, but generally most were caught up in the general enthusiasm over surgical solutions to medical conditions. The *New York Times* editorialized in 1949 that "surgeons now think no more of operations on the brain than they do of removing an appendix." The brain was "just a big organ ... no more sacred than the liver."[106] In 1947 the title of a *Life* magazine article read, "Operation to Cure Sick Minds Turns Surgeon's Blade into an Instrument of Mental Therapy." The *Life* article used Freudian terminology to argue that by severing the nerve connections between the prefrontal areas and the rest of the brain, the neuro-surgeon was freeing the mind from the tyrannical superego. Reporters dazzled by the seeming march of medical science overlooked this awkward mixing of psychoanalysis and brain surgery.[107]

Yet positive press coverage alone could not account for lobotomy lasting as long as it did. Clinical results suggested that, although from time to time surgeons operated on mental patients whose conditions did not warrant the procedure, other patients did actually improve after psychosurgery. In the 1930s a middle-aged Florida druggist tried to commit suicide twice and was institutionalized for a year and a half with severe depression. Forty days after the operation he was well enough to be sent home. His wife claimed his core personality had actually improved because of the lobotomy. Surgeon James Watts liked to display on his wall a poem written post-operatively by one of his patients:

> Gentle, clever your surgeon's hands
> God marks for you many golden bands
> They cut so sure they serve so well
> They save our souls from Eternal Hell

An artist's hands, a musician's too
Give us beauty of color and tune so true
But yours are far the most beautiful to me
They saved my mind and set my spirit free.

Relatives of patients, after years of stress from living with and caring for them, frequently implored psychiatrists to operate. Every time John Fulton returned from a trip, he faced a stack of letters from strangers pleading with him to perform a lobotomy. Relatives and patients themselves seemed to realize the operation could not produce a complete cure but were content if the procedure ended suicide attempts, violent outbursts, and destructive rampages. The magnitude of and mystery surrounding the operation often drew doctors, patients, and families together in a kind of collaboration in which the usual power gradients disappeared. No one was more eager to perform a lobotomy than Walter Freeman, but sometimes even he found himself being pressured by relatives to do something. So high was family demand for the operation for loved ones that researchers warned of the "great danger that lobotomy may become too popular."[108]

By no means were all psychiatrists supportive of lobotomy. Certain physicians, including Moniz and Freeman, were overly zealous in their advocacy of the operation, and their motivations were not above reproach. Freeman ultimately paid a stiff price for his stout defense of the procedure: his biographer has written that he "ranks as the most scorned physician of the twentieth century," next to Nazi doctor Josef Mengele.[109] A psychiatrist at the McLean Hospital in Massachusetts, a well-financed private hospital, admitted that "usually" lobotomies were done to "quiet people down."[110] Yet for many psychiatrists, lobotomy was a "last resort" for mostly incurable patients whose quality of life (and that of their desperate families) was abysmal. Most would have agreed with the Israeli David Bental that in the vast majority of cases lobotomy was the "lesser of two evils." It was either experiment with lobotomy or watch patients and families endure misery.

A striking feature of lobotomy was the higher incidence of operations for women. From January 1, 1949, to June 30, 1951, of all U.S. patients who underwent lobotomies 60 percent were women.[111] At hospitals such as the McLean, which had an active psychosurgical program, lobotomies on women outnumbered those for men. However, women residents also outnumbered men at the McLean by 2 to 1.[112] Many of the male residents had been diagnosed with drug and alcohol disorders, categories deemed unsuitable for lobotomy. Typically hospitalized women patients were not career women, and their doctors tended to think that a lobotomy stood a chance of returning them to their "normal" lives as housewives or dutiful daughters, whereas the operation might mean the end of a businessman's career. The higher incidence of lobotomy for women actually reflected psychiatrists' hope – not desperation – that the operation could help female patients.

The history of lobotomy and the other somatic therapies aptly captured the climate within the mental health field in the first half of the twentieth century. In retrospect these years were a turbulent transition period in the quest for mental health. The search for psychological wellness had taken enormous strides since the days of Dorothea Dix. The boundaries of medical knowledge were expanding rapidly against a backdrop of war, unrest, and political experimentation. Researchers conquered both new afflictions and diseases that had plagued humankind for centuries. Despite demoralizing frustrations at almost every turn, many mental health professionals were gripped at the same time by a resilient confidence that similar breakthroughs in the war against mental illness loomed on the horizon. While some succumbed to pessimism and apathy, others kept their faith in medical science and glimpsed a bright future behind the gloomy clouds that seemed to envelop the search for sanity. Still others, haunted by human suffering, were motivated by a keen desire to make people better.

As medical caregivers struggled with the challenges of treating mental diseases, governmental involvement in mental health services grew slowly but steadily. Policy makers repeatedly affirmed that it was in the interests of states to improve the physical and mental health of their populations, and the masses seemed to agree, as the first signs of a populist belief in an entitlement to mental health surfaced in the twentieth century. At the grassroots level, families too became increasingly involved in the process that saw asylums admit people with mental disabilities in mounting numbers as the twentieth century unfolded. Similarly, popular demand for medical care for conditions such as neurasthenia and hysteria – though typically confined to the affluent classes and the so-called worried well – rose in the course of the new century alongside a broadening public hunger for emotional well-being. Compared with the multi-billion-dollar sales industry in drug manufacturing at the end of the twentieth century, drug company profits a century earlier were modest; nonetheless, they were still a harbinger of the large role pharmaceutical corporations would play in the mental health field after mid-century.

Last, but not least, the expansion of the media in the form of radio, movies, newspapers, and popular magazines either trumpeted advances in psychiatric science and treatments or sensationalized the shortcomings of mental health care services. The basic message was the same, however: modern societies had an obligation to suffering humanity to end unhappiness and psychological distress through state investment in research, training, and services. In the post-1945 Cold War era this consensus in favor of bureaucracy, expertise, public administration, state welfare, and self-improvement was not immune from attacks, but its high standing at the outset of the twenty-first century suggested strongly that it enjoyed a kind of providential status that never failed to astonish its numerous critics.

FIGURE 1. Philippe Pinel (1745–1826) removing the chains from the inmates of Paris's Salpêtrière hospital in 1795. This picture depicts an epochal event in the quest for mental health, suggesting that with the arrival of the new discipline of psychiatry the mentally ill were emancipated from centuries of ignorance, cruelty, and brutal treatment. Yet scholars insist that it was not Pinel but a colleague who actually liberated the Salpêtrière's patients. Reproduced by permission of the Centre for Addiction and Mental Health Archives, Toronto.

FIGURE 2. Dorothea Dix (1802–87). No one did more to advance the cause of improved mental health care on both sides of the Atlantic Ocean than Dix, herself tormented by depression and anxiety for much of her adult life. Like so many other proponents of the asylum at the time, Dix was also an unflagging activist for school and prison reform. Reproduced by permission of the Centre for Addiction and Mental Health Archives, Toronto.

FIGURE 3. Dr. Joseph Workman (1805–94). Workman, the medical superintendent of the Toronto asylum from 1853 to 1875, was, like so many nineteenth-century advocates of asylum-based "moral treatment," a Unitarian who believed that the reformist crusade to build mental hospitals was part and parcel of a non-sectarian and non-dogmatic approach to religion. Reproduced by permission of the Centre for Addiction and Mental Health Archives, Toronto.

FIGURE 4. Queen Street Asylum, Toronto, front grounds, Fall–Winter, ca. 1910. By this time in history, in country after country mental hospitals such as the Toronto asylum had become highly visible institutions on the urban landscape. Reproduced by permission of the Centre for Addiction and Mental Health Archives, Toronto.

FIGURE 5. Capping ceremony, nursing students, Queen Street Asylum, Toronto, ca. 1906. By the early twentieth century more and more mental hospitals were staffed by trained female psychiatric nurses, an indication of the steady growth in professional disciplines involved in the quest for mental health during the twentieth century. Reproduced by permission of the Centre for Addiction and Mental Health Archives, Toronto.

FIGURE 6. Freud group. In 1909 the Viennese neurologist Sigmund Freud visited the United States for the first time, launching the history of psychoanalysis in twentieth-century American life. Pictured in this photo taken at Clark University in Massachusetts are Freud (front row left), Clark University president G. Stanley Hall (front row center), the Swiss-born psychiatrist Carl Jung (front row right), and Freud's followers A.A. Brill, Ernest Jones, and Sandor Ferenczi (left to right back row.) Reproduced by permission of the Centre for Addiction and Mental Health Archives, Toronto.

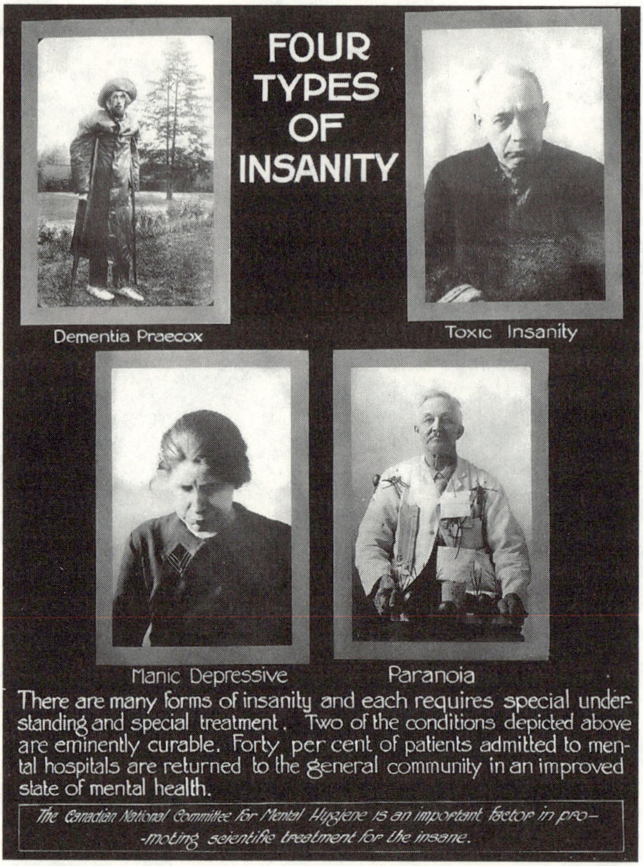
FOUR
TYPES
OF
INSANITY
Dementia Praecox
Toxic Insanity
Manic Depressive
Paranoia
There are many forms of insanity and each requires special understanding and special treatment. Two of the conditions depicted above are eminently curable. Forty per cent of patients admitted to mental hospitals are returned to the general community in an improved state of mental health.
The Canadian National Committee for Mental Hygiene is an important factor in promoting scientific treatment for the insane.

FIGURE 7. "Four Types of Insanity." This Canadian National Committee for Mental Hygiene poster from the early twentieth century depicts the four essential categories of mental illness as defined by medical experts. The CNCMH was just one of numerous organizations around the industrialized world that tried to convince the public and professions that not all forms of mental illness were incurable. Reproduced by permission of the Centre for Addiction and Mental Health Archives, Toronto.

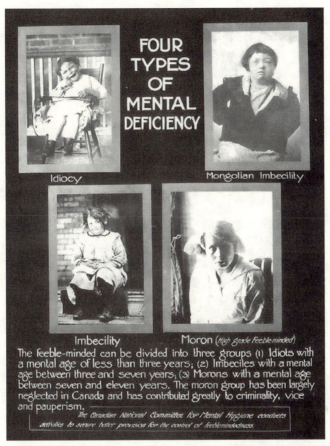

FIGURE 8. "Four Types of Mental Deficiency." A CNCMH poster reflecting the growing interest during the early twentieth century in what today would be called the "developmentally delayed." Officials in the mental hygiene movement often urged governments to confine these groups to special institutions or subject them to eugenic measures such as sterilization. Reproduced by permission of the Centre for Addiction and Mental Health Archives, Toronto.

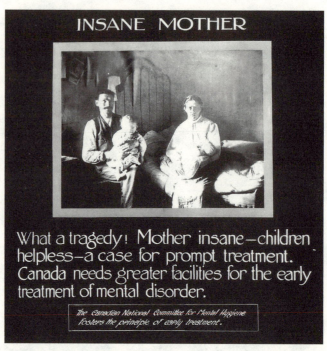

FIGURE 9. "Insane Mother." The CNCMH, like other mental hygiene organizations, preached that early detection and prompt treatment were keys to preventing the spread of mental disorders in families such as this one. Reproduced by permission of the Centre for Addiction and Mental Health Archives, Toronto.

FIGURE 10. The Allan Memorial Institute, Montreal, ca. 1975. In the post-1945 era "the Allan," as it was often called, stood out as one of the leading institutes for neurological research in the world. In 1943 the heirs of Sir Hugh Allan, a wealthy Montreal businessman, donated the building to Montreal's McGill University and Royal Victoria Hospital. It was there that Donald Ewen Cameron performed his infamous "psychic-driving" experiments. Reproduced by permission of the Centre for Addiction and Mental Health Archives, Toronto.

FIGURE 11. Brock Chisholm (1896–1971). A consummate maverick, Chisholm nonetheless occupied several top positions of power during the World War II and Cold War eras, including director general of the World Health Organization (1948–52). Chisholm became notorious for his advocacy of world government as the best vehicle for achieving global mental health. Reproduced by permission of the Centre for Addiction and Mental Health Archives, Toronto.

FIGURE 12. Heinz Lehmann (1911–89), German-born Canadian psychiatrist who played a leading role in the pharmaceutical revolution that swept psychiatry in the 1950s and beyond. Best known for his use of chlorpromazine in the treatment of schizophrenia, Lehmann became an international celebrity and target of anti-psychiatric protesters. Reproduced by permission of the Centre for Addiction and Mental Health Archives, Toronto.

4

A Bottomless Pit

The period stretching from World War II to the dawn of the twenty-first century was a time of tremendous ferment, conflict, and flux in the history of mental health policy and practice. In the 1950s governments began closing down mental hospitals by the droves, releasing countless patients into the community. Fifty years later the quest for mental health had come full circle, only this time the asylum was a casualty of history, not its savior.

On other fronts, lawmakers pledged unprecedented resources for mental health research, programs, and services. Researchers discovered remarkable new medications for psychosis and mood disorders, reached innovative insights into brain chemistry, and made impressive strides in evolutionary neuro-biology. New technologies of neuro-imaging enabled scientists to scan the brain and view anatomical and physiological phenomena never before seen.

Over the same period the population was aging steadily and a consumer revolt in medicine fundamentally altered the relationship between doctors and patients. The pharmaceutical industry spent millions trying to convince physicians, the public, government bureaucrats, and health insurance companies that their products were safe and effective, a campaign that helped send rates of prescription drug use soaring. Illegal drug use also spread, making addiction a central concern in the mental health field. The definition of psychiatric disease itself succumbed to inflationary pressures as more and more mental and behavioral states were labeled medical disorders. Never before in history were more people diagnosed as depressed, deluded, anxious, addicted, or addled. All the while, a mammoth industry of scientists, clinicians, and therapists expanded rapidly to meet a seemingly insatiable popular demand for psychological wellness.

By the end of the century an unprecedented number of people around the world were receiving some form of psychiatric or psychological treatment. Yet something else had changed. To many observers, the therapeutic sensibility – the dependence on the psychological sciences to ease personal unhappiness – extended into almost every nook and cranny of society. For the first time in history millions believed they were entitled to mental wellness and that emotional *unwellness* was an acceptable response to the conditions of modern existence. By the turn of the new century the quest for mental health had been democratized as never before. As stakeholders once again mobilized to reform mental health care in the early twenty-first century, they faced challenges that previous reformers could barely have imagined.

SYKEWAR

The transition to a therapeutic culture had been under way for some time, but it picked up speed thanks to a world war that altered the course of modern history. May 8, 1945, when Nazi Germany surrendered to the Allied powers, is often referred to as "Zero Hour." It must certainly have seemed so to many inhabitants of a devastated central Europe, especially Germans who viewed the end of the war as a liberation from the past as much as a crushing military defeat. Yet to those Allied powers whose lands were relatively unscathed by war, 1945 was less a new beginning than an excellent opportunity to apply the lessons learned from recent advances in science, medicine, technology, and public administration. For many in the mental health field, the stakes in the battle against mental disease appeared to be as high as those in the struggle to defeat Hitler and Imperial Japan. In the eyes of these experts, victory in the war over mental health looked to be just as attainable.

Much of this optimism stemmed from the perception that World War II had taught some valuable lessons about mental health. A major difference between the first and second world wars was that the usual lines separating the battlefront and the home front all but vanished during World War II, the deadliest armed conflict in human history. During World War I only a small fraction of the 10 million who died between 1914 and 1918 were civilians, but during World War II the civilian loss of life was enormous. Hundreds of thousands of civilians perished in bombing raids, including the dropping of atomic bombs on the Japanese cities Hiroshima and Nagasaki in the summer of 1945. The former Soviet Union's civilian death toll alone exceeded 20 million. Some 5 million non-combatant European Jews were killed in Nazi death and labor camps. Experts at the time argued that the lessons of total war had spawned a new kind of psychiatry that promised to heal the emotional wounds of entire peoples.

When world war broke out in 1939, army services generally were better prepared for the toll war exacted on soldiers' and civilians' nerves. The discovery of shell shock during World War I had alerted national governments to the need for better screening, training, monitoring, and leadership of recruits, as well as the usefulness of psychiatric expertise in determining different levels of intelligence. Experience from World War I also led psychologists and psychiatrists to doubt the wisdom of mass pension schemes for war-related emotional disorders. In post-1918 Germany, medical experts viewed the Bismarckian scheme of social insurance as a "malingerers' charter" that encouraged the labeling and recognition of *kriegsneurosen* while pushing the nation toward bankruptcy.[1] In 1939 a panel of British psychologists wrote:

> There should be no excuse given for the establishment of a belief that a functional nervous disability constitutes a right to compensation. This is a hard saying. It may seem cruel that those whose sufferings are real, whose illness has been brought on by enemy action and very likely in the course of patriotic service, should be treated with such apparent callousness. But there can be no doubt that in an overwhelming proportion of cases, these patients succumb to "shock" because they get something out of it. To give them this reward is not ultimately a benefit to them because it encourages the weaker tendencies in their character. The nation cannot call on its citizens for courage and sacrifice and, at the same time, state by implication that an unconscious cowardice or an unconscious dishonesty will be rewarded.

The warning in the psychologists' report was clear: if governments made it possible for people to "get something out of" succumbing to shock, then the country would be turned into "one vast raving Bedlam."

When war came, mental disorders proved to be by far the most glaring source of discharges from the British army. British military psychiatrists were slow to adopt selection and screening, but once they did they followed a mix of approaches based on the principles of prevention, deterrence, therapy, and drug treatment. A variety of factors account for the different rates of British psycho-neurosis between the two world wars: leadership and training had improved, doctors knew better what to expect, World War II was a "good war" without the shattered illusions of the earlier war, and demoralizing trench warfare was less prevalent in 1939–45. But equally the British decisions to eschew the term "shell shock" and refuse pensions for psychiatric casualties (until 1944) suggest that the United Kingdom's "pitiless psychology" struck a balance that other national approaches to military psychiatry failed to match.[2]

By contrast, Germany's armed forces tended to endure more battle stress than did the victorious Western Allies but recorded comparatively few psychiatric casualties. Allied psychiatrists claimed that German POWs appeared to be comparatively free of war neurosis. The Germans believed that wartime psychological disorders were due less to the war experience itself than to the desire to flee danger and receive financial compensation. German methods were based heavily on strict discipline (Germans shot more than 15,000 of their own soldiers for cowardice), and the incidence of suicide among the ranks was alarmingly high. For these and other reasons, it is likely that a good many German psychiatric casualties suffered in tragic silence.

At the other extreme, the U.S. armed forces quickly discovered that their reliance on screening did not prevent them from experiencing high casualty rates for mental disorders. Eventually, almost 1.9 million recruits were rejected by psychiatric screening, a full 12 percent of all recruits, but an additional 550,000 were discharged for "neuro-psychiatric" reasons, close to half of all discharges for health reasons. The grand total of all U.S. personnel formally disqualified from military service because of psychological disorders was 2.5 million.

As astounding as these statistics are, they take on new meaning when examined in greater detail. In a six-month span in 1944, the psychiatric casualty rate among U.S. combat divisions in Europe rose as high as 75 percent under intense combat conditions. Future U.S. president Dwight D. Eisenhower (1952–60), commander in chief of Allied Supreme Headquarters, talked about the "lost divisions" due to mental breakdown. His war experience certainly shaped his later thinking as president when he mused about the Cold War being a "Mind's Race" as well as an arms race. Elsewhere Eisenhower called the Cold War a "sykewar," a World War II code name for psychological warfare.[3] To Eisenhower, like many in the mental health field, victory in a future war would come down to who had the sanest men in arms. Governments that ignored the mental health of their citizens ran the risk of annihilation.

SAVED BY PSYCHOLOGY

Eisenhower's interpretation of the Cold War as a "sykewar" revealed the hefty influence of the Menningers, William and Karl, from Topeka, Kansas. Known popularly as "Dr. Will" and "Dr. Karl," they were at the forefront of the effort to convince the public to reconsider its conventional attitude toward health if human beings hoped to survive the new age that was dawning. The Menningers, along with their father, Charles, were world-renowned psychiatrists who managed Winter Veterans' Administration Hospital, founded Topeka's Menninger Clinic, and trained scores of psychiatrists from the United States and abroad. Karl wrote the best sellers *The Human Mind* (1930), *Man Against Himself* (1938), and *The Vital Balance* (1965). During World War II William Menninger was the U.S. army's chief of psychiatry. In 1948 *Time* magazine featured Will on its cover and called him "psychiatry's U.S. sales manager."[4] The title was apt because in upcoming years no one did more to "sell" psychiatry to Americans than Will and the other Menningers.

The Menningers emerged from the war as the nation's most respected authorities on mental health. They advocated an eclectic approach to mental health that combined both cutting-edge, cosmopolitan trends and old-fashioned American empiricism, which said that as long as it seemed to work it was worth using. Menninger-style psychiatry was ideally suited for a nation that valued forward-looking technocratic expertise, yet still clung emotionally to an idealized past of small towns, neighborly familiarity, and grassroots civic involvement. The fact that the Menningers hailed from midwestern Topeka rather than Manhattan or Boston helped to smooth their acceptance as America's favorite psychiatrists.

Yet as much as they identified with the nation's heartland, the Menningers were dedicated to breaking with the past, notably psychiatry's institution-based history stretching back to the nineteenth century. Though personally conventional, Will Menninger became the leader of a young generation of U.S. psychiatrists who longed to branch out beyond the walls of the state hospital. On the eve of World War II three-quarters of all U.S. psychiatrists were employed in state hospitals, but ten years later that number had dwindled to 17 percent. In earlier days mental health experts had talked about taking psychiatry into the community. The big difference in the post-1945 era was that many psychiatrists imagined that the key to improving mental health was a clean break with the asylum. Many up-and-coming psychiatrists had similar military backgrounds, valued private practice over hospital service, were enamored of Freudian-style psychotherapy, and were not as wedded as the old guard to the traditions of asylum psychiatry. Their experiences with treating war neuroses in combat zones left them optimistic about the possibilities of curing patients. They asserted the resounding superiority of what they called social psychiatry to the whole idea of state hospital medicine.

Social psychiatry became highly politicized against the backdrop of a postwar world seemingly teetering on the brink of war between communism and Western-style democracy. For the second time in thirty years, opinion makers – notably in the United States – insisted that the world be made safe for democracy once again. This time many expected mental health policies to play a major role in winning the war for the minds of men and women.

To realize the goals of social psychiatry the Group for the Advancement of Psychiatry (GAP), a collection of committees within the American Psychiatric Association (APA), was formed in 1946. Will Menninger, who spearheaded GAP's founding, capitalized on wartime imagery when he called it a "mobile striking force for American psychiatry," prepared to invade fields of endeavor that the supposedly "do-nothing" APA had historically shunned.[5] Psychiatrists were urged to get "out of the hospitals and clinics and into the community," where they would lead the campaign for "individual and communal health." Psychiatrists needed to "renovate" their specialty by focusing on "social problems and social needs," Will Menninger said in 1947. GAP psychiatrists trained their sights on "child and adult education, social and economic factors which influence the community status of individuals and families, intergroup tensions, civil rights and personal liberty."[6] Reflecting the can-do optimism of postwar America, GAP invited members of the other "helping professions" – clinical psychologists, social workers, psychiatric nurses, and the like – to join it in changing the world.[7]

The distinctive version of politicized psychiatry fashionable in the 1940s was evident in the teachings of Brock Chisholm, who became notorious as the "man who killed Santa Claus." Chisholm was a psychiatrist who during World War II was Canada's deputy minister of health and also served as director general of medical services for the entire Canadian army. In 1948 Chisholm was named the first director general of the World Health Organization, earning him the unofficial title of "doctor to the world."[8] Chisholm was a fervent backer of the WHO's new (and open-ended) definition of health as not merely "the absence of illness, but a state of complete physical, mental, and social well-being."

Chisholm had other, more controversial views, including his theory that Santa Claus was "an offence against peace." In 1945 he told an Ottawa audience that

> any child who believes in Santa Claus has had his ability to think permanently destroyed.... Can you imagine a child of four being led to believe that a man of grown stature is able to climb down a chimney.... He will become a man who has ulcers at 40, develops a sore back when there is a tough job to do, and refuses to think realistically when war threatens.

According to Chisholm's no-nonsense way of thinking, this form of parenting created human beings incapable of thinking on their own and made them "easy meat for demagoguery and mob orators."

Essentially Chisholm traced all the ills of the world to the family: parents, unless they diligently followed the advice of experts like Chisholm, were to blame for war, poverty, hatred, intolerance, and injustice. Chisholm told wartime audiences that mothers had spoiled their sons, making them unfit for the psychological strain of battle. "From earliest childhood a boy is trained not to run risks so as not to break his mother's heart." Poor parenting skills, he insisted, not the actual conditions of war, were responsible for the proportion of those suffering from mental breakdown in Canada's armed forces reaching 25 percent.[9]

In attacking Canada's mothers, Chisholm was relying on the theory of "momism," a popular concept during the quarter-century between World War II and the Nixon presidency among psychiatrists who were experienced in dealing with men in uniform. Edward Strecker, a onetime APA president, agreed that mothers put their nations at risk. Strecker claimed that mothers made their sons immature when they failed to "untie the emotional apron string." At the same time many North American psychiatrists subscribed to the notion of the "schizophrenogenic mother," introduced by the Freudian Frieda Fromm-Reichmann, a refugee from Nazi Germany. Fromm-Reichmann's theory stated that schizophrenia was caused by overprotective yet emotionally cold mothers.[10]

Chisholm's Santa Claus speech was one tactic in his larger campaign to popularize a new approach to mental health in the atomic age. More outspoken than the Menningers, Chisholm shared GAP's belief that world war had revolutionized the study and practice of psychiatry. He thought it necessary to construct an entirely new world order based on a revolutionary interpretation of citizenship that stressed emancipation from traditional mores. Chisholm's colleague, University of Pennsylvania psychiatrist Kenneth Appel, insisted that conservatism itself was a personality disorder. Arthur Schlesinger, Jr., claimed American conservatives were guilty of "schizophrenia." Left-of-center social scientists, including David Riesman, Nathan Glazer, and Richard Hofstadter, defined conservatism as a problem of abnormal psychology, a failure of intolerant, uninformed, and uneducated individuals to adjust to the complex modern world. People's primary loyalty ought to be to humankind in general, not to family, tribe, church, or country. Psychiatry's job, Chisholm and Appel believed, was to help train a new generation of world citizens. The prospects for peace, prosperity, and security hinged on a scientifically grounded approach to mental health that radically changed the emotional lives of every man, woman, and child. As the psychologist Abraham Maslow declared, "The world will be saved by psychologists – in the very broadest sense – or else it will not be saved at all."[11]

Chisholm's bold calls for developing a "new kind of human being" on the basis of psychological knowledge did not enjoy widespread support. Yet for a brief moment after World War II, it appeared that there might be the political will to wage a war in favor of mental health on a global scale. Chisholm's basic message that the key challenge facing medical experts was the pursuit of psychological well-being rather than curing people with mental disabilities fared better and represented a major watershed in history: the search for sanity was now as vital a quest as the effort to treat those already ill.

The new version of social psychiatry spread beyond America's borders and across much of Europe outside the Iron Curtain. In West Germany, memories of medicine during the Third Reich discredited the biological reductionism of Nazism and sparked attempts to treat the whole patient. This patient-centered form of social psychiatry often emphasized "community" living, the environmental origins of mental disease, and the use of psychological types of treatment. The reach of social psychiatry varied from one country to another, depending on the opposition it encountered from psychiatrists who preferred biological therapies. But there was no mistaking its politicized nature wherever its advocates were successful in putting ideas into practice. To its defenders social psychiatry was democracy in action and deserved the full backing of governments at all levels.

THE AFFLUENT SOCIETY

Back in the United States, GAP captured the headlines, but there too its efforts did not go unopposed. Many members of the APA disliked its radical direction. GAP's adversaries defended psychiatry's links to biological medicine and tended to be skeptical about the grand claims of psychotherapists.[12] The tensions between GAP's followers and biologically oriented psychiatrists would simmer for years, only to end in the 1970s when biological psychiatry emerged victorious.

In the meantime, to realize its self-proclaimed, groundbreaking destiny, GAP openly cultivated close ties with the media. The 1940s and 1950s were years in America's history dominated by the techniques of advertising and public relations. An older industrial culture of production and saving was giving way to one of sales, services, and consumption, a new bureaucratic age highlighting human relations. In his *Lonely Crowd* (1950) sociologist David Riesman maintained that this transition from industrial to post-industrial culture affected the American social character, producing an "other-directed" personality type that persistently sought to conform to the values of "peer groups" and the media. Psychologist Erich Fromm called the "other-directed" type the "marketing personality."

Trust and amiability, public relations experts testified, were necessary to "sell" products to the American public, and GAP psychiatrists, being open to innovation, welcomed the opportunity to "sell" psychiatry and the "product" of mental health. GAP's cultivation of the media was pioneering and far-sighted. Television had just arrived, radically expanding the possibilities of spreading information about mental health. The fine line between addressing real needs and stimulating demand for services was gradually fading in a day and age of rapidly changing communications technology.[13]

In the midst of an economic boom unlike any other in history, Americans increasingly viewed mental health as another valued consumer product. In the mid-1950s the average American had twice as much real income to spend as in the prosperous 1920s and also had more time to spend that income. Most workers enjoyed at least two weeks of vacation per year. Economist John Kenneth Galbraith argued in *The Affluent Society* (1958) that Americans, spurred on by mass advertising, were frantically buying consumer goods, including automobiles, televisions, and dishwashers, all the while unwisely plunging into debt. Despite the millions who still lived in poverty, the rising age expectancy for Americans combined with the perception of material progress to convince many people that their quality of life would only get better and psychiatry – like modern industry – could help them achieve such a goal.[14]

The "selling" of mental health based on wartime clinical experience paid off in the late 1940s as the federal government launched the largest hospital-building program in American history. Under the Veterans

Administration (VA), sixty-nine veterans' hospitalswere constructed, each with its own psychiatric unit. Sixteen veterans' psychiatric hospitals were also built. The number of psychiatric cases in all VA hospitals doubled between 1940 and 1948. VA hospitals became hotbeds of psychiatric training and research. They were also sites of escalating consumer demand, as veterans and their family members sought assistance for the emotional challenges they faced during the transition to peacetime. Marital tensions and parenting difficulties tended to be the most common complaints. As demand mounted, waiting lists for clinical services grew longer and longer. To psychologist Carl Rogers, the counseling that veterans and their families received not only helped them adjust to peacetime living, but also made them better democratic citizens. A client was no longer "just another G. I. Joe," Rogers wrote, but someone who "begins to resume selfhood as a specific, unique individual." This type of counseling, according to Rogers, was nothing less than an exercise in "democracy" itself.[15]

World war thrust the issue of mental health onto the national and international stage in another pivotal way. In 1946, amid a crescendo of veterans' demands for expanded services and complaints about the sorry state of military mental health, the U.S. Congress passed the National Mental Health Act (NMHA), laying the groundwork for the National Institute of Mental Health (NIMH). The steady increase in the NIMH budget over its first decade and a half (from $9 million in 1949 to $189 million in 1964) mirrored the bipartisan perception in Washington that mental health research was a key national priority. The NMHA and the NIMH marked the first time in the nation's history that the federal government became a prime agent of reform and innovation in mental health policy. It would not be the last.

TEAMWORK

As psychiatrists took stock of the many changes wrought by the world war, they noticed that the mental health care field was getting increasingly crowded. To some in organized medicine, this proliferation of mental health professions was a natural development. The medical director of the National Committee for Mental Hygiene noted:

> As the psychiatrist left the institution ..., the further he proceeded into the community, the more he began to see new material, to be challenged by problems he had never been called upon to face before, to be confronted by questions to which there were no ready answers. As

he studied these problems and his relationship to them, certain things
became evident both on the social and technical side – in the first place,
that he could not continue to maintain a proud professional attitude, a
dictator who from his professional height observed and gave out edicts
to the more humble; that he was already beyond his depths; that he
has reached the limits of his knowledge, and must now take his place
humbly with other workers that together they might extend the borders
of knowledge and find solutions for problems that thus far in human
history had remained unsolved.[16]

The rise of the mental hygiene movement, by introducing the notion of a
"team" of mental health workers, justified the inclusion of not only other
medical specialists such as endocrinologists, pediatricians, and neurologists, but psychologists, nurses, educators, and social workers as well.
Child guidance, the effort to use science to discover why children showed
up in juvenile courts, was another new profession consisting of people
without medical training who claimed expertise in areas that overlapped
the mental health sphere.

Few mental health–oriented disciplines that emerged in the twentieth century could match the professional success of marriage counseling. For centuries people had been consulting their priests, physicians,
village elders, and the like about their family problems, but only in
the twentieth century did a profession appear whose primary purpose
was to offer expert advice about family matters, especially relations
between spouses. The origins of marriage counseling lay in the eugenics
and mental hygiene movements, and dated back to Weimar Germany
(1919–33), where reformers founded clinics designed to treat married
men and women with complaints about their conjugal relations, including reproduction and contraception. When World War II intensified
debate over America's divorce rate, notably because of the popularity of
war marriages and the return of soldiers to their families at war's end,
marriage counseling began to flourish. The link between the war and the
rise of marriage counseling was reflected in the 1942 founding of the
American Association of Marriage Counselors, the first national organization dedicated to establishing standards for training and licensing,
shortly after the bombing of Pearl Harbor. During the 1950s America's
divorce rate dipped slightly, but as it began to climb again after the 1960s
marriage counseling continued its striking growth. By the end of the
twentieth century there were tens of thousands of marriage counselors,
therapists, and social workers in the United States and abroad. Marriage
counseling was one of the foremost professions within the enormous
"caring industry."[17]

The expansion of marriage counseling was stimulated by the growth of the media, principally television. Paul Popenoe, the founder of one of America's first marriage counseling clinics, the Los Angeles–based American Institute for Family Relations, was a frequent guest on Art Linkletter's television program *House Party*, dispensing advice on how to stay married and what to expect before tying the marital knot. Popenoe, who invented computer dating, reached a huge audience because Linkletter's show enjoyed an audience of millions of viewers (many of whom were housewives), and for decades he authored a column on marital advice in the women's magazine *Ladies Home Journal*.[18]

The development of marriage counseling dovetailed with the emergence of sex counseling as a discipline and similarly benefited from the expansion of communications technology. When Alfred Kinsey's *Sexual Behavior in the Human Male* (1948) and *Sexual Behavior in the Human Female* (1953) were published, the media lavished considerable attention on his findings, which suggested that Americans failed to live up to their own standards of sexual conduct. In the 1960s physician William Masters and psychologist Virginia Johnson took up where Kinsey left off, offering therapy for couples with sexual dysfunctions. Their faces appeared in a wide variety of magazines, including *Time* and *Playboy*, and they were guests on numerous television talk shows, another media innovation of the 1960s. By the 1970s hundreds of sex clinics had sprung up across the United States, sparking calls for licensing and credentialing standards in sexual therapy. Yet despite wide differences in theory and clinical methods, practitioners in the field agreed, first, that a key component of mental health was sexual gratification and, second, that men and women in committed relationships needed expert advice to deal with their difficulties. High demand for marriage counseling suggested that the viewpoint that conjugal happiness was achievable through professional intervention was widely shared throughout American society. As public faith in marriage counseling grew, couples with shaky relationships who did not seek expert guidance ran the risk of appearing less than committed to their partners than those who did. Thus, over the course of the twentieth century, marriages, as one U.S. newspaper declared in 1959, became "society's business" as never before.[19]

Also benefiting from this shift in the quest for mental health was the discipline of psychology. For most of their early history, psychologists strove to free themselves from the field of academic philosophy, but until they did they had little experience treating patients. In the 1930s professional turf wars between Psychology and Psychiatry broke out. Psychiatrists openly questioned psychologists' claims to be able to relieve mental suffering. In 1933 the APA president accused psychologists of launching an "invasion" of the field of mental medicine without the skills to back it up.[20]

Yet wartime shortages in mental health personnel boosted the status of psychologists, as they conducted research, assisted in mobilizing and training military personnel, and devised diagnostic tests and motivational materials. After the war many psychiatrists, impressed with what psychologists had been able to accomplish in military settings, welcomed them as partners in "psychiatric teams," but as Will Menninger stressed, psychiatrists insisted on being the "quarterback."[21]

Wartime successes in returning servicemen to combat and civilian life laid the foundations for the sixfold growth in membership of the American Psychological Association between 1940 and 1960. Over the same time period the number of members involved in actual clinical work soared from 272 to more than 2,500. Meanwhile, the media celebrated the exploits of prominent psychologists such as Erich Fromm, Carl Rogers, Abraham Maslow, and Rollo May – to say nothing of psychiatrists practicing psychoanalysis – as psychology steadily shaped attitudes toward addiction, child rearing, and even religion. Indeed, some U.S. theologians, including Protestant Norman Vincent Peale and Rabbi Joshua Liebman, used psychological theories to transform religion into a form of therapy. Peale and Liebman were just two of the more well known post-1945 clergymen to de-emphasize sin and guilt and redefine their pastoral work in terms of psychological counseling as a means of achieving personal growth and "peace of mind" (the title of Liebman's 1946 book).[22]

In the 1950s and 1960s psychologists and psychiatrists unsuccessfully tried to negotiate a truce that settled where one discipline's jurisdictional boundaries ended and the other's began. The right of psychiatrists to prescribe medications remained a pivotal difference between the two professions. For the rest of the century, as biological psychiatry began its ascendancy, uneasy relations festered, in contrast to the relatively tranquil relationship between psychiatry and social workers and psychiatric nurses. Meanwhile the ranks of non-medical personnel increased dramatically thanks to the escalating demand for mental health services and the proliferation of community mental health programs. At the end of the twentieth century the field was glutted with various professions, occupations, and interest groups, many of which had different visions of how to pursue the quest for emotional wellness.[23]

By the mid–twentieth century, then, it was clear that total war had profoundly shaped the quest for mental health. War led national governments to mobilize their populations, breaking down conventional distinctions between the civilian and military sectors of society. Organizations and institutions across the spectrum of American society deemed mental health to be synonymous with the nation's political ideals. Even private matters such as love and marriage, one expert insisted, were a "national concern." Leaders in the field insisted that Cold War Americans needed "not simply peace of mind but strength of mind."[24] War had created conditions that experts claimed had to be addressed in the interests of national security and prosperity, while also providing psychiatrists and psychologists with abundant opportunities for study, practice, and self-promotion. Their military experiences convinced them that the search for sanity had the tremendous potential to transform the everyday lives of people in America and around the world.

MOOD MEDICINE

While Brock Chisholm, GAP, and the Menningers preached their message that mental health was too important a matter to be left to ordinary people, crucial events were transpiring elsewhere that would similarly expand the definition of emotional illness. By the summer of 1952 the inhabitants of the neighborhood surrounding the Sainte-Anne mental hospital in Paris's Fourteenth Arrondissement knew something was up inside the old asylum. Every spring the hospital's windows were thrown open and the sounds of the agitated patients flooded the streets outside. Yet in 1952 a comparative calm prevailed. Whenever Sainte-Anne psychiatrist Jean Thuillier encountered local merchants, he was asked, "What are you doing with the patients up there? We don't hear them anymore." "I'm not killing them," Thuillier replied defensively.[25]

Actually, what Thuillier and his chief, Jean Delay, were doing was administering the latest drug for combating severe mental disabilities. Delay and his assistants were experimenting with a new compound derived from research into antihistamines by the Rhône-Poulenc pharmaceutical company. The drug was called chlorpromazine, the first of the phenothiazine anti-psychotics. Its most remarkable chemical property was its ability to calm patients without sedating them. The research that produced chlorpromazine, in the words of Hungarian-born psycho-pharmacologist Thomas Ban, "dragg[ed] psychiatry into the modern world."[26]

Starting in Paris at the Sainte-Anne hospital, chlorpromazine use spread to hospitals in Lyon and Basel. In Germany, as in France, the medication – launched as Megaphen – proved to be most popular among younger asylum psychiatrists willing to experiment with new treatments.[27] The scene quickly shifted to Canada. In 1953 Ruth Koeppe-Kajander, training in psychiatry at the London (Ontario) mental hospital, obtained permission to give the drug to twenty-five patients. Later in 1953 she reported that patients on the medication lost their agitation but not their consciousness. That same year German-born Heinz Lehmann, a psychiatrist at Montreal's Douglas Hospital, was relaxing in his bath when he first read the European reports about chlorpromazine. Intrigued, he ordered supplies of the drug, administered it to seventy patients, and with Canadian psychiatrist Gorman Hanrahan proclaimed its effectiveness.[28]

Chlorpromazine was licensed in the United States by the Food and Drug Administration (FDA) in March 1954 and distributed by Smith, Kline and French under the trade name Thorazine (Largactil in Britain). Lehmann's international notoriety was cemented in 1957 when he shared the prestigious Albert A. and Mary Woodward Lasker prize. Lehmann's exploits helped to make Montreal's McGill University, where he taught, one of the leading centers for psychiatry in the world, along with Topeka's Menninger Foundation and the Maudsley Hospital in London.

The coming of Thorazine was a groundbreaking event in the quest for mental health. Thanks to Thorazine and other new drugs, a profound change in the way people lived their lives and thought about their own feelings was about to sweep the world over the course of the second half of the twentieth century. Millions of people began popping prescription psychiatric pills. The pharmaceutical industry rapidly became a multi-billion-dollar business with impressive lobbying clout in the corridors of political power and the revenue to pay for mass advertising of its products. Smith, Kline and French made $75 million in 1955 alone, a lot of money in those days.[29]

In 1945 about 1 percent of the U.S. population sought psychiatric therapy. By 1980 prescription drug use had bumped that figure up to a full 10 percent.[30] The efforts of Brock Chisholm and the Menningers laid the ideological foundations of therapism, the doctrine that an unprecedented number of people suffered from bona fide mental illnesses and required treatment from a range of expert healers. But the pharmaceutical revolution transformed therapism into a mainstay of everyday life for huge swaths of the population.

Lost amid the excitement over the new medications was the fact that drug treatment of people with severe mental disabilities was far from new. Early in the nineteenth century the synthesis of organic compounds gave rise to the pharmaceutical industry, as giant companies such as Bayer and Ciba extended their dye-making operations to include the manufacture of drugs. The oldest, widely used sedative in medicine was potassium bromide, a favorite drug of asylum psychiatrists in the second half of the nineteenth century. Its anti-convulsant properties were a big asset, but its toxicity was a major drawback. Chloral hydrate, introduced in 1869 as a therapeutic agent by German professor of pharmacology Otto Liebreich, had even more powerful sedative features and dominated drug therapy until the mid–twentieth century. By the early twentieth century chloral hydrate ("knock-out drops") was psychiatrists' drug of choice for their hospitalized patients – it helped inmates sleep, a vital consideration for over-worked staff members. It was also handy for people to use at home so they would not require admission to an asylum; novelist Virginia Woolf, for example, took the drug in the 1920s.

Chloral hydrate's unpleasant taste and the odor it left on the breath did not prevent countless men and women from habitually using it and becoming addicted to it, as well as to barbiturates, such as Veronal, first marketed in the United States in 1903. It was only when the tranquilizer Miltown was introduced in 1955 that prescriptions for chloral hydrate fell out of favor (though barbiturate use remained robust until the 1980s).

Once Thorazine arrived on the scene, chloral hydrate quickly became a pharmacological dinosaur. The immediate effect of Thorazine on many patients was astounding. Patients who had been hospitalized for years suddenly improved so much that they could be returned to their families. One French psychiatrist described a farmer, hospitalized for five or six years, who underwent "almost a resurrection" when he started taking the new medication. U.S. psychiatrist Donald Klein later recalled a patient who had not said a thing in thirty years, but after taking chlorpromazine asked a hospital staff member, "When am I getting out of here?" "It was Rip Van Winkle," Klein observed, "an honest to God miracle." Other public hospital psychiatrists rejoiced that for the first time in memory they could have potted plants, glassware, and other breakable objects on the wards, because patients were no longer violent. Chlorpromazine replaced paraldehyde, legendary for producing the foul smells many psychiatrists remembered years later about life in asylums. To Winfred Overholser, medical superintendent of the mammoth St. Elizabeths

Hospital in Washington, D.C., Thorazine and similar drugs heralded the end of "Bedlamism."[31]

Thorazine's arrival, coinciding with the hoopla over the polio vaccine, penicillin, and other medical "magic bullets," suggested that chlorpromazine was a similar wonder drug. However, the euphoria began to wear off once the new anti-psychotics started to have worrying side effects, especially in the United States, where dosages sometimes reached 350 mg a day, in contrast to Europe, where dosages of 150 mg were considered healthy. In the 1960s it became obvious that patients who took the drug over the long term exhibited odd tongue, jaw, and cheek movements, symptoms that mimicked Parkinsonism. Clinicians began calling these involuntary side effects "tardive dyskinesia." Patients disliked these symptoms so much that once released from the hospital they soon stopped taking their medication. Knowledge about what was and was not an unhealthy dose gradually increased, but meanwhile excitement over Thorazine tended to wane over the balance of the twentieth century.[32]

PEACE OF MIND PILLS

People with milder mental symptoms were also affected by scientific discoveries in pharmaceutical laboratories. Before the 1950s people with "nerves" had relied on over-the-counter nostrums that were often laced with alcohol or opium. Despite mounting official alarm over overdoses due to unregulated self-medication, Americans in the first half of the twentieth century ingested a variety of medicines to calm their anxieties, make them happier, and help them sleep. Those containing the sedative bromide were popular, as was the barbiturate Veronal, marketed as a sleep-inducing agent.

Production and sales of barbiturates leapt during World War II as army physicians used them liberally to help dying, wounded, fatigued, or shell-shocked troops. Then in 1954 Miltown, the brand name for meprobamate, hit the market. Miltown, the first of the so-called minor tranquilizers, was discovered by Czechoslovak-born Frank Berger, who worked in the laboratories of the makers of Carter's Little Liver Pills. Berger liked the word "tranquilizer" because it distinguished meprobamate – a sedative – from the barbiturates. Soon, the press was hyping tranquilizers as "peace of mind pills." As one psychiatrist later commented, Miltown "*was* the revolution."[33]

Miltown, named after a hamlet in New Jersey near Berger's lab, was hailed as the "penicillin of psychiatry." Celebrities happily sang its praises.

Comedian Milton Berle told *Time* magazine that "[i]t's worked wonders for me. In fact, I'm thinking of changing my name to Miltown Berle." Miltown, dubbed a "dry martini," was served at "Miltown parties" across suburban North America. No drug had ever been in such demand in the United States or enjoyed so much media fanfare.[34]

Miltown's fame lasted only a few years. It was followed by the even safer benzodiazepines Librium in 1960 and Valium in 1963. The benzodiazepines were the brainchild of Leo Sternbach, who, like Frank Berger, moved to the United States as a refugee from Nazi anti-Semitism. Valium soon became the most widely prescribed drug in recorded history. As he faced one Cold War crisis after another, U.S. President John F. Kennedy took Librium to calm his nerves. Studies in 1979 and 1981 showed that about one in ten adult Americans had taken a tranquilizer one or more times during the previous year.

Some commentators claimed that Americans were more tranquilized than people in other parts of the world, but studies showed that adults in countries such as Belgium, Denmark, France, Germany, and the Netherlands ingested more benzodiazepines than the average American. As benzodiazepine use tapered off in the United States and Great Britain in the 1980s, per capita tranquilizer consumption increased in France and Japan. In 1998 a psycho-pharmacologist attributed the French fondness for benzodiazepines to the fact that the French were "more relaxed" than Anglo-Americans in their attitudes toward taking pills to calm nerves. In Japan cultural values did not discourage people from reporting anxiety symptoms, so doctors appeared even more willing than their U.S. colleagues to prescribe benzos.[35]

Meanwhile, Miltown represented a watershed in two respects. It was lauded for being non-addictive and safe, without any "hangover" effects. Additionally, Miltown, unlike barbiturates, was not toxic enough to be fatal if ingested in either accidental or intentional overdoses. For "seekers of fast relief," "instant happiness" seemed just a swallow away.[36]

With the arrival of Miltown, anti-anxiety drugs also ceased to be sold over the counter. Prior to World War II prescription-only drugs were limited to narcotics, and for the most part the market in drugs was free. In 1951 the U.S. Food and Drug Administration, thanks to the Humphrey–Durham amendments to the 1938 Food, Drugs, and Cosmetics Act, announced that all new drugs would be available by prescription only. The thalidomide scandal of the early 1960s ended debate over consumer access to drugs. Thalidomide, a sedative and tranquilizer, was launched in 1957 by a German firm, sold over the counter, and ingested by thousands of pregnant women. Four years later shocking news surfaced in Germany, Canada, Australia, and Africa of severe birth defects due to thalidomide use. The thalidomide tragedy might have happened even with closer medical oversight, but after the uproar over thalidomide there was little chance that psychiatric drugs would be available without a physician's prescription.[37]

The thalidomide event shook public faith in industry's pledge to provide "better living through chemistry." The horror over thalidomide coincided with the publication of Rachel Carson's *Silent Spring* (1962), a searing indictment of the health effects of pesticides and herbicides manufactured and marketed by chemical companies. Three years later consumer advocate Ralph Nader published *Unsafe at Any Speed*, which attacked the automobile industry's tendency to emphasize design over safety. Nader was not simply an old-style muckraker who exposed abuse and corruption in government and the business world; he applied pressure on the public and private sectors to guarantee consumers rights to safety, informed choice, and redress. Nader's activism thrust consumerism into the national spotlight, and his relentless and uncompromising attacks on businesses and government led to the founding of new federal watchdog agencies such as the Occupational Safety and Health Administration, the Environmental Protection Agency, and the Consumer Product Safety Commission. In the name of protecting the consumer rights of average citizens to safety and security, government in the 1960s expanded its role in the everyday lives of Americans and millions around the world.

Adding to stories of corporate culpability was the 1970 FDA decree that high-estrogen oral birth control pills were unsafe, followed by Wisconsin Democrat Gaylord Nelson's widely viewed U.S. Senate hearings into "the Pill." Public confidence in industry to provide safe and effective drug products has remained shaky ever since, exerting pressure on the FDA and its counterparts in other countries to safeguard public safety by stringent testing of new drugs.

The FDA's high visibility during the debates over thalidomide and the Pill helped to catapult it into a position of increasing power for the rest of the twentieth century. It went from an underfunded and relatively obscure government agency entrusted largely with enforcement responsibilities to a huge federal bureaucracy dedicated to regulating the pharmaceutical industry.[38] Accompanying the expansion of the FDA's power in Washington and over industry was its growing function as a source of public information on the risks and benefits of new products, including psychiatric drugs. The FDA's burgeoning watchdog role meant that the state's involvement in the mental health field took a giant step forward.

One example of the FDA's reach was its controversial decision to declare meprobamate – Miltown – a dangerous drug subject to abuse, despite testimonials in its favor by several leading psycho-pharmacologists, including Thomas Ban, who admitted prescribing it into the 1980s. "It's a very good drug," Ban protested. "In outpatient psychiatry it's the best thing that ever happened."[39]

Another example of the FDA's clout involved the drug clozapine, discovered in 1958 when a Swiss company synthesized a group of compounds that proved effective against treatment-resistant schizophrenia. Patients with tardive dyskinesia who took clozapine often saw their symptoms vanish. Yet clozapine did not receive FDA approval until 1989, entering the U.S. market the next year, due to government concerns about cost containment, as well as scares about the drug suppressing bone marrow production of infection-fighting white blood cells. Lawsuits against clozapine's manufacturer for its high price tag further delayed its availability until 1992. The history of clozapine, a success story of psychopharmacology, illustrated how the historical context surrounding drug development changed abruptly after the 1960s. As new drug applications became more and more subject to bureaucratic regulation, the chances of effective drugs swiftly making it to the market shrunk as time went on.[40]

PSYCHEDELIC MEDICINE

The search for a wonder drug that could produce better and faster treatment and thus free up badly needed hospital beds led to the studies of English psychiatrist Humphry Osmond into the effects on patients of *d*-lysergic acid diethylamide (LSD). While living in England, Osmond had befriended Aldous Huxley, the author of *Brave New World* (1932). Huxley's 1954 book, *The Doors of Perception*, was based on his experiments with mescaline, a hallucinogenic drug to which Osmond had introduced him. (Rock star Jim Morrison later named his band after the title of Huxley's book.) In a 1957 letter to Huxley Osmond coined the term "psychedelic."

In years to come Harvard Professor Timothy Leary became known as the guru of LSD, but Humphry Osmond deserves the title as much as anyone. After moving to Canada, Osmond began collaborating with the Canadian psychiatrist Abram Hoffer, who shared his passion for research into the biochemistry of mental diseases. In 1943 Albert Hoffman, a young Swiss chemist, had accidentally discovered LSD's properties when he came in contact with the compound and began having bizarre and disturbing sensations. A few years later the chemical company that had bottled LSD sent a sample to Osmond and Hoffer, who quickly became convinced that LSD not only might cure schizophrenia, but might also reveal the biological nature of severe mental illness. Osmond and Hoffer agreed that taking hallucinogenic drugs opened up a whole new dimension of psychological experience that could prove both therapeutic and enlightening. One of their colleagues enthusiastically remarked, "Psychedelic drugs are to psychology what the microscope is to biology or the telescope is to astronomy."

Osmond and Hoffer viewed themselves as pragmatists following the trial-and-error paths blazed by researchers such as Henri Laborit, Ugo Cerletti, and Manfred Sakel. Osmond and Hoffer were willing to push the boundaries of accepted research, but they were disappointed to learn that other researchers, while willing to use chemicals to control patients' symptoms, objected to their claims that psychedelic drugs revolutionized psychiatric treatment.[41] Additionally, as the heady 1960s unfolded, LSD – or "acid," as it was often called – became closely identified with anti-establishment politics. LSD advocates including Timothy Leary and the rock band the Beatles lauded it for its supposed ability to unlock the mysteries of the mind and help its users achieve personal freedom.

In Scottish psychiatrist R. D. Laing's hands, LSD became a weapon with which to attack the psychiatric establishment, despite Osmond's and Hoffer's protests that it should be no such thing. In the words of a critic, "Amid the succession of psychiatric prophets who compelled attention during the sixties and early seventies it was R. D. Laing who dominated the scene longest, as arch-seer and prophet-in-chief."[42] Not only did Laing take LSD himself, he shared it with patients during therapy sessions. To Laing, LSD was a portal into a universe of enlightenment that revealed how the world of the mundane senses was false and dehumanizing.

PSYCHIC DRIVING

The public relations surrounding LSD were starkly different than the hoopla surrounding Miltown, which enjoyed the fulsome praise of the media, the entertainment industry, advertising firms, and organized medicine. LSD, by contrast, was quickly stigmatized as politically subversive. Laing, Leary, and others popularized LSD as a counter-cultural drug that young people swiftly adopted in their protests against established institutions, including organized medicine. Leary toured campuses urging university students to "turn on, tune in, and drop out" and alarmed public health authorities enough that in 1966 LSD was banned in California. The next year all other states banned the drug, followed by most other countries in the Western world. By that date, in the eyes of mainstream society LSD was linked to youth suicide, homicide, and campus unrest. Yet banning LSD only made it seem more subversive to a younger generation intent on challenging the status quo. By the late 1960s LSD, a product of scientific research, was a casualty of the political conflicts bred by the generation gap.

Osmond and Hoffer's psychedelic project showed the fuzzy line between failure and success in mental health research. Early on they concluded that LSD-induced hallucinations mimicked those of delirium tremens, the "rock-bottom" experiences that allegedly frightened many alcoholics into sobriety, so they advocated LSD's use in the treatment of alcoholics. Alcoholics Anonymous co-founder "Bill W." admired their work with problem drinkers, noting especially LSD's ability to introduce spirituality into the treatment of alcoholism. Pro-LSD psychiatrists who treated alcoholics reported 50 percent recovery rates. Psychedelic research in general enjoyed widespread support from patients, their families, and community organizations. Forty years later historian Erika Dyck contacted a handful of Osmond and Hoffer's patients, who told her that they were still happy they had participated in these trials.⁴³

The destiny of LSD was intertwined with military investigators' interest in it as a kind of "truth serum" that could be used to interrogate spies, which in turn led to the infamous experiments conducted by Scottish-born psychiatrist D. Ewen Cameron of McGill University's Allan Memorial Institute. Though his reputation was in tatters a decade after he died in 1967, during his lifetime Cameron was a global leader in psychiatry. In 1943 he started research at the Allan Memorial Institute, one of the foremost psychiatric institutes in the world. Before serving as the president of the World Psychiatric Association and the Canadian and American Psychiatric Associations, he was a member of the Nuremberg medical tribunal that sat in judgment on Nazi doctors accused of human rights abuses during World War II.

While at McGill, Cameron devised the therapy of "psychic-driving," which entailed electro-shock and insulin-induced coma in an effort to erase patients' bad memories and psychological patterns. Cameron's assistants made audio cassettes of positive messages, which they then played back to patients for days on end, what Cameron called "de-patterning." He also gave LSD to some patients in an effort to gain information about their lives. Even before Cameron left the Allan Institute in 1964, colleagues were raising questions about his methods. It was revealed that some of the funding for his experiments came from the Central Intelligence Agency (CIA). There is little doubt that Cameron and his team were aware that their research was of interest to the U.S. military in its search for effective "brain-washing" techniques. Eventually the CIA settled out of court with more than two hundred of Cameron's former patients.

Cameron was domineering and impatient, always "looking for short cuts [and] trying to speed up the treatment process," former colleague Thomas Ban remembered.[44] But the 1950s were a day and age when the boundaries between treatment and research, like those between voluntarism and involuntarism, were often not clear. It was a time of adventurism in medical research, when the hits received all the press and the misses were mostly ignored. Public confidence in medical scientists like Cameron was high. The backlash against Cameron's research helped pave the way to the introduction in later years of peer review, consent forms, ethics committees, and the vetting of funding, all designed to prevent abuses of human subjects in medical experiments. Some were left wondering if these safeguards simply added layers of bureaucracy that ultimately stifled freedom and creativity in mental health research. What the mounting concerns over biomedical research did do, however, was reveal the swelling popular demand that scientists and clinicians be more transparent in their professional activities. The belief that the medical establishment should be free to run its affairs as it alone saw fit was rapidly losing public support.

ANTI-PSYCHIATRY

The stories about Ewan Cameron's research fed a mounting, widespread uneasiness in many countries that the evolving relationships among government, industry, researchers, universities, the courts, and organized medicine threatened personal freedoms and public safety. Critics variously attacked psychiatrists, mental hospitals, shock therapies, the pharmaceutical industry, the laws governing mental patients, and the medical model of mental disease. Many of these attacks had been rehearsed earlier in history, but their general tenor and tone in the 1960s and 1970s were unprecedented in scope and magnitude. Despite its initial radicalism, however, the overall legacy of the anti-psychiatry movement, rather than to topple the mental health establishment, was to make it by the end of the twentieth century more inclusive than ever before.

One of the most accurate barometers of anti-psychiatry sentiment was the movies. Up to the 1970s Hollywood's depiction of psychiatry – for example, in *Spellbound* (1945), with Ingrid Bergman – had generally been positive. That trend ended abruptly with the 1975 film adaptation of Ken Kesey's 1962 novel, *One Flew over the Cuckoo's Nest*. Directed by Milos Forman, the film won five Oscars. The central character, Randle McDaniel, played by actor Jack Nicholson, defies the chain of command in the mental hospital where he is housed. He is later lobotomized as a way for the hospital administration – embodied in the stern Nurse Ratched – to show inmates who is boss.

A similar anti-psychiatric theme surfaced in the 1987 Argentine film *Hombre mirando al sudeste* (Man facing southeast). One day a new patient mysteriously appears on the ward of a bleak Argentine psychiatric hospital. Announcing himself as a visitor from "another world," the patient – calling himself Rantés – proceeds to overturn the established order inside the asylum. He tries to cure his psychiatrist of his loneliness and alienation, thereby reversing the power gradient between doctor and patient. Rantés feeds, clothes, and cures his fellow patients, who naturally view him as superior to the asylum's doctors. The hospital's administrators decide this subversive climate cannot continue, and they order the staff to medicate Rantés, who dies shortly thereafter.

One Flew over the Cuckoo's Nest, like *Hombre mirando al sudeste*, reveals how far psychiatry's image had plunged in only a few short years. In the 1950s the press tended to celebrate advances in psychiatry, but by the 1970s psychiatry was frequently depicted as a threat to both emotional health and personal liberty. Psychiatry, in this interpretation, serves the interests of the powerful by punishing those who question authority or deviate from society's norms. Canadian-born sociologist Erving Goffman argued in his 1961 *Asylums* that mental hospitals closely resembled prisons and similar "total institutions." Just like a prisoner, Goffman wrote, a mental patient endured a "sentence" in the asylum, "totally exiled from society." The asylum, according to followers of Goffman, was a favorite vehicle of repression for totalitarian governments.[45]

One sign that 1960s anti-psychiatry was different from earlier hostility toward the profession was that, by the 1960s, the mainstream churches had tended to make their peace with mental medicine. In the past some religious institutions, notably the Roman Catholic Church, had disputed psychiatry's monopoly over the care of people with mental disabilities. Historically Catholics had disagreed with psychiatry's view of sin, exorcism, and demonic possession. However, by the 1950s Pope Pius XII announced that he accepted Freudian psychoanalysis so long as it did not conflict with church doctrine. As time went on, Catholic clergy increasingly collaborated with psychotherapists when dealing with the everyday challenges of counseling parishioners.[46]

Instead, twentieth-century religious criticism of psychiatry tended to come from unorthodox groups, such as the Church of Scientology, founded in 1954 by science fiction writer L. Ron Hubbard. By the early twenty-first century Scientology claimed about 8 million followers worldwide. No religious group has taken as negative a view of psychiatry as Scientologists, who believe that a regimen of vitamins and exercise is more helpful to depressed people than are prescription drugs. In 1969 Hubbard remarked that "there is not one institutional psychiatrist alive who ... could not be arraigned and convicted of extortion, mayhem, and murder."[47] For years Scientology lobbied elected officials in the United States to limit the use of Ritalin, a drug frequently administered to children who have difficulty concentrating. Scientology's stance on mental health care became front-page news in 2005 when actor Tom Cruise, a church member, appeared on the U.S. morning television program *The Today Show*. With countless viewers tuned in, Cruise alleged that psychiatry was a "pseudo-science" and that psychiatrists irresponsibly prescribed drugs to millions of people. When questioned on this point, Cruise burst out, "You don't know the history of psychiatry, I do."[48]

Joining Scientology in its attacks on psychiatry was physician Thomas Szasz. Born in Budapest, Hungary, in 1920, Szasz emigrated to the United States in 1938, completed his medical training at the University of Cincinnati, trained as a psychoanalyst in Chicago, and from 1956 to his retirement in 1990 was a professor of psychiatry at the State University of New York in Syracuse. Szasz created a stir in 1960 by calling the medical model of mental illness a "myth." To Szasz, mental illness was fundamentally different from cancer or arteriosclerosis and thus no disease at all. Szasz dubbed belief in the reality of mental illness, like belief in witches or other "magical" concepts, a "social tranquilizer" or "I-wish-it-were-true type of fantasy" that the problems of living could somehow be cured through the intervention of professionals named psychiatrists rather than surmounted by personal courage and integrity.

In 1969 Szasz co-founded with the Church of Scientology the Citizens Commission of Human Rights, a watchdog group dedicated to investigating and exposing psychiatric violations of human rights. Szasz made it clear that his alliance with Scientology was purely strategic and did not mean he endorsed the church's doctrines. Szasz's links to the libertarian movement and one of its pivotal leaders, Murray Rothbard (1926–95), were stronger. As Szasz wrote in 2004, "Psychiatry sits uneasily in the belly of libertarianism." Rothbard, a follower of Austrian economist Ludwig von Mises, who defended free markets and the individual's unhampered exercise of private property, wrote for William F. Buckley's conservative *National Review* and at his death was Distinguished Professor of Economics at the University of Nevada, Las Vegas.[49] Rothbard hailed Szasz's *The Myth of Mental Illness* as "a highly original and unique work" and noted Szasz's "gallant and courageous battle against the compulsory commitment of the innocent in the name of 'therapy' and humanitarianism." For his part, Szasz stressed the many similarities between his own thought and Rothbard's libertarian, anti-government philosophy.[50]

Thinkers from other parts of the political spectrum echoed Szasz's sharp criticism of psychiatry, its claims to expertise, and the mounting societal tendency to seek professional treatment for emotional difficulties within expanding state bureaucracies. In 1966 University of Pennsylvania sociologist Philip Rieff lamented the emergence of "psychological man," a "man of leisure, released by technology from the regimental discipline of work so as to secure his sense of well-being." The appearance of this personality type, Rieff argued, was a revolutionary occurrence in history. In Rieff's mind, therapists taught "psychological man" to think he was discontented and to seek out therapy in an effort to become happier. Rieff warned that the "triumph of the therapeutic" had grave political consequences because it diverted individuals from the public tasks of the community to the private pursuit of personal well-being.[51]

Christopher Lasch, a history professor at the University of Rochester and the author of a series of books, including the *Culture of Narcissism* (1977), shared Rieff's loathing of everyday Americans' reliance on expert advice in an effort to improve individual emotional health. Lasch wrote:

> Plagued by anxiety, depression, vague discontents, a sense of inner emptiness, the "psychological man" of the twentieth century seeks neither individual self-aggrandizement nor spiritual transcendence but peace of mind, under conditions that increasingly militate against it. Therapists, not priests or popular preachers of self-help or models of success like the captains of industry, become his principal allies in the struggle for composure: he turns to them in the hope of achieving the modern equivalent of salvation, "mental health."

Like Rieff, Lasch claimed that the "therapeutic outlook" of the twentieth century "trivializ[ed] politics" by convincing people that exploring one's inner life through "personal growth" was a more effective way of changing the world than participating in the political process.[52]

Less subtly than either Rieff or Lasch, conservative groups – notably in the United States – dubbed psychiatry the "thought control brigade." In 1958 one author in *American Mercury* told of his "posing as a communist for the FBI for nine years" and discovering that a large percentage of the U.S. Communist Party consisted of "psychiatrists, psychologists, medical doctors and social, health and welfare workers."[53] Conservative activists singled out Brock Chisholm, accusing him of being a covert Communist and advocate of "brain-washing." To some on the political right Chisholm's statement that psychiatry had to "now decide what is to be the future of the human race" smacked of the "same finesse in execution that the Communists in Russia have used and are now using."[54] The rightist attack on psychiatry in the 1950s united a motley crowd of both respectable and fringe groups, including the John Birch Society (JBS) and the Daughters of the American Revolution. U.S. anti-communist hostility to psychiatry was robust enough that in 1965 *Look Magazine* warned of "the far right's fight against mental health."[55]

Yet as the conservative movement began its ascendancy in U.S. politics in the 1970s, distrust of psychiatry began to wane as a conservative cause. By the 1980s most U.S. conservatives had become much more selective in their attacks on psychiatry. Eager to attract voters to the Republican Party, they distanced themselves from anti-psychiatric groups such as the JBS and libertarians such as Szasz and Rothbard. When they did criticize psychiatry, they increasingly blamed its mistakes on the influence of the leftist, counter-cultural radicalism of the 1960s, which, they alleged, distorted psychiatry's scientific mission, making it a political agenda bent on ending injustice, poverty, and crime. Late-twentieth-century conservatives tended to argue that psychiatry should be reformed, not overthrown. They assailed what they called the impact of "political correctness" on psychiatry and urged the public – particularly Americans – to recover the old ideals of stoicism and self-reliance. Yet despite conservatives' passion and eloquence in attacking "psychological man," the "therapeutic outlook" kept gaining ground as the new millennium approached.[56]

UNSOUND MINDS

When anti-communist opponents of psychiatry summoned up the specter of Soviet mental health policy, they were drawing on a powerful comparison. Under dictator Joseph Stalin (1929–53) Soviet psychiatry had been heavily politicized. Stalin's better-known meddling in science involved his open support for the theories of the biologist Trofim Lysenko, who defended the doctrine of the inheritance of acquired characteristics to explain evolution. Stalin promoted Lysenko's ideas because they were consistent with Marxist philosophy and enabled him to apply firm control over the Soviet scientific community. For similar reasons Stalin imposed the theories of Ivan Petrovich Pavlov on Soviet psychiatry. Pavlov won the Nobel Prize in Physiology in 1904, and his experiments showing that ringing bells could make dogs salivate thrilled many psychologists, who imagined his theories about behavioral conditioning could be applied to human beings. Pavlov's heavy emphasis on physiology and conditioned reflexes suited orthodox Marxist doctrine.[57]

Alongside the ideological conformity of Stalinist medicine, another sinister aspect of Soviet psychiatry's politicization was the USSR's incarceration of political dissidents. After the 1917 Russian Revolution, which brought the Bolshevik Party to power, the forced hospitalization of political dissidents was rare, if only because the government felt no need to rely on psychiatry to deal with its perceived enemies. Under Lenin and Stalin the political police either executed those who questioned authority or imprisoned them in the sprawling state concentration camp system. In any case, Soviet psychiatry was in disarray following the revolution and civil war (1918–21), with few psychiatrists and mental hospitals in which to incarcerate dissidents. Under the Stalinist terror, a psychiatric diagnosis could actually save someone from a firing squad or a long labor camp sentence. As one dissident testified:

> For several weeks [in 1947] I was kept in jail. From there I was sent for a psychiatric examination to the Serbsky Institute of Forensic Psychiatry in Moscow. There I was declared "not responsible" for my actions and interned in a Leningrad prison hospital. I remained in this institution for about a year. In the conditions of Stalin's era, I was inclined to consider this confinement not so much a measure of repression, but rather as a chance of escaping a much harsher punishment.[58]

Stalin's death in 1953 led to a relative relaxation of outright police terror in the USSR, but a more subtle form of repression involving Soviet psychiatry began to unfold. Communist ideology implied that no one in his or her right mind could object to life in Soviet Russia, supposedly an ideal state. According to Stalin's successor, Nikita Khrushchev, there was no such thing in the Soviet Union as "political prisoners, only persons of unsound mind." Psychiatric incarceration became a way to suppress political opposition. Soviet psychiatrists who persecuted dissidents tended to work in major academic centers where the KGB – the political police – were clustered. In the 1980s the Soviet Union had 5.5 million patients labeled "socially dangerous," nearly 2 percent of the entire population.

Soviet psychiatry suffered from other problems that resulted in the abuse of patients: its refusal to acknowledge non-biological causes of mental disease, over-diagnosis of schizophrenia, and over-reliance on outdated treatments such as lobotomy, insulin shock sleep therapy, and "wet wraps," in which patients were wrapped in wet bed linen. Until 1992 there were no laws protecting psychiatric patients in Russia, leaving ample room for human rights abuses. Yet whether it was due to communist ideology or the backwardness of Soviet psychiatry, the propensity of psychiatry to act as an accomplice of the state in the USSR intensified fears elsewhere of what could happen if other governments became heavily involved in mental health care.

NIGHTMARES OF DEPENDENCE

In addition to worries about the threat of psychiatry to individual freedom, concerns over drug use were fueling a backlash against the mental health care field by the 1970s. Initially the chief doubts about tranquilizers were related not to their medical or social hazards but to their prices, which some Americans complained made them too expensive for lower-income families. In 1960 a U.S. senator accused pharmaceutical companies of price gouging and urged them to make tranquilizers more readily available. Some practitioners insisted that pills were no substitute for compassion or psychotherapy, and others warned about physicians' carelessness and drug manufacturers' thirst for profit. Yet up to the 1970s consumers were blamed as much as anyone for the mounting use of prescription pills. Patients were not "passive recipients" of medical or commercial browbeating, one U.S. physician maintained. Despite his efforts to convince the public that pills were sometimes not *the* answer, patients continued to flood his office "demanding medication to relieve their anxiety." In 1956 Carter Laboratories discovered it could not manufacture Miltown fast enough to meet public demand.[59]

In 1966 the rock band the Rolling Stones wrote an ode to Valium entitled "Mother's Little Helper," which referred to a "typical" middle-class woman:

> Running for the shelter
> Of a mother's little helper

> And it helps her on her way
> Gets her through her busy day.

U.S. psychiatrist and author Robert Coles chastised affluent Americans who "devour a nondescript assortment of pills ... in a naive and frantic search for a careless, silenced mind." To another observer, Americans seemed to believe that "this life cannot be lived without drugs."

Shortly thereafter, however, the blame game shifted gears. Prescription drug users – especially women – were increasingly portrayed as victims of psychiatrists, family doctors, and pharmaceutical manufacturers rather than over-indulgent seekers of fast relief. When beloved actress Judy Garland died in 1969 at the age of forty-seven from a sleeping pill overdose, the public tended to blame the drugs, not her. Women's magazines ran stories about the dangers of tranquilizer use, and former first lady Betty Ford, citing her own dependence on drugs and alcohol, encouraged others to get treatment for their addictions. In 1975 *Ms.* magazine, co-founded by feminist Gloria Steinem in 1971, drew the attention of its readers to the potential of Valium and other drugs to produce dependence. In 1979 Senator Ted Kennedy chaired U.S. congressional hearings on tranquilizer use, including testimony from patients who had suffered tranquilizer withdrawal. "These drugs," Kennedy declared, "have produced a nightmare of dependence."[60]

Alarm over drug dependence also stemmed from mounting worries about illicit drug use. In the 1970s America's attention shifted from heroin addiction to marijuana and cocaine abuse. Marijuana's spread throughout the nation's schools and universities made the issue a particular concern for parents. In 1979 two-thirds of young people between the ages of eighteen and twenty-five said they had tried marijuana at least once. But it was the explosive growth of cocaine abuse in the 1980s that created the main drug crisis of that period, an "uncontrolled fire" in the words of U.S. President Ronald Reagan. In the form of "crack," a potent, smokable, rock-like form of the drug sold in small vials for only a few dollars apiece, cocaine went from being a drug of the well-to-do, college-educated set to that of the poor and homeless.[61] Cocaine addiction caused anxiety, mood swings, and paranoid delusions and hallucinations, notably the sensation of bugs crawling just beneath the skin, during either intoxication or withdrawal. Dermatologists, psychiatrists, plastic surgeons, and family physicians reported sharp spikes in the number of patients suffering from such symptoms. In 1985 the American Academy of Psychiatrists in Alcoholism and Addictions was founded, renamed in 1996 the American Academy of Addiction Psychiatry. By then, substance abuse and addictions constituted one of the fastest-growing fields in psychiatry.

The impetus behind the backlash against prescription drugs came mainly from the women's movement. Data such as those from a 1975 U.S. survey showing that 72 percent more women than men used tranquilizers politicized women's health care advocates. When the rates of female visits to physicians, women's referrals to surgery, women's diagnoses with certain psychological disorders, and women's drug prescriptions surpassed those for men, activists dismissed the idea that women were sicker than men and instead concluded that medicine had "betrayed" women. The 1984 edition of the best-selling *Our Bodies, Ourselves* 1971 stated that physicians routinely refused to listen to or believe women, withheld knowledge or lied to them, and "offered them tranquilizers or moral advice instead of medical care or useful help from community resources." Physicians "prescribed drugs which hooked [women], sickened them, changed their entire lives," *Our Bodies, Ourselves* declared.[62]

The attacks of the burgeoning women's movement on the mental health care field were a chapter within a much broader series of events that convulsed most of the industrialized world in the 1960s and 1970s. Wave after wave of counter-cultural protests assailed long-standing mores and institutions. Against the backdrop of an unpopular war in Southeast Asia, activists for African American civil rights and women's reproductive freedom paraded in the streets and often clashed with the forces of law and order. Laws restricting abortion and birth control were toppled in country after country. Campus radicals burned draft cards, held mass sit-ins, conducted strikes that closed classrooms, and protested war-related corporate recruiting efforts. Race riots broke out in American cities in the summers of 1965 and 1966. In Quebec the so-called Quiet Revolution challenged the Roman Catholic Church's power in the province and jump-started the modern-day drive toward Quebec independence. Mexican American and Native American militants followed the example of the Black Power movement in celebrating racial pride. In 1970 the first Earth Day was held around the world, heralding the rise of environmentalism. Soon rifts among these various movements developed, with feminists calling Black Power activists male chauvinists and heterosexual and homosexual feminists accusing each other of intolerance. Yet for a brief time unity trumped disunity, and together these various currents constituted a powerful challenge to the status quo in numerous countries, including organized medicine and its growing ties to government, higher education, and industry.

In the eyes of its critics, the sins of the medical field went beyond its subordination of women. Through its monopoly over the mental health care system, the medical profession allegedly ignored the needs of minorities, marginalized alternative forms of healing, and made the public increasingly dependent on "expert" advice, thus weakening individual self-reliance. Former Roman Catholic priest Ivan Illich in his 1976 best seller, *Medical Nemesis,* claimed that organized medicine was actually dangerous to public health. To many on the political left, organized medicine was just another type of "big business" that sought to preserve age-old inequalities.

Mental health issues were often at the nub of political radicalism. In their song "For What It's Worth" the rock group Buffalo Springfield blamed Americans' "paranoia" for their supposed resistance to liberating change. Betty Friedan, author of the feminist classic *The Feminine Mystique* (1963), borrowed freely from psychologists Abraham Maslow, Carl Rogers, and Karen Horney to argue that women suffered from the "problem that had no name." Maslow, a Brandeis University professor of psychology who taught that human beings seek self-actualization through a hierarchy of needs and motivations, convinced feminists like Friedan that women's personalities were not fixed at adolescence by biological urges but could grow and develop through the various stages of life. Told by psychiatrists that they should seek fulfillment through their husbands and children, women in Friedan's view still hungered deeply for personal authenticity. Their higher, non-material needs went unsatisfied, Friedan insisted, when women "forfeited" themselves in favor of their families. To forget how "pointless" her existence was, Friedan argued, the typical suburban housewife resorted to pills. "You wake up in the morning, and feel as if there's no point in going on another day like this. So you take a tranquilizer because it makes you not care so much," she wrote. Other feminists, including Kate Millett, used psychology to deconstruct how masculine power "socialized" women, sharply defined sex roles, and distorted female identity. "We have had our mental and emotional feet bound for thousands of years," a radical feminist angrily asserted.[63]

Relying heavily on postwar psychology to advance their liberationist mission, however, did not keep radicals from heaping abuse on the field of mental health. When women were advised to go into psychotherapy to overcome their unhappiness, some feminists protested that therapy implied that women were sick, that oppression was all in their heads. Looking for a more political form of action, some women gravitated toward consciousness raising (CR), but advocates of CR found it difficult to distinguish it from "group therapy." What was the right balance between individual healing and the achievement of collective political goals? Which school of psychology was best suited to feminist CR? What theories of psychology were liberating and which were merely tools of oppression? Could men practice feminist therapy too? The ferment of the women's movement in the 1970s tended to overshadow the fact that consensus on the answers to these questions was elusive.

More crucially, though the women's movement insisted that most psychology and psychiatry were dehumanizing, it repeatedly relied on "psychologizing" to unmask how powerful elites supposedly produce "false consciousness" and serial unhappiness in socially disadvantaged individuals and groups. By the 1970s the "therapeutic outlook" appeared to be so firmly rooted that even radical opponents of the status quo resorted to fashionable theories of psychology to explain why society functioned the way it did.

PSYCHO-POLITICS

France in particular was a hotbed of this kind of counter-cultural approach to studying modern society, dubbed "psycho-politics" by its admirers. When French students and workers took to the streets in May 1968, they triggered a series of protests elsewhere in Europe. Prominent among the heroes of the student revolutionaries were the philosopher Michel Foucault and the psychiatrist Jacques Lacan. Foucault and Lacan rejected talk about society "influencing" autonomous individuals and instead argued that most oppression happens when individuals internalize official codes of conduct. Modern society, according to Foucault, systematically yet subtly polices the self through the so-called helping professions, notably education and medicine. Foucault's *Madness and Civilization* (1961) blamed modern civilization's emphasis on reason and technology for the growing institutional confinement of the mentally ill. Foucault's argument that the march of modern civilization has caused a corresponding decline in toleration of the mentally ill appealed to many in the 1960s who distrusted psychiatry's power, loathed asylums, and believed that at one time in history people with mental disabilities enjoyed greater freedom and validation.

Unknown outside a small circle of Parisians before 1966, Jacques Lacan exploded onto the international stage during the revolutionary year of 1968. For Lacan, language was chiefly to blame for stamping the mind in such a way that the individual unwittingly conformed to the social order. To the student revolutionaries who adored him and his own students later at the University of Vincennes outside Paris, he was the "prophet of paranoia." Lacan's interest in the paranoid mentality dated back to his days as a medical student at Paris's Special Infirmary for the Insane at the Prefecture of Police, where he saw patients with delusions of persecution and grandeur. Lacan wished to do for paranoia what R. D. Laing did for schizophrenia: depict paranoids as more sane than so-called sane people.

Since his death in 1981 Lacan's influence has faded, but during his lifetime he was the key figure in the popularization of Freudian psychoanalysis in postwar France. Lacan's brand of psychoanalysis came with a typically idiosyncratic spin. Unlike other psychoanalysts who followed Freud's format of strict fifty-minute therapeutic sessions, Lacan's treatment sessions sometimes lasted no more than five minutes. Lacan's iconoclastic version of psychoanalytic doctrine, coupled with his support for striking students in May 1968, reinforced his image as a radical thinker who had laid the foundations for the highly politicized French antipsychiatric movement.[64]

French adherents of psycho-politics also included Frantz Fanon, a black psychiatrist from Martinique. Fanon translated his personal brushes with racism into a full-fledged theory about the effects of colonization on the psyche. Fanon's ascent to international stardom took place against the backdrop of France's bloody war against Algerian nationalists (1954–62), whom he openly supported. Fanon died of leukemia in 1961, at the age of thirty-six, just as his book *The Wretched of the Earth* was published. Fanon's training as a psychiatrist was central to his political views. Based on his treatment of both torturers and their victims during the Algerian war of independence, Fanon argued that anti-colonial violence had a cleansing and liberating effect. Fanon's work was hailed by leading French cultural figures such as philosopher Jean-Paul Sartre, who in his preface to *The Wretched of the Earth* admiringly wrote that "violence, like Achilles's lance, can heal the wounds that it has inflicted." Sartre and countless others celebrated Fanon because of their belief that a violent break with the past was necessary to achieve a just society.[65]

The theories of Foucault, Lacan, and Fanon attracted countless followers and helped to spawn a brand of anti-psychiatric hooliganism that sometimes turned violent. During the 1968 student revolts in Paris, Jean Delay's office was ransacked and he was forced to retire. Beginning in 1969 the Department of Psychiatry at Tokyo University was occupied by protestors for ten years, bringing all research to a halt. Dutch psychiatrist

Herman van Praag needed a police escort to get to work. During a 1971 debate over the validity of psychiatry at Montreal's McGill University, a member of the audience threw a cream cake into Heinz Lehmann's face (unperturbed, Lehmann kept speaking as if nothing had happened).[66] Only fifteen years earlier, acclaim for the new drugs had resounded across the continents. Now the same psychiatrists who had championed these medications were threatened with bodily harm in what were once considered sanctuaries of scholarship and teaching.

Activists, whether or not influenced by the theories of Lacan, Foucault, or Fanon, quickly discovered that such aggressive protests could intimidate the psychiatric profession. At the 1970 and 1973 American Psychiatric Association annual meetings, gay rights advocates staged noisy demonstrations protesting the APA's definition of homosexuality as deviant. One activist angrily ordered the APA to "[s]top it, you're making me sick."[67] In 1974 the APA voted to cease defining homosexuality as a psychiatric illness. The spectacle of the APA changing its doctrine under threats from protestors emboldened Vietnam War veterans to pressure the APA to elevate post-traumatic stress disorder to the status of a full-fledged disease in 1980, thereby making them eligible for VA benefits. By kowtowing to special-interest protestors, the APA defused some animosity toward the profession but in the process suffered a serious blow to its reputation as a scientific discipline. Public pressure, by compelling psychiatrists to change their diagnostic system, had revealed how much the quest for mental health was becoming democratized as the century wound to a close.

PATIENTS INTO CONSUMERS

Overall these attacks on psychiatry were part of a fundamental shift in the relationship between doctors and their patients. The first big such change had occurred in the nineteenth century when people with mental disabilities gradually became known as "patients." Near the end of the twentieth century the word "patient" itself quickly fell out of favor, replaced by the more business sounding "consumer" or "client." This shift in vocabulary reflected a subtle but important change: the power gradient between patient and doctor, once heavily tilted toward physicians, was now more evenly balanced. Laypeople, like consumers in other respects, demanded full disclosure and satisfaction from their health caregivers. In Britain, government health departments consulted mental patients' groups on health care policy issues, sometimes more closely than psychiatrists themselves. Some U.K. psychiatrists confessed that they found the situation uncomfortable, but as governments' reliance on "clients" showed no signs of abating in the new century, the specialty realized that such policy decisions would be made with or without it. As the twenty-first century opened, a more democratic form of decision making in the mental health field was fast becoming a reality.

As another sign of the times in the mental health field, some patients referred to themselves as "survivors." In using the term, patients and their advocates depicted themselves as wary victims of an inherently unjust, adversarial system. Comparisons were made between World War II Holocaust survivors and people who had suffered abuse or neglect at the hands of the mental health care system. U.S. psychiatrist Peter Breggin – often called the "conscience of psychiatry" by admirers – captured the mood of the anti-psychiatric movement with his 1991 book, *Toxic Psychiatry*. Breggin and others protested against laws governing the committal of patients to mental hospitals, accused psychiatrists of psychologically and physically abusing patients, and argued that electro-convulsive therapy and psycho-surgery were inhumane. Courts in the 1970s and 1980s moved to protect patients' rights – chiefly to refuse treatment or hospitalization – based on the belief that psychiatrists and hospitals were the biggest obstacles to a patient's recovery. Many psychiatrists, viewing with dismay how poorly patients fared living on the streets without their medication, protested that court decisions meant that patients were "dying with [their] rights on."[68]

As the century wound to a close, more and more patients demanded a collaborative and egalitarian relationship with their doctors , and this sentiment particularly applied to mental health care. A "post-modern" consumer of mental health care products was emerging, someone who was acutely sensitive to his or her own emotions and sensations and more willing than his or her predecessors to define symptoms as illness. The post-modern patient felt alienated from the medical profession, yet still used doctors to obtain drugs.[69] There was no mistaking the shift in general attitudes: by the 1980s more and more people believed that prescription drug therapy was an individual right, and their doctors had a kind of constitutional obligation to provide them with such treatment.[70] Typically, post-modern patients were better informed about health issues than their ancestors and enjoyed a more open relationship with their doctors, but by the end of the twentieth century both patients and doctors eyed each other more warily than in earlier generations.

A milestone in this fast-moving sequence of events was the 1979 founding of the National Alliance for the Mentally Ill (NAMI). Based in Washington, D.C., this advocacy group consisted of parents and friends of those with severe mental disabilities. By 1996 NAMI had 130,000 members and chapters in every American state. NAMI started out as an organization of angry people who felt psychiatry had seriously short-changed chronically ill and handicapped persons. Its charter boldly asserted that laypersons could run the group without professional leadership, and it adamantly opposed theories that depicted families as "villains" responsible for the mental illness of their relatives.

Yet NAMI was a lot less anti-psychiatric than it looked at first glance. The organization supported the view that mental illness was first and foremost a biological condition, and therefore the mentally ill should be treated with the best medical care. NAMI claimed that people with mental disabilities were like cancer or heart disease patients. The only difference was that mental patients suffered from a sick brain. NAMI demanded not less medical treatment for people with mental disabilities, but more.

The NAMI point of view had seeped into popular discourse by the late 1990s when Tipper Gore, wife of U.S. Vice President Al Gore, told the press that her problems were due to "a clinical depression, one that I was going to have to have help to overcome. What I learned about it is your brain needs a certain amount of serotonin and when you run out of that, it's like running out of gas."[71]

To the president of the APA in 1990, NAMI's "passionate espousal of biological psychiatry" was a vindication of the profession. By providing a model for other disease-specific advocacy groups – for example, those for social phobia and obsessive-compulsive disorder – NAMI helped to foster cozy relations between patients' organizations and the pharmaceutical industry. Indeed, with half of its funding coming from pharmaceutical companies, NAMI had no sympathy for Szasz's theory that mental illness is a myth.[72]

Led by NAMI, most of the anti-psychiatry movement made its peace with the mental health establishment. Despite the differences among the various anti-psychiatry groups, by the end of the twentieth century they had coalesced into a sort of "big tent," consumerist coalition. Over the years activists had watched as their original alliances with other radical movements from the 1960s – feminist, gay, student and African American – melted away, so they decided to dispense with the confrontational tactics popular in the 1960s and 1970s. The term "survivor" fell out of favor because of its sensationalist overtones, and anti-psychiatry evolved from a campus-based to patient-based movement. The coming of the Internet enabled the many advocacy groups to reach out to millions around the world and form a kind of global community with increasing political clout. The impact of the consumerist mental health movement was visible as early as 1991 when the United Nations General Assembly adopted its Principles for the Protection of Persons with Mental Illness and Improvement of Mental Health Care, and in 2002 the Scientology-funded Citizens Commission on Human Rights successfully petitioned the UN secretary-general to report annually to the General Assembly on the progress of human rights, including those of people with mental disabilities. NAMI and its British counterpart, the Mental Health Foundation, may not have agreed with the myriad other organizations in this movement on all mental health issues, but hidden beneath the rhetoric separating such groups was the consensus that the best way for the successors of the anti-psychiatry movement to achieve their goals was to eschew radicalism and adopt grassroots lobbying and legislative advocacy efforts to promote reform rather than revolutionary change. By the new millennium, mental health care professionals may not have been thrilled with the emergence of mental health consumerism, but they had to accept that in the space of a few short decades this version of consumerism had profoundly undermined the hierarchy that had historically governed the field. As the new century opened, the quest for mental health was becoming increasingly pluralist and diverse in composition.[73]

PROZAC NATIONS

Through its acceptance of biological psychiatry, the mental health consumerist movement aided industry in transforming depression into a major epidemic in the late twentieth century. In 1975 a prominent U.S. researcher had asked rhetorically, "Is everyone depressed?" At the time it seemed like a good question.[74] Prior to the 1950s, clinical depression was thought to be a rare condition. The long-standing consensus was that there were firm distinctions between run-of-the-mill melancholy and disabling depression. The former was considered to be either a Galenic temperament or a mere problem of everyday living – in common parlance, having the blues. Most psychiatrists followed Emil Kraepelin's lead in viewing depression as a symptom of manic-depressive disorder. Some in the 1950s touted the new anti-depressant imipramine (Tofranil) as a means of making patients feel "better than well," but at the time there appeared to be no groundswell of opinion in favor of taking potent chemicals to achieve such an emotional state. The word "anti-depressant" to designate certain drugs was not coined until 1952 and did not catch on until the mid-1960s.[75]

Yet in 1980 depression officially became a mental disease. An emotional condition as old as time itself was suddenly transformed into the common cold of mental illness. What had caused such an abrupt change? Was it a case of science discovering a disease that had simply gone undetected for millennia? Were sufferers of depression finally coming out of the closet and receiving the care and compassion they so justly deserved?

The truth is that as the market for benzodiazepines collapsed, the pharmaceutical industry took dead aim at depression. In 1973 U.S. benzodiazepine use peaked at more than 80 million prescriptions. By 1986 it had fallen to 61 million. Yet the industry already had a new series of drugs, called the selective serotonin re-uptake inhibitors (SSRIs), which increase the level of the neurotransmitter serotonin, believed to affect mood. Pharmaceutical companies such as Eli Lilly and Smith Kline gradually concluded that the SSRIs, discovered back in the 1950s, could be marketed as anti-depressants and in due course patented Zoloft, Praxil, and Prozac. Each had its own chemical structure, but all were touted as fighting depression. First demand for SSRIs had to be stimulated, though, and that meant changing the course of history by elevating depression to the status of a widespread, clinically recognized biological illness. In a revolutionary step, the pharmaceutical industry sold a drug by selling a disease first.[76]

The "selling" of depression happened so fast that only insiders seemed to notice. Within a few short years experts were warning that depression was a world health emergency. Between the 1950s and the turn of the century, estimates of the frequency of depression jumped a thousand-fold. The highpoint was the 1990s, dubbed "the age of depression" by historian David Healy. By the end of the 1990s, at any given time 2 to 3 percent of men and 4 to 9 percent of women in America were reportedly depressed. Worldwide, depression affected 120 million people. The WHO Regional Office for Europe called it a "social and economic time-bomb." By the new millennium it was the most common global psychiatric disorder, the fourth-leading contributor to the global burden of disease, and the most common women's mental health problem.[77]

Depression's higher incidence among women than men sparked lively debate over the theory that women's hormonal systems play a key role in depression. The links between depression and suicide also raised grave concerns. All in all, the global attention paid to depression by the early twenty-first century represented nothing less than a major revolution in the history of mental health care. Sorrow, an emotional state that millions had endured for centuries, was now a mental illness.

The striking rise in the incidence of depression worldwide and the availability of new drugs to treat it led psychiatrist Peter Kramer in 1993 to celebrate Prozac as an example of "cosmetic psycho-pharmacology," the idea that even "normal" people were entitled to take medication if it made them feel less sad or more confident in social settings. Industry tells us, "Since you only live once, why not do it as a blond?" Kramer argued, so why not live life as a "peppy blond?" Later Kramer insisted he was being ironic, but his irony was lost amid the media excitement over the whole idea of feeling "better than well."[78] In 1994 *Newsweek* magazine asked, "Want to boost your self-esteem, focus better on your work, tame the impulse to shop until you drop, shrug off your spouse's habit of littering the floor with underwear ... or keep yourself from blurting out your deepest secrets to the first stranger who comes along?" The new anti-depressants, *Newsweek* stated, could give you a "made-to-order, off-the-shelf" new personality.[79]

By 1999 Prozac had become the third-best-selling prescription drug. "Britain Becomes a Prozac Nation," the *Times* announced in 2007 after British doctors wrote more than 31 million prescriptions for SSRIs in 2006 alone. In Japan, where sales of benzodiazepines remained strong, Prozac made few inroads into the marketplace until the end of the century, but in the United States, which accounted for 70 percent of world sales, Prozac was hailed as the pill that cured not only depression, but also shyness, panic attacks, and obsessive-compulsiveness. In the early twenty-first century, anti-depressant sales were even on the rise in Japan, leading one American observer to note that "one of the most powerful aspects of globalization" was the growing influence of U.S. psycho-pharmacology.[80]

The vast expansion of the diagnosis of depression was most likely linked to an actual rise in the incidence of the condition. Throughout the industrialized world and in many developing countries in the twentieth century, populations were aging as birthrates declined, and depression in the elderly was an all too real problem. However, when the escalating rate of depression is compared with the sharp increase in the diagnosis of many other mental disorders at the same time, the availability of anti-depressants appears to have been the crucial factor. A British mental health expert told the *Times* in 2007 that doctors were "guilty of a knee-jerk reaction in prescribing pills.... The mindset of GPs will have to change so that they consider counseling and other forms of therapy as a frontline treatment."[81]

Yet counseling and cognitive behavior therapy, long touted as effective against mild to moderate forms of depression, are time-consuming and expensive. Over the last third of the twentieth century, third-party health insurers scaled back their coverage of psychiatric services, pressuring physicians to provide only short-term treatment aimed at symptom relief. In the eyes of government and private insurance companies, psychiatry had the unenviable reputation of being a "bottomless pit," an insatiable consumer of resources and health care dollars.[82] In 1994 the executive director of the Mental Health Association of Minnesota lamented that "insurers would just as soon cover us from the neck down." A 1995 editorial in the *American Journal of Psychiatry* reported that psychiatrists "are urged to prescribe 'cheap' antipsychotics or antidepressants instead of those with fewer side effects and to reduce or eliminate the time spent in psychotherapeutic contact with our patients so that these 'services' can be given by less costly 'providers.' "[83] All these factors combined to make anti-depressants a "quick fix" and depression a largely man-made epidemic as the new millennium dawned.[84]

ONE WORLD, ONE PSYCHIATRY

The meteoric expansion of the depression diagnosis was part of a radical upheaval in the way psychiatrists classified mental illnesses as a whole. Since the nineteenth century, physicians had tried to organize the huge symptom pool of psychiatry – obsessions, delusions, hallucinations, phobias, and mood swings – into neat categories, a process that one psychiatrist in 1981 mordantly called the "endless reshuffling of the same old cards." What complicates the situation is that the boundaries between many psychiatric syndromes – for example, schizophrenia and the affective disorders – are often unclear. In the nineteenth century many psychiatrists got caught up in lively debates over how to distinguish one mental disease from another, but without any concrete knowledge about biological causes they time and again failed to find consensus. Emil Kraepelin's bold diagnostic system based on two primary diseases – dementia praecox and manic-depressive disorder – sparked further discussions, but Kraepelin's theories enjoyed a mixed reception in the early twentieth century.[85]

For the most part, however, there was little sense of urgency surrounding the topic of psychiatric diagnosis as the twentieth century unfolded. Regular physicians might administer penicillin for pneumonia and antibiotics for infection, but until psychiatrists had specific drugs for distinct varieties of mental illness, attempts at classifying mental diseases seemed to many clinicians as meaningless as debating how many angels could dance on the head of a pin. The ascent of psychoanalysis in the first half of the twentieth century also caused interest in psychiatric classification to ebb. Most mental illnesses – including schizophrenia – were believed to be due to maladjustment or dysfunctional family dynamics, and so were dubbed "reactions" or varieties of hysteria. What difference did it make, many psychiatrists asked, what you call a condition when the true task for the healer is to find the underlying psychological cause? Matters were not improved when studies showed that psychiatrists in different countries diagnosed schizophrenia at widely dissimilar rates. The French, for example, tended to dislike the concept of schizophrenia, while the Americans repeatedly astonished their British colleagues with their fondness for the diagnosis. What was the point of labeling a mental state one way or another if diagnosis was a matter of personal or national taste?

Indifference to psychiatric diagnosis was so pervasive in the 1960s that U.S. psychiatrist Robert Spitzer recalled that at professional conferences "academic psychiatrists interested in presenting their work on descriptive diagnosis would be scheduled for the final day in the late afternoon. No one would attend. Psychiatrists simply were not interested in the issue of diagnosis." Conference-goers apparently worried more about catching early flights out of town than about the boundaries between, say, paranoia and schizophrenia. As late as the 1970s many psychiatrists were still taking a nonchalant attitude toward diagnosis.[86]

Meanwhile, however, Kraepelin was not forgotten. With the passage of time more and more psychiatrists were attracted to his belief that mental diseases existed in nature like cancer, tuberculosis, or diabetes, just waiting to be discovered by exhaustive clinical and laboratory research. Psychiatrists, quoting Plato in *Phaedrus*, called the process "cutting nature at the joints."

The renewed interest in psychiatric diagnosis led to concerted efforts to reform the American Psychiatric Association's *Diagnostic and Statistical Manual of Mental Disorders* (DSM), sometimes referred to as U.S. psychiatry's "bible." The first two editions of the DSM appeared in 1952 and 1968 and were sprinkled liberally with psychoanalytic jargon.

DSM-I and DSM-II stressed the psychological mechanisms underlying mental illness, casting doubt on the theory that separate mental diseases actually existed.

Yet for years discontent had been brewing within U.S. psychiatry over the "psycho-social model" that underpinned the theory of social psychiatry and dated back to the Menningers and the Group for the Advancement of Psychiatry. This model held that psychological illness occurred because of the individual's failure to adapt to his or her environment. Some psychiatrists denounced the psycho-social model as "soft-headed" and "pseudo-psychiatry." Others feared that adherence to the model politicized the profession and negated its claims to scientific impartiality. In 1976 the president of the APA stated that social psychiatry, in "carrying psychiatrists on a mission to change the world, had brought the profession to the edge of extinction."

Leading the campaign to prepare DSM's third edition for 1980 was the "St. Louis school," a group of clinicians and researchers at Washington University. The central member of the school was Robert Spitzer, who headed a task force that from 1974 to 1978 worked on writing DSM-III. Spitzer believed psychiatry's true mission was the discovery of biologically real mental diseases, not social reform. Spitzer wanted the new DSM to more closely resemble European psychiatry's traditional interest in diagnosis and put an end to American psychiatry's love affair with psychoanalysis. "With its intellectual roots in St. Louis instead of Vienna, and with its international inspiration derived from Kraepelin, not Freud," Spitzer and colleague Ronald Bayer unabashedly declared, "the task force was viewed from the outset as unsympathetic to the interests of those whose theory and practice derived from the psychoanalytic tradition."[87] Thanks to the efforts of Spitzer's task force, when DSM-III appeared in 1980 psychiatric classification was back in vogue and Freudianism was fast losing its grip on U.S. psychiatry.

Yet the effort to reform diagnosis in psychiatry was quickly overtaken by politics and economics. Psychiatrists who wanted to channel Kraepelin's spirit in the 1960s believed doing so would mean the triumph of "observation" over "theory" in the classification of mental diseases, but they discovered that the insurance and pharmaceutical industries were exerting their own influence over diagnostic psychiatry.[88] To Spitzer's opponents, DSM-III was a "capitulation to computers and insurance company requirements." Indeed, in the 1970s insurance companies had begun cutting back coverage for outpatient visits and hospital stays. If government and private insurers were going to pay to treat mental disabilities, they wanted to know how and why psychiatrists diagnosed these conditions. A diagnostic system that stressed precise description and standard criteria would dispel the industry view that psychiatry was a "bottomless pit." A standardized diagnostic system would also make it easier for researchers to qualify for funding grants.[89]

The effort to introduce science into psychiatric diagnosis, however, did not prevent psychiatry from becoming a "bottomless pit." The list of mental diseases kept multiplying with dizzying speed. DSM-II expanded the number of diagnoses from 106 to 182. DSM-III contained 265 separate mental illnesses. The fourth edition, published in 1994, was 400 pages longer than the third and listed three times as many disorders as the first DSM-I in 1952. DSM-V, scheduled for 2012, was forecast to be even longer. Those who wanted to find a medical name for their emotional conditions – and thus get coverage for treatment – had only to leaf through the DSM, a striking testament to psychiatry's populism in the early twenty-first century. Practitioners may have thought the coming of neo-Kraepelinian psychiatry meant the triumph of science over theorizing, but they soon realized that other factors were also shaping the classification of mental diseases.

Initially, foreign psychiatrists – notably in Britain – resisted using the DSM. They tended to prefer the WHO's International Classification of Diseases (ICD). In 1981 Michael Shepherd, a leading British psychiatrist, predicted that "serious students of nosology will continue to use the ICD," but the coming years returned a different verdict. By the mid-1990s the process begun by DSM-III had culminated in the convergence of the DSM and ICD. At the 1996 Madrid meeting of the World Psychiatric Association, its banner read, "One World, One Language." Psychiatry was becoming globalized, with a common scientific language – English – and common diagnostic system whose foundations had been laid by DSM-III. Many European practitioners, proud of their own national traditions in the field, resentfully believed that what had happened to psychiatry was more a case of American imperialism than of globalization. At the outset of the twenty-first century foreign psychiatrists lamented that an "Americanization of mental illness" was occurring, a process in which U.S. psychiatry exported its disease categories – for example, depression, post-traumatic stress disorder, and anorexia – to other parts of the globe, not just because of Western drug company marketing and advertising, but also because American researchers and institutions ran most scholarly journals and hosted the leading conferences in the field. One critic called it "homogenizing the way the world goes mad," but that was just another way of saying that by the end of the twentieth century U.S. psychiatry and the DSM reigned supreme.[90]

A VAST FAILURE

The multiplying number of DSM mental disorders – what Peter Kramer called "diagnostic bracket creep" – not only "medicalized ordinary unhappiness," argued Harvard University professor of psychiatry Arthur Kleinman, but also trivialized the suffering of people with severe mental disabilities. One such person was Maxine Mason, a forty-six-year-old woman from Queen's, New York, who on November 17, 1994, died at the Rockland Psychiatric Center.[91] Those glancing at her obituary most likely did not recognize Mason by her real name. To millions of readers, Mason was better known as Sylvia Frumkin, the subject of reporter Susan Sheehan's Pulitzer Prize–winning 1982 book, *Is There No Place on Earth for Me?*

First serialized in the *New Yorker*, Sheehan's poignant story recounted how she followed Mason for two and a half years as Maxine, diagnosed in 1963 as a schizophrenic at age fourteen, bounced back and forth between her parents' home, community group homes, private psychiatric facilities, and state hospitals. In the process, Mason went on and off medications, periodically endangering herself and repeatedly plunging the lives of her parents and her sister into chaos. Though "treatment resistant" – about 15 percent of schizophrenics fail to respond positively to any medication – Mason was prescribed various dosages of drugs by a series of psychiatrists, who frequently mistook her symptoms for different diseases. Maxine Mason could be endearing, belligerent, noisy, incoherent, or rude, but to Sheehan, Mason's plight as a mental patient was a desperate plea for help. In her fleeting, lucid moments, Mason wondered aloud if she could ever find emotional peace. Her hard-pressed family, like so many other families throughout history compelled to take care of their sick relatives, wondered the same thing.

The sad events of Maxine Mason's life were enmeshed in a policy revolution that spanned the era between Sputnik and Watergate and helped to pave the way for the ascendancy of therapism. This revolution in mental health care has been dubbed "deinstitutionalization," the process that saw hospital administrators discharge patients into the community. The revolution had begun during World War II when conscientious objectors – some of whom were Quakers – leaked stories to the press about the substandard conditions in U.S. state hospitals. After the war major publications carried exposés of state hospitals with headlines such as "Bedlam USA." The deplorable conditions in asylums were not unique to the United States. One Canadian psychiatrist remembered how the asylum in Weyburn, Saskatchewan, "stunk [*sic*] like something out of this world.... The whole basement was a shambles, naked people all over the place lying around, incontinent."[92]

Indeed, one of the first steps in the history of deinstitutionalization took place in the Canadian province of Saskatchewan, where in 1944 voters elected Thomas Clement ("Tommy") Douglas their premier. Douglas promptly began overseeing a massive overhaul of the province's health care system. By 1961, when he left provincial politics, Tommy Douglas's reforms had commanded the attention of friend and foe alike, but everyone agreed that he had made Saskatchewan the homeland of socialized medicine and a leader in mental health care reform.

Douglas was a Scottish-born Baptist minister with a taste for political reform, including state health insurance, or Medicare. To Douglas, Medicare was one pillar in a major reorganization of public welfare. Within months of taking power, Douglas's government agreed to pay all costs of hospital care for those suffering from mental disabilities. Emphasizing the prevention of mental illness, he believed that a mental hospital should be a place of last resort and tirelessly encouraged changes in public attitudes toward people with mental disabilities. He backed plans to move patients out of mental hospitals and into smaller homes scattered throughout the province. Between 1963 and 1966, for example, there was a 72 percent reduction in the inmate population at the Weyburn Hospital, one of the province's two public mental hospitals. No other asylum in the world matched that rate of patient discharge. Douglas's policies were yet another demonstration that sweeping mental health care reform often took place within the crucible of egalitarian political experimentation.[93]

Aiding the release of patients into the community was the discovery by hospital psychiatrists that many patients reacted positively to the first anti-psychotic drugs. Between 1955 and 1980 the resident population in U.S. mental hospitals tumbled from 558,922 to 130,000. In England and Wales the number of asylum patients was 150,000 in 1954, but abruptly fell to 75,000 by 1980, a decrease of 50 percent. In the Canadian province of Ontario, asylum patients went from a peak of 19,000 in 1960 to about 5,000 in 1976, even as the number of staff members and psychiatrists rose. Similar trends unfolded in Austria, Switzerland, Luxemburg, and both Germanies after 1970. In Italy in 1978 the so-called Law 180 abolished all psychiatric hospitals, due largely to the efforts of psychiatrist Franco Basaglia, who as director of the mental hospital in Trieste had led the campaign to close that institution.

Deinstitutionalization was limited to mainly Western industrialized countries. In many developing countries, institutional mental health care hardly existed in the first place. In Japan the number of psychiatric beds actually rose in the second half of the twentieth century, and in some South American nations asylum-type beds were simply replaced by beds in psychiatric inpatient units in general hospitals. The extent of deinstitutionalization differed from one country to another and from one American state to another. Yet the end result was basically the same in developed countries: the asylum was dethroned as the dominant resource for the treatment of people with mental disabilities. To many in the mental health field, such people were better off in the community.

A quarter-century later, however, deinstitutionalization – in the words of the *New York Times* – was "a vast failure." All too often, people like Maxine Mason were unable to find a place in society. When non-compliant, they became part of a revolving-door process that saw them cycled in and out of hospitals until they were lost to follow-up, an amorphous group drifting from hostels to prisons to the street. To avoid side effects they often stopped taking their medication. Routinely, they were victims of petty criminals looking for cigarettes or loose change. The homeless mentally ill were "like rabbits forced to live in company with dogs," according to one newspaper report.[94] Whether they committed violent crimes or were just nuisances on city streets, many found their way into jails or similar "secure units," prompting talk about a "reinstitutionalization" of the mentally ill by the end of the twentieth century.[95] To some observers, it appeared as if little had changed since the days of Dorothea Dix.

OVERKILL AND OVERSELL

How had deinstitutionalization reached this state of affairs? In the United States, the coming of deinstitutionalization had coincided with the presidency of John F. Kennedy and the heavy intervention of the federal government in mental health policy. The early 1960s were a turning point in the history of health in general. Prior to World War II few governments had departments of health, an unsurprising state of affairs at a time when everything seemed to indicate that overall health was improving by leaps and bounds. If thanks to medical science people were getting healthier all the time, why did governments need to get more involved? In sharp contrast to the early twenty-first century, when health issues regularly grabbed media attention, the press rarely covered health stories before the 1950s.

Yet the first stirrings of coverage of mental health issues in the 1950s and 1960s helped to propel personal health matters out of the shadows and into the spotlight. The Kennedys themselves publicly acknowledged the sad story of the president's sister Rosemary, who had been diagnosed as mildly retarded and had undergone a failed lobotomy. With the Kennedy White House leading the way, people slowly started to believe that they no longer needed to feel ashamed about personal sickness, even mental illness.

Kennedy was the first president ever to address Congress on mental health issues. His administration set up a task force that produced the Mental Retardation Facilities and Community Mental Health Centers (CMHC) Construction Act of 1963. Kennedy highlighted the general philosophy behind the legislation when he stressed the importance of prevention as well as the role of "harsh environmental conditions" in triggering mental illness. The major aim of the CMHC Act, Kennedy remarked, was a 50 percent reduction in state hospital populations "within a decade or two." The CMHC Act of 1963 called for the construction of 1,500 community mental health centers. More than two decades later, however, less than half that number had been built. Daniel Moynihan, later Democratic senator from New York, had worked on Kennedy's task force. In 1989 Moynihan asked: "What if, on the occasion of the bill signing in 1963, someone had said to President [John F.] Kennedy: 'Wait. Before you sign the bill you should know that we are not going to build anything like the number of community centers we will need.... The hospitals will empty out, but there will be no place for the patients to be cared for in their communities. A quarter-century hence the streets of New York will be filled with homeless, deranged people"? Moynihan's answer: Kennedy would have put down his pen and refused to sign.

To Moynihan and others, the shortage of community centers was the chief reason for the failure of deinstitutionalization, but there were other factors to blame. In time, those CMHCs that were built "drifted away from their original purpose" to provide "counseling and crisis intervention for predictable problems of living," complained one APA president. The coming of CMHCs dovetailed with the growth in third-party insurance plans. Individuals with emotional disturbances rather than severe mental illnesses increasingly patronized the CMHCs. The mounting emphasis on psychotherapy in CMHCs mirrored the trend of treating people suffering from "maladjustment" rather than chronic, debilitating mental diseases. Planners may never have been happy with the total number of CMHCs, but deinstitutionalization also failed because the original aim to make them community-based, service-provider institutions for the severely ill fell far short of success.[96]

It would be tempting to conclude that the breakthroughs in drug therapy in the 1950s were the biggest single cause of deinstitutionalization. Yet the availability of new medications only partly accounts for the emptying of mental hospitals and the rise of the community mental health movement. In Britain asylum populations had started dropping before chlorpromazine came on the scene. The belief that many patients did better in the community than in the asylum and that community-based prevention strategies were the best weapons against mental illness were at least as important as the coming of Thorazine. In Britain, as at some U.S. hospitals, efforts had been under way before the introduction of chlorpromazine to make hospitals less authoritarian and more rehabilitative. Asked to choose between the new anti-psychotic drugs and the new "social facilities" available in asylums, England's Aubrey Lewis replied famously that he would have "no hesitation ... : the drugs would go."[97]

The drop in asylum populations, the closing of mental hospitals, and the exodus of patients "into the community" happened because minds had been dazzled by cutting-edge ideology in the first place. As an NIMH official conceded in 2004, the entire community mental health care movement had suffered from "overkill and oversell."[98] Earlier, in 1971, the World Health Organization had heralded "the trend towards caring for the mentally ill in the community wherever possible and recognition of the need to consider the patient in the context of his social environment .... The approach is the antithesis of custodial care in large isolated institutes and of an exclusively medical approach which seeks to treat mental illness in the same terms as a physical disease."[99] The idea that people with mental disabilities had to be freed from the custodial clutches of psychiatrists blinded caregivers to what was happening on the ground. A Canadian psychiatrist recounted:

> Deinstitutionalization was an incredible thing, and when I talk about it in retrospect I can't believe what I am saying, but there I was honestly saying that all you had to do was load them with neuroleptic drugs and send them out into the community. We began reading ... how hospital screws people up. So we took tens of thousands of patients and threw them out of the hospital without any support system. We said there was going to be follow-up, but the fact of the matter is that nobody really

understood, so the bureaucrats were delighted to get them out of the hospital ... and only in 1975 and later did we say: "Hey, this is crazy, what about housing, what about recreation?"

Another practitioner conceded that psychiatrists suspected something was wrong at the time, "but we had the attitude that it was the community's responsibility and not the hospital's responsibility once they were discharged. We believed that the worst possible place a person could be was in the big institution.... But we didn't realize we weren't sending them out to a nice boarding home with Ma and Pa looking after them but to God knows what." Civil servants in the 1970s were equally loath to protest. One remembered his point of view at the time: "What the hell do they [the mentally ill] want from us? Once they are out of the hospital they're on their own, they're just normal citizens, we won't interfere with that. It's not our job to provide services for these people." "People aren't wrong in assuming that the government was being insensitive," he confessed.[100]

The idea that "hospitals screw people up" found converts among politicians eager to cut costs. In 1975 the Ontario minister of health vehemently denied that "dollars and cents" were behind the shift to community care, but the perception persisted that governments liked the policy because it saved taxpayers money. Since then studies have found that deinstitutionalization does not save money overall, but in the 1970s, when governments began paying for the massive expansion of public welfare in the 1960s – notably Medicaid and Medicare (1965), housing programs, food stamps, Social Security – programs that offered the prospect of trimming costs in other areas were bound to enlist strong support.

Last but not least, the term "deinstitutionalization" was misleading. The fall of the asylum was as much a transfer of patients from one institution to another as it was a release of people with mental disabilities into the community. The coming of Medicaid in the United States enabled the states to shift elderly and poor residents to nursing homes, triggering a steep drop in the number of aged patients in state hospitals. During the 1960s the population in U.S. nursing homes jumped from 470,000 to more than 900,000. By 1985 more than 600,000 nursing home residents were diagnosed as mentally ill, at a cost of $10.5 billion. The quality of care in nursing homes varied so much that some commentators wondered aloud whether these elderly patients would have been better off back in the asylum. By that point in history the grim conclusion that deinstitutionalization had failed people such as Maxine Mason was starting to dawn on even its most ardent backers.[101]

By the end of the century deinstitutionalization had run its course, bringing the age of the asylum to a largely unmourned end. As Philip Rieff had predicted, the "triumph of the therapeutic" had become a reality. The emphasis of the quest for mental health had shifted from the Maxine Masons of the world to the "worried well," the countless men and women who sought "peace of mind" through prescription drugs or various types of counseling and psychotherapy. Few any longer shared the belief of Brock Chisholm and GAP that psychiatry alone could end racial conflict or achieve world peace. Instead, the end of the century witnessed the growing belief that emotional well-being was a consumer product, a matter of private taste and personal choice. Political parties, far from discouraging this trend toward personal fulfillment, were actively promoting it as the century wound to a close, with both Britain's New Labour and Conservative parties calling for the state-led cultivation of happiness as an end in itself. Policy makers celebrated the transition from the traditional governmental role of redistributing material wealth to a form of emotional welfare that served psychological needs.

Yet amid all the talk about the emergence of a therapeutic state, unhappiness kept growing at a worrisome pace. The warnings of Christopher Lasch and others that therapism, far from quenching the thirst for mental well-being, would only exacerbate it, took on added relevance as the twenty-first century opened and more and more people reported that they could bear their emotional pain no longer.

5

Emotional Welfare

As deinstitutionalization unfolded over the last decades of the twentieth century, millions of individuals like Gail Andrews increasingly occupied center stage in the quest for mental health. Andrews's personal issues had little in common with people such as Maxine Mason. Indeed, at first glance Gail Andrews had it all: a middle-aged professional living in Toronto in the early twenty-first century, she was trilingual, well read, a long-distance cyclist, and an accomplished musician. She had a great job as a senior executive at a major accounting firm. Other companies tried to recruit her as a partner.

Despite all this good news, Gail Andrews lived a life of emotional torment. Like millions in the early twenty-first century, Gail suffered from "social anxiety disorder" (SAD), aptly called "crippling shyness." Although by all measures she was a professional success, nearly every situation that triggered her anxiety was work related: leading workshops, giving presentations, doing "power lunches," even taking phone calls. Her fear of social performance left her "never able to relax." In 2008 she told a reporter, "If you really knew me, you wouldn't like me ... at all."[1]

At the turn of the millennium millions of people around the world reported feeling like Gail Andrews. They complained about being wracked by anxiety about social interactions, what the drug industry called being "allergic to people." Defined as a feeling of apprehension or fear accompanied by a range of physical symptoms including sweating, dizziness, fainting, nausea, or heart palpitations, anxiety afflicted almost 20 million adult Americans by the early twenty-first century. Though the rate of anxiety disorders varied from one country and culture to another, reported anxiety levels had mounted ominously in successive birth cohorts since the end of World War II. In 2001 the National Institute of Mental Health declared anxiety the most common mental health problem in the United States. In 2002 the World Mental Health Survey reported that anxiety was the most prevalent mental health problem around the globe. Every day countless people the world over swallowed prescription drugs to curb their anxiety. In 2006, in the United States alone, doctors wrote more than 71 million prescriptions for anti-anxiety drugs. SAD had evolved from a disorder limited to urban settings in First World countries into a global concern.

The great turning point in the history of the anxiety diagnosis came in 1980 when the third edition of the *Diagnostic and Statistical Manual of Mental Disorders* separated depression and anxiety and subdivided anxiety into a series of disorders that included SAD (or social phobia), generalized anxiety disorder (GAD), obsessive-compulsive disorder (OCD), panic disorder (PD), specific phobias, and post-traumatic stress disorder (PTSD). Researchers reported that OCD and SAD were equally common in men and women, but women were more likely than men to suffer from GAD, PD, PTSD, and specific phobias.

Few events better captured the stage the quest for mental health had reached by the new millennium than the striking rise in the incidence of anxiety disorders. This "age of anxiety" – as it was dubbed – was the product of a kind of "perfect storm" of events and trends in medicine, culture, society, industry, politics, education, language, and the media, all of which dovetailed to accelerate the democratization of mental health at an unprecedented pace. Canadian journalist Patricia Pearson, writing about her own battle with SAD, argued that the symptoms of anxiety at the end of the twentieth century were due to a culture that celebrates fierce, winner-take-all competition, notably on college campuses, in the information industries, and in the corporate business world. According to Pearson, the message that there is "no shame in shamelessness" puts a premium on grabbing all the attention we can, thereby fostering an acute fear of failure in countless people who temperamentally find it difficult to emulate the Donald Trumps of the world. Living within a culture that privileges "hucksterism," Pearson maintained, breeds "intense anxiety."[2]

Yet other trends helped to produce high levels of crippling anxiety, notably the culture of vulnerability fostered by the self-help and recovery movement. According to some observers, society's chief institutions – schools, government, medicine, corporations, and the media – taught people that anxiety was an *acceptable* response to life in the modern age. The prevailing ethos of society tended to validate victimization and powerlessness as much as vanity, self-promotion, or cutthroat assertiveness. When people in the late twentieth century experienced the emotional and physical symptoms of anxiety, they underwent a "flight into illness" similar to what late-nineteenth-century men and women experienced when they suffered from "neurasthenia," only in much greater numbers. In the words of historian Edward Shorter, the symptoms of anxiety became "socially and medically correct."[3]

Anxiety has had a long history. In 1525 St. Thomas More first used the term, writing that only Jesus Christ himself died "without grudge, without anxietie [*sic*]." The poet John Keats called it "wakeful anguish." For centuries the symptoms of anxiety were believed to be commonplace in people's lives, but in the late nineteenth century physicians began describing patients who complained that in certain social situations or settings – open or closed spaces, speech making, workplaces, and the like – they had trouble breathing, their hearts started pounding, their pulses raced, their palms sweated, their limbs tingled, their heads ached, and their stomachs felt as if butterflies were swarming inside. The first signs of clinical anxiety coincided with the "age of progress," a time when many of the old dangers that had threatened humanity for centuries – starvation, epidemic disease, high infant mortality – began to abate. Overall standards of living were on the rise, culminating in the post–World War II era in a state of affluence and prosperity in America never before seen in history. The striking advances in life expectancy, education levels, and disposable income freed up time for people, who seemed to use it to fret and worry.[4]

The trend toward labeling everyday anxiety a sickness became a stampede during the Cold War. Within a few decades, countries including the United States were reporting that as many as 10 percent of their respective populations suffered from social anxiety. At the turn of the twenty-first century, the anxiety diagnosis was thriving across the Atlantic Ocean as much as in North America. The French, typically hailed for their joie de vivre, were reputed to be the world's biggest consumers of tranquilizers and anti-anxiety pills, with nearly one in five men and women taking anti-depressants.[5]

Social anxiety disorder shares symptoms with those of many other psychiatric conditions, including "agoraphobia," first diagnosed in 1876 as a dread of public places. The definition of agoraphobia broadened in the twentieth century to mean panic attacks in any place or situation where someone feels unsafe or trapped. Anxiety is also a prominent feature of mild depression, hypochondria, anorexia nervosa, and obsessive-compulsive behavior. Body dysmorphic disorder (BDD) – the "distress of imagined ugliness" – was known in Europe as "dysmorphophobia," a term coined in 1891. BDD is another condition accompanied by anxiety, although its primary symptom is the delusional belief that there is something wrong with one's physical appearance.[6]

Yet no matter how much the SAD diagnosis overlaps other conditions, the consensus at the beginning of the twenty-first century was that anxiety-related disorders constituted discrete diseases and posed a major obstacle to the quest for mental health. Psychiatrists tended to think that most people delayed seeking treatment, thereby making their conditions worse. The public, mental health experts insisted, simply did not realize how sick it truly was.

CONSPIRACISM

For the countless people reporting higher levels of anxiety than ever before in the early twenty-first century, the concept and terminology of stress, introduced in the 1930s by the Vienna-born physiologist Hans Selye, had special resonance. As an endocrinologist at McGill University and the Université de Montréal, Selye studied how the body responded to environmental stimuli. He called this process of physiological adaptation "stress," but people seemed to prefer using the term to describe the external factors that triggered bodily and mental changes in the first place. Public opinion also confused stress with depression, fatigue, or tension. These disturbances were not stress, Selye insisted, adding that stress was "not so much what happens to you, but the way you take it."[7] Nonetheless, soon millions were using it to explain how circumstances beyond their control caused their psychological unease.

"Anxiety," like "stress," became a commonplace term during the second half of the twentieth century. In 1950 American composer Leonard Bernstein named his Second Symphony after W. H. Auden's Pulitzer Prize–winning 1947 poem "The Age of Anxiety." The buildup of nuclear weapons, the energy crises of the 1970s, the appearance of AIDS in the 1980s, the horrors of Bosnia and Rwanda in the 1990s, the threat of climate change and global warming, the international economic meltdown of 2008: these and other developments convinced millions that it was natural to be anxious in a world of grim uncertainty, diminishing natural resources, deadly ethnic violence, runaway killer diseases, massive job losses, and imminent environmental catastrophe.

Polls after the terrorist attacks on the World Trade Center and Pentagon on September 11, 2001, reported that stress and fear levels were rising in numerous countries. Americans told pollsters that after 9/11 they were more suspicious of people around them and uncomfortable in public places. A poll conducted by the National Sleep Foundation shortly after 9/11 found that almost seven out of ten Americans experienced some form of sleep disturbance in the period following the attacks. The September 11 attacks prompted the Office of Mental Health to predict that 2 million New Yorkers would need counseling. Travelers on London's subway were much more vigilant after the terrorist bombings of 2005. In 2006 one in three people in the United Kingdom said they harbored suspicious fears about other people. Such attitudes reflected the distress felt by millions living in the shadows of international terrorism.

Worries about terrorism exacerbated conspiratorial thinking. Already noticeable before 9/11, the "paranoid intellectual temper" of inveterate mistrust, reductive suspicion, and heroic irony spread even further after airliners crashed into the Pentagon and the twin towers of the World Trade Center.[8] Prior to 9/11 commentators had noted the upsurge in what author Daniel Pipes has called "conspiracism," the visceral readiness to believe that all history can be reduced to plotting on the part of powerful individuals or organizations. Conspiracy theories about President John F. Kennedy's 1963 assassination continued to circulate decades later. Conspiracism seemingly motivated the militiamen who in 1995 bombed the federal building in Oklahoma City. In the 1990s many African Americans believed that the CIA practiced genocide by purposely introducing crack cocaine and AIDS into inner-city neighborhoods. Conspiracism even invaded the White House. In 1998, at the height of her husband's scandal involving aide Monica Lewinsky, then first lady Hillary Rodham Clinton blamed a "vast right-wing conspiracy" for Bill Clinton's difficulties as president. After 9/11 even highly educated people were convinced that the attacks on the World Trade Center and Pentagon were the work of either the Bush White House or Israel's Mossad intelligence agency.[9]

The taste for unmasking conspiratorial agendas was spread by developments in communications technology, particularly the coming of the Internet. Next to fear, paranoia may be the most communicable mentality, and it has plenty of opportunities to proliferate in cyberspace, where customary boundaries between people and things vanish, leaving individuals feeling insecure and anxious.[10] Movies, such as director Oliver

Stone's overwrought 1991 film *JFK* about Kennedy's assassination, told audiences that their governments plot to subvert justice and spread lies. According to their critics, the news media also deserve some of the blame for propagating a culture of fear that incessantly reminded the population of its vulnerability and victimization.[11] Television, radio, newspapers, and Web sites served up a steady diet of stories about natural disasters, violent crime, drug-resistant "killer bugs," and insensitive government agencies. In the multi-channel universe these stories have been told over and over again to audiences that show few signs of being able to shut their eyes and ears. Paranoid fears seem to flourish in the modern-day global village, fanning anxiety to unprecedented levels.

THE UPJOHN ILLNESS

Developments in psycho-pharmacology also accounted for the reported elevated levels of anxiety. "As often happens in medicine," psychiatrist David Healy has written, "the availability of a treatment leads to an increase in recognition of the disorder that might benefit from that treatment."[12] The great fanfare surrounding the introduction of tranquilizers in the 1950s and 1960s made it appear to people who felt anxious that relief was just a prescription away. Advertising and marketing agencies trumpeted the virtues of anti-anxiety medications, a factor that became more pronounced once direct-to-consumer advertising began in the 1990s in the United States and New Zealand. The drugs appeared to promise "an end to trouble-making tension."[13] Physicians' over-prescription of tranquilizers, often driven by pressure from the pharmaceutical industry's "detail men" who provided physicians with free samples and accompanying literature, also helped to stimulate the consumption of benzodiazepines.

The mounting publicity surrounding minor tranquilizers had concrete consequences. In 1980 the DSM-III said good-bye to the theory that anxiety-related panic and social phobia were simply neurotic symptoms and defined them instead as official, full-fledged psychiatric diagnoses, raising hopes that insurers would cover the costs of treating their condition.

By the 1980s society's honeymoon with tranquilizers was over, as critics increasingly warned about rising addiction, but its *marriage* to "mood medicine" was still intact. Indeed, just as authors were putting their finishing touches to DSM-III, the Upjohn Company was preparing to market the new benzodiazepine alprazolam (Xanax) as a drug for panic disorder. By the 1990s Xanax was one of the hottest psychiatric drugs around. To those who sincerely believed in Xanax's virtues, it was a godsend, but to insiders panic disorder was the "Upjohn illness." Once again, the pharmaceutical industry had affected the history of psychiatric diagnosis, almost overnight transforming panic disorder from one of the least to one of the most recognized mental illnesses. At the same time, drug companies bolstered the notion that each anxiety diagnosis is a biological reality by introducing new medications, such as the serotonin re-uptake inhibitor sertraline for post-traumatic stress disorder. As the 1990s came to an end, the commercial power of the pharmaceutical companies to change the course of history was a troubling reality to many in the mental health field.

Drug therapy was not the only form of treatment that sustained the anxiety diagnosis. BDD patients often resorted to surgery or dermatological help to allay their anxiety over their imagined bodily defects. Some people with social phobia chose surgery when they felt publicly humiliated over their chronic facial blushing. In 2002 a Toronto administrative assistant in her thirties told the media how she turned beet red in social situations. "I get really uncomfortable because … I'm thinking they're probably wondering 'Why is she doing that?'" After trying anti-depressants, tranquilizers, and hypnosis, she opted for endoscopic thoracic sympathectomy by clipping (ETS), which, by destroying certain portions of the sympathetic nerve trunk, inhibits blushing. The fact that medical insurance in Canada and other jurisdictions covered ETS encouraged doctors and patients to invoke the anxiety diagnosis more readily.[14]

Thus, the politics of reimbursement have helped to popularize anxiety disorders as they have the depression diagnosis. The development of new drugs influenced the official recognition of psychiatric disease categories because patients had a better chance at third-party reimbursement for pharmaceutical treatment, especially in contrast to long-term and intensive psychotherapy. Both patients and clinicians benefited from a DSM diagnosis, jokingly called an "insurance claim" by some mental health industry insiders.[15]

MILKING THE SYSTEM

No anxiety-related diagnosis demonstrated more vividly how the politics of reimbursement exerted an influence on the history of mental health than post-traumatic stress disorder. The symptoms of PTSD, a condition characterized by the emotionally painful re-experiencing of a horrific event, include nightmares, flashbacks, irritability, severe anxiety, and crippling phobias. World War II was a turning point in the history of PTSD because it overturned the World War I theory that psychiatric breakdown could be prevented by better selection and monitoring of recruits and paved the way for experts' view that "every man had his breaking point." In contrast to the situation in the 1919–39 era, Cold War governments discovered that it was difficult to deny veterans third-party disability benefits for having served their countries – for example, the U.S. Department of Veterans Affairs compensation program.[16]

In 1980 PTSD became an official diagnosis in the wake of the Vietnam War when advocates of the disease successfully lobbied for its inclusion in the DSM-III's section on anxiety disorders. In 1982 the *Journal of Nervous and Mental Disorders* estimated that 500,000 to 700,000 veterans suffered from PTSD out of the 3 million who served in the Vietnam theater of war. A 1990 government study claimed that half of all veterans were PTSD victims, even though only 15 percent actually served in combat units.[17]

PTSD skeptics alleged that its chief advocates were anti-war, "self-serving psychologists and psychiatrists" who wanted to "milk" Veterans Affairs. Indeed, PTSD proponents included the Vietnam Veterans Against the War.[18] The PTSD diagnosis enabled some veterans to attach meaning to their Vietnam experiences and helped to boost their self-esteem when the challenges of adjusting to peacetime proved highly stressful. Yet the theory that traumatic events caused emotional illness swiftly spread beyond the community of Vietnam veterans to groups within the women's movement that saw PTSD as a handy diagnosis to apply to victims of rape, domestic violence, child abuse, and sexual assault. In 1992 Harvard Medical School professor Judith Lewis Herman wrote that "the most common post-traumatic disorders are those not of men but of women in civilian life." Before long, therapists sympathetic to Herman's viewpoint were putting into practice her theory that there was a real "war between the sexes.... Hysteria is the combat neurosis of the sex war."[19] Armed with the PTSD diagnosis, experts such as Herman redefined the private relations between men and women as public health issues amenable to professional intervention.

PTSD proved to be a lucrative diagnosis. U.S. veterans receiving disability checks for PTSD jumped from 120,000 in 1999 to 216,000 in 2004. That increase alone accounted for an additional $2.6 billion in benefits. In 2003 those who qualified for the PTSD diagnosis were entitled to as much as $2,100 per month, tax free. In the end analysis, the U.S. government discovered what the British government learned about shell shock in the wake of World War I: reimbursement policies can heavily affect the destiny of a psychiatric diagnosis and the emotional health of millions.

VICTIMIZATION

The widening of the PTSD diagnosis to include people in civilian life was a critical factor in the growing emphasis on victimization in late-twentieth-century society. The standard interpretation of PTSD was that its sufferers were victims twice over: first, at the hands of the original perpetrators and then at the hands of an indifferent society that supposedly disregarded people's pain.[20] PTSD thus revealed how anxiety disorders dovetailed with the emergence of the self-help and recovery movement (SHRM). This movement stretched back to the early twentieth century, when the popularity of mental healing began to take root in educated social circles. Books such as Dale Carnegie's *How to Win Friends and Influence People* (1937) and Norman Vincent Peale's *The Power of Positive Thinking* (1952) continued the tradition of self-help. Peale was joined by fellow U.S. clergymen Billy Graham and Bishop Fulton J. Sheen, who similarly applauded the virtues of happiness for a well-rounded life.

The dam broke in 1967 with Thomas A. Harris's smash, *I'm OK – You're OK*. After Harris, authors of such books became virtual gurus, notably "Doctor Phil" McGraw, Tony Robbins, Deepak Chopra, and Robert Fulghum. Daytime television programs, including *Oprah* and *Donahue*, were watched by millions and provided forums in which these self-appointed experts spread their teachings. Mainstream magazines such as *Redbook* and *Ladies' Home Journal* ran countless stories on how to improve the quality of one's emotional life. In 2003 alone, between 3,500 and 4,000 new self-help books were published.

The main themes of SHRM were vulnerability, powerlessness, victimization, and authenticity. Though the proponents of SHRM differed on a range of issues, they tended to preach that almost everyone lived in a hostile world, filled with multiple addictions, menacing relatives and friends, mendacious governments, wicked corporations, fanatical terrorists, and the like. In such a world, SHRM advocates argued, there were untold millions who silently paid a steep emotional price trying merely to survive. The SHRM industry, composed of countless therapists, counselors, workshoppers, personal coaches, and social scientists, claimed to be able to help these millions recognize that they were not to blame for their psychological and physical symptoms, they deserved better emotional health, and they could enjoy a much higher sense of self-esteem and self-worth.

The message was that people were sicker than they thought and had a right to mental health.[21]

At one time unhappy people would have been told to stop blaming others for their misery and get on with their lives. By contrast, SHRM taught that there were medical labels that not only explained symptoms of anxiety, but valorized them as well. If, for example, you sweat profusely, your head spins, your stomach churns, and your heart races when you get ready to deliver a speech, you suffer from a bona fide medical condition and need only seek expert, professional help to feel better. SHRM made it acceptable for highly stressed people to adopt certain sick roles rather than use their willpower to overcome their symptoms, as countless human beings had done for generations and generations. Where once self-reliance and emotional toughness were highly prized, the adoption of emotional sickness as a kind of badge of personal honor had stamped American life by the early twenty-first century.

MEMORY WARS

If rugged, stoical individuals seemed to be a vanishing breed in the late twentieth century, there were other serious stakes as the victimization movement gained momentum. The belief that society was full of victims in dire need of recovery paved the way for recovered (or repressed) memory theory. According to Judith Herman and other mental health professionals, the majority of both psychiatric inpatients and outpatients were actually victims of "physical or sexual abuse or both." Drawing on Freudian concepts, Herman claimed that victims rarely remember such events of abuse. Patients initially may even deny what happened, so the therapist's challenge is to recover the memories through dialogue and construct a "fully detailed, written trauma narrative." Cure is complete, she maintained, only once the patient accepts this "narrative," makes it public, and confronts her abuser.[22]

By the 1990s the recovered memory movement was advancing by leaps and bounds. In 1988 Ellen Bass and Laura Davis published *The Courage to Heal*, which only a few years later had sold 800,000 copies. Bass and Davis argued that one-third of all girls had been sexually abused by the age of eighteen. Noted African American women such as Maya Angelou, Toni Morrison, and Oprah Winfrey bolstered the movement by recounting tales of childhood sexual seduction at the hands of older men. Major television networks broadcast programs uncritically publicizing recovered memory. Defenders of the theory proclaimed that society was full of survivors of incest. Thousands of vulnerable, emotionally fragile men and women entered therapy.

Amid the flurry of stories about childhood incest and sexual abuse, a troubling variant of the narrative began attracting headlines. In 1983 the McMartin pre-school trial mesmerized the English-speaking world. Teachers at the prestigious Los Angeles school were accused of molesting hundreds of their young pupils and threatening them with torture if they ever spoke out. As prosecutors built their case, further charges that the teachers formed a satanic cult and child pornography ring multiplied rapidly. Initial press coverage seemed to take the defendants' guilt for granted.

Finally, in 1990, after spending $15 million to try to convict the mother and son who ran the pre-school, the prosecution decided not to seek a third trial. Yet by then the McMartin case had spawned similar trials in the 1980s as thousands of Americans – mainly women – reported being victims of such abuse.[23] Numerous women alleging satanic abuse complained of multiple personality disorder (MPD), renamed in 1994 dissociative identity disorder by the APA, the condition in which a single person displays different personalities or identities. First popularized by the 1973 novel *Sybil*, MPD emerged in the 1980s as a full-fledged movement all of its own, but its defenders, like those from the recovered memory and SRA movements, typically invoked childhood sexual (and often satanic) abuse as the key cause of what was once called "split personality."[24]

Members of the recovered memory and SRA movements have accused skeptics of being "on the side of the molesters, rapists, pedophiles, and other misogynists." One English therapist equated SRA denial with Holocaust denial.[25] Nonetheless, these tactics ultimately failed to intimidate critics, who formed their own organizations, notably the False Memory Syndrome Foundation in the United States and the False Memory Syndrome Society in Britain. Individuals who belonged to these groups sought firmer regulations of psychotherapy, including bigger restrictions on insurance coverage and the criminalization of false accusations. They objected that memory gets shakier over time, that it can easily be distorted by a therapist's suggestions, and that leading questions from adult authority figures can get children to say virtually anything. A crushing blow to the SRA movement was the serial failure of police forces on both sides of the Atlantic Ocean to find a shred of forensic evidence to back up accusations of satanic ritual murders or human sacrifices.[26]

The peak of the recovered memory movement occurred when fears about satanic cults, serial murderers, pedophile rings, child pornography, illicit drug pushers, and the like were rife in U.S. popular culture. Intense media coverage of these fears fostered belief in the existence of conspiracies aimed chiefly at children. The tide started to turn, however, in the 1990s as patients began suing their therapists for malpractice, in many cases winning sizable settlements. Amid accusations that therapists were keeping patients in treatment indefinitely to maximize insurance payments, insurance companies increasingly cut back health coverage for psychotherapy. One company paid out $2.5 million for a single patient who in therapy came to believe that her mother had trained her at age thirteen to be a high priestess of a satanic cult that ritualistically sacrificed newborns.[27] Most therapists found that high malpractice insurance premiums made it impossible to perform recovered memory therapy.

These reactions on the part of the insurance industry helped to take the sting out of the bitter "memory wars" of the 1980s and 1990s. However, in 1995 one critic of the recovered memory movement marveled at the "extraordinary speed with which it has come to dominate the mental health debate in North America, and to move rapidly up mental health agendas in other countries."[28] Litigation may have sent a chill through the recovered memory movement, but the notion that society was full of emotionally battered people desperately in need of healing through no fault of their own seemed to be firmly planted in the popular culture of the early twenty-first century.

GENDER

SHRM, the pharmaceutical revolution, and the culture of victimization were responsible for the emergence of an illness-affirming popular culture that by the end of the twentieth century had helped to normalize the anxiety diagnosis, but a major change in the status of women revealed how popular culture could also *breed* illness. The personal example of Gail Andrews and women's greater statistical risk for most anxiety disorders reflected a socioeconomic trend that roughly coincided with the rise in the incidence of anxiety. Beginning in the 1970s women – primarily in developed countries – entered the paid workforce in increasing numbers and in better jobs than ever before. Economic necessity, improved educational credentials, and affirmative action hiring largely accounted for these patterns. The expanding presence of women in higher education was both cause and effect of women's greater visibility in the paid workforce.

By the 1990s U.S. women held more than a third of all corporate management positions and accounted for nearly one-fourth of all doctors and lawyers. In recent years half of all U.S. law students have been women, and since the mid-1980s more women than men have received bachelor of arts degrees.[29]

In other industrialized countries the situation was similar. Although many women over the past several decades also entered the ranks of the working poor, women tended to dominate part-time employment, and women's wages lagged behind those of men, many other women made inroads into the non-traditional sectors of the economy, including highly qualified positions in corporations and government. In Canada in the 1990s, women accounted for more than one-half of the growth in jobs demanding a university education. The number of women in business and finance more than doubled in the 1990s, and women managers increased by 40 percent over the same decade. In developed countries in general, women represented half of all enrollments in post-secondary education in 1990, and that percentage continued to rise into the twenty-first century. In many countries women were enrolling in medical school in increasing numbers, leading some researchers to talk about a "feminization of medicine" in the twenty-first century.[30] In Britain in 2006, more women than men were training to be doctors. Between 1990 and 2003 the number of full-time, Canadian women university teachers jumped by more than 50 percent. (By contrast, the number of male full-time university teachers fell by 14 percent.) In North America and Western Europe 40 percent of all post-secondary teachers were women. Nothing remotely like this had ever happened in all of women's history.

The connection between rising levels of anxiety and the history of women is one part social and the other part biological. Clearly, men as well as women suffered from anxiety. However, the larger number of women than men who complained of anxiety matches what physicians have been saying for centuries about psychosomatic illnesses. Historically, women have reacted to stress more somatically than men. Women have been more predisposed than men to convert emotions into bodily sensations, and indeed there may be a genetic basis to this tendency.[31]

Biology dovetails with social pressures. Governments, Hollywood, the media, social scientists, and lobbyists for women's issues have tended to applaud highly educated women in the corporate world. Women have been told they can "have it all," that they can balance family and professional career. If middle-class women who both raise families and pursue careers outside the home felt anxious, drug industry advertising told such women that all they needed to be a "supermom" was a "little chemical help." Peter Kramer called Prozac a "feminist" drug.[32]

However, the message that gender need not be an obstacle to women's professional success sometimes founders on the shoals of real life, as mirrored in the data showing that more women than men seek medical relief for their anxiety-related emotional and physical symptoms. In GAD the sex ratio was roughly two women to one man. The stark contrast between the ideal of the high-achieving career "supermom" and the many, inevitable frustrations at home and in the workplace most likely was a persistent source of distress for the countless women who have entered the academic, corporate, entertainment, and government worlds in recent decades. Anxiety may be the price women pay for their social and economic gains of the past century.

Thus, by the early twenty-first century a host of social, medical, and biological circumstances had converged to produce an upsurge in anxiety. The overall environment of modern-day life – a subtle interplay of scientific theory and cultural values – bestowed a kind of legitimacy on the pool of anxiety-related symptoms. The contents of this symptom pool have been in a perpetual state of negotiation among a variety of stakeholders, opinion makers, and vested interest groups in government, industry, medicine, education, law, and the media, who have sought to bend and shape psychiatric diagnoses over time. The result in the case of the anxiety diagnosis was the widespread belief that at the onset of the new century millions were too emotionally crippled to get through life without professional help.

THERAPEUTIC GOVERNANCE

The rise of the anxiety diagnosis by the early twenty-first century was one of several signs that the quest for mental health had reached yet another crossroads. The WHO's 2001 report, the EU's new strategy on mental health, George W. Bush's New Freedom Commission on Mental Health, and Canada's Mental Health Commission were among the most striking indications that officialdom on both sides of the Atlantic Ocean was mobilizing for another major campaign in the search for sanity. By the early twenty-first century the consensus among national and international governments appeared to be that the staggering toll of mental disabilities on their populations dictated that much more had to be done in the pursuit of mental health. Where once democratic governments had been concerned primarily about their citizens' material needs, in the new millennium they appeared more interested in providing *emotional* welfare systems within which their citizens could seek healing and self-fulfillment.[33]

Governmental resolve to provide people with mental disabilities with the services they seemingly needed in the new millennium was buoyed by the growing international recognition that mental health was a fundamental human right. The 2008 United Nations Convention on the Rights of Persons with Disabilities described people with mental disabilities as "subjects with rights, who are capable of claiming these rights, and making decisions for their lives based on their free and informed consent as well as being active members of society.... [A]ll persons with all types of disabilities must enjoy all human rights and fundamental freedoms."[34] The WHO's official mandate was to convince the 64 percent of countries that in 2005 still did not have any mental health legislation that protected the rights of people with mental disabilities to pass such laws. Over the course of the twentieth century no two countries' experiences in the mental health field were identical, yet at the dawn of the twenty-first century globalization in the form of the UN and WHO was spreading the egalitarian idea of mental health as a basic human right from one end of the world to the other.[35]

Alongside government leadership in the campaign to achieve full rights for people with mental disabilities was the mounting popular craving in the early twenty-first century for emotional wellness. Rates of psychiatric medication usage and the reported rise in people diagnosed with mental disorders were so striking that one U.S. journalist in 1997 wondered whether or not the country was "officially nuts."[36] All the while the media – ranging from radio and television to new digital communications technologies – fed this craving for mental health with unremitting messages about how to recognize and treat emotional disorders. Unquestionably, such messages disseminated some useful medical knowledge, but they also helped to stimulate self-absorption and feelings of vulnerability and victimization, notably in countries like the United States. What began two centuries ago as a trickle of interest in mental health had by the early twenty-first century evolved into a kind of torrential crusade in the name of emotional well-being.

In short, the predictions that "psychological man" would become the dominant personality type looked increasingly prescient as the new century began to unfold. "Psychological man" appeared to thrive in societies characterized by the five A's: "affluenza," aging, addictions, advertising, and administration. The current stage of the quest for mental health and the ascendancy of "psychological man" were the culmination of numerous currents in history stretching back to the eighteenth century and intertwined with the growth of mass politics, the rise of the modern bureaucratic nation-state, the spread of consumerism, and more recent trends toward globalization. The quest for mental wellness accelerated over the course of the twentieth century thanks to historically unprecedented levels of disposable income and leisure time, which – along with the rise of the mass media and advertising – have made populations more inclined to consume goods and services than ever before. The history of the quest for mental health suggests that these circumstances are key conditions for therapism and populist demands for mental health services. Therapism's doctrines of emotional openness, powerlessness, non-judgmentalism, and dependence on expert advice may conflict with character traits that earlier generations honored, but the wide-ranging acceptance of therapism as the world entered the twenty-first century testifies to its revolutionary capacity to overturn long-standing traditions of self-reliance in favor of managerial, bureaucratic controls.

Incontestably, elites in government, medicine, law, industry, education, and the media have served their own interests by playing key leadership roles in the quest for mental health. Opinion makers in the mental health field have often encouraged populations to believe they were sicker and more dependent on professional help than they really were. From time to time experts and lawmakers have disregarded informed personal choice. Psychiatrists have advocated therapies that have not always been in the best interests of people with mental disabilities but that have rationalized their professional claims to monopolistic control over mental health services. Sometimes bureaucracies such as the Food and Drug Administration have fought power struggles that ultimately have not improved public safety. Powerful drug companies have spent millions of dollars on the mass advertising of psychiatric drugs in the late twentieth century in order to stimulate the consumption of pharmaceutical medicines. Corporations share some of the blame for "condition branding," that is, teaching the masses that their emotions are diseases requiring medication. When in 2002 Miami Dolphins football player Ricky Williams appeared on *The Oprah Winfrey Show* to tell her audience that he suffered from painful shyness, few knew that the pharmaceutical corporation GlaxoSmithKline was paying him to admit to his anxiety in front of the cameras.

However, the "therapeutic outlook" is not the result of a conspiracy. Historically consumers of mental health products and services have been far from passive. The history of democracy, beginning with Rousseau and his celebration of peoples' inalienable rights to health and happiness, has stimulated mass demands that governments along with industry and the professions provide the health and welfare that populations deserved. This relationship between governments and the governed has been defined as much by duties imposed on peoples as benefits bestowed on them. Yet despite some eloquent voices raised in protest, the search for psychological health has typically been a bottom-up as much as a top-down process. As author Frederick Crews has noted, the drug industry did not create Oprah's show. The millions who over the years daily watched her program and followed her own life struggles with emotional and physical challenges were united in their expectation that Oprah and her guests would help them "achieve a happier you." Drug companies and the professions may have "turbocharged" emotional needs, but the popular hunger for self-improvement extends far and wide and back through time. Americans in particular have rarely needed prodding to resort to science, medicine, and technology to make them feel happier and less nervous. This state of affairs would have been impossible unless millions shared a common faith in the gospel of mental health.[37]

In the early twenty-first century, as governments and industry target almost all age groups for mass psychiatric drug use, we are reminded of Tocqueville's warning back in the 1830s that "servitude" and "wretchedness" rather than "freedom" are the typical destiny of societies that pursue democratic goals, and no goal has a more democratic lineage than mental health. The quest to make people less anxious, depressed, obsessive, and delusional had not made them less sorrowful, yet as Frank Furedi and others have pointed out, these outcomes have not prevented the therapeutic ethos from becoming a part of everyday common sense. Opinion makers inside and outside of government advocate "therapeutic governance," the notion that the state should intervene in the management of the most subjective aspects of individual personality, such as feelings and personal values. Some educators have called this a training process in becoming "emotionally literate." In 2000 a U.S. professor of public administration lauded therapeutic governance as a Rousseauian method for "re-uniting the self that modernism has sought to split apart."[38] Once states were geared primarily toward economic production, but in the twenty-first century experts hailed the reorientation of governance in favor of meeting the emotional needs of vulnerable citizens who struggle to cope with the demands of life. Officialdom in corporations, government, law, and education praises this shift in policy as not only a benign but a positively enlightened and overdue reform for a society that above all else views personal emotions as the key cause of all social problems, including poverty and crime. The history of the twenty-first century will determine whether or not state management of mental health leads to emotional conformism or to liberation from the "rooted sorrows" that have tormented minds like Samuel Johnson's through the ages.

Notes

Introduction

1. "Mental Illness Is Europe's Unseen Killer, Says European Commissioner for Health and Consumer Protection," http://www.medicalnewstoday.com/articles/18827.php.
2. One historian has called this coalition the "medical–industrial complex." Herzberg, *Happy Pills in America*, p. 16.
3. Sommers and Patel, *One Nation Under Therapy*, p. 8. By the early twenty-first century, an enormous "caring industry" had arisen in the United States, involving some 77,000 clinical psychologists, 192,000 clinical social workers, 105,000 mental health counselors, 50,000 marriage and family therapists, 17,000 nurse psychotherapists, and 30,000 life coaches. In addition, there were 400,000 nonclinical social workers and 220,000 substance abuse counselors. See Ronald W. Dworkin, "The Rise of the Caring Industry," *Policy Review*, no. 161, http://www.hoover.org/publications/policy-review/article/5339?sms_ss=mailto.
4. Steve Salerno, *SHAM: How the Self-Help Movement Made America Helpless* (New York: Crown, 2005, p. 39).
5. Oliver James, *The Selfish Capitalist: The Origins of Affluenza* (London: Vermillion, 2007).
6. Kramer, *Listening to Prozac*, p. 15.
7. Historian and psychiatrist David Healy borrows the term "pharmageddon" from health care policy analyst Charles Medawar to describe what he calls the "psychopharmaceuticalization of everyday life," the widespread medication of unhappiness throughout Western society. Medawar defines pharmageddon as "a gold standard paradox: individually we benefit from some wonderful medicines while, collectively, we are losing sight and sense of our health." Quoted in David Healy, *Mania: A Short History of Bipolar Disorder* (Baltimore: Johns Hopkins University Press, 2009), p. 249.
8. Furedi, *Therapy Culture*.

9. Barzun, *From Dawn to Decadence*, p. 773. See also Paul Edward Gottfried, *After Liberalism: Mass Democracy in the Managerial State* (Princeton, NJ: Princeton University Press, 1999).

10. Alexis de Tocqueville, *Democracy in America*, ed. Richard D. Haffner (New York: Mentor, 1956), p. 317.

Chapter 1. A New Egalitarianism

1. David Gordon, "Soft Despotism, Democracy's Drift: Montesquieu, Rousseau, Tocqueville, and the Modern Prospect," http://mises.org/misesreview_detail.aspx?control=358.

2. Frank E. Manuel, *The Age of Reason* (Ithaca, NY: Cornell University Press, 1951), p. 68.

3. Porter, *Mind-Forg'd Manacles*, 164; Neil McKendrick, J. H. Plumb, and John Brewer, *The Birth of a Consumer Society: The Commercialization of Eighteenth-Century England* (Bloomington: Indiana University Press, 1982).

4. Porter, *Mind-Forg'd Manacles*, pp. 10, 99.

5. Roy Porter, " 'The Hunger of Imagination': Approaching Samuel Johnson's Melancholy," in Bynum, Porter, and Shepherd (eds.), *Anatomy of Madness*, vol. 1, pp. 78, 81.

6. Tocqueville, *Democracy in America*, p. 40.

7. Micale, *Approaching Hysteria*, pp. 19–22.

8. William F. Bynum, "The Nervous Patient in Eighteenth- and Nineteenth-Century Britain: The Psychiatric Origins of British Neurology," in Bynum, Porter, and Shepherd (eds.), *The Anatomy of Madness*, vol. 1, p. 93; emphasis in the original.

9. Edward Shorter, *Bedside Manners: The Troubled History of Doctors and Patients* (New York: Viking, 1986), pp. 211–40.

10. Harold Nicolson, *The Age of Reason* (London: Panther, 1968), p. 535.

11. Ibid., p. 538.

12. Simon Schama, *Citizens: A Chronicle of the French Revolution* (New York: Vintage Books, 1989), p. 161.

13. Goldstein, *Console and Classify*, 101.

14. Darnton, *Mesmerism and the End of the Enlightenment in France*, 40.

15. Ibid., 62.

16. Ibid., 97.

17. William F. Bynum, *Science and the Practice of Medicine in the Nineteenth Century* (Cambridge: Cambridge University Press, 1994), pp. 56–59; see also Johann Peter Frank, "The Civil Administrator – Most Successful Physician," trans. Jean Captain Sabine, *Bulletin of the History of Medicine*, 16, 1944: 289–318, p. 297.

18. Goldstein, *Console and Classify*, 276–77.

19. Ignatieff, *A Just Measure of Pain*, pp. 148–49.

20. Ibid., p. 151.

21. Scull, *Social Order / Mental Disorder*, p. 222.

22. Ibid., p. 90.

23. Ibid.
24. Porter, *Mind-Forg'd Manacles*, pp. 214, 277.
25. William F. Bynum, "Rationales for Therapy in British Psychiatry, 1780–1835," in Scull (ed.), *Madhouses, Mad-Doctors, and Madmen*, p. 43.
26. Scull, *Social Order / Mental Disorder*, p. 112.
27. Gollaher, *Voice for the Mad*, p. 3.
28. Grob, *The Mad Among Us*, p. 46.
29. Gollaher, *Voice for the Mad*, p. 129.
30. Ibid., 209.
31. Glenn, *The Myth of the Common School*, p. 158.
32. Ibid., p. 149.
33. Ibid., pp. 89–90.
34. Goldstein, *Console and Classify*, p. 100.
35. Gollaher, *The Myth of the Common School*, p. 145.
36. Rothman, *The Discovery of the Asylum*, p. 129.
37. Gollaher, *Voice for the Mad*, p. 344.
38. Ibid., pp. 178–79.
39. See Weisz, *Divide and Conquer*; see also Reiser, *Medicine and the Reign of Technology*, p. 144.
40. Ackerknecht, *Medicine at the Paris Hospital*, p. 32.
41. Ibid., p. xi.
42. Weisz, *Divide and Conquer*, p. 113.
43. Goldstein, *Console and Classify*, pp. 82–83, 87.
44. Goldstein, *Console and Classify*, pp. 97, 99, 105; see also Colin Jones, "The 'New Treatment' of the Insane in Paris," *History Today*, 30, 1980: 5–10.
45. Joseph Ellis, *After the Revolution: Profiles of Early American Culture* (New York: W. W. Norton), 2002, pp. 61–62.
46. Angus McLaren, "Phrenology: Medium and Message," *Journal of Modern History*, 46, 1974: 86–97, p. 90.
47. Goldstein, *Console and Classify*, p. 255.
48. Angus McLaren, "A Prehistory of the Social Sciences: Phrenology in France, *Comparative Studies in Society and History*, 23, 1981: 3–22, p. 7.
49. Cooter, *The Cultural Meaning of Popular Science*, pp. 179–80.
50. Ibid., p. 78.
51. Ibid., p. 21.
52. Ibid., p. 164.

Chapter 2. Bricks and Mortar Humanity

1. Peter McCandless, "'Build! Build!' The Controversy over the Care of the Chronically Insane in England, 1855–70," *BHM*, 53, 1979: 553–74, p. 557.
2. Pick, *Faces of Degeneration*, pp. 119–20; see also Eugen Weber, *Peasants into Frenchmen: The Modernization of Rural France, 1870–1914* (Stanford, CA: Stanford University Press, 1976).
3. Glenn, *The Myth of the Common School*, pp. 36–37.
4. Carlton J. H. Hayes, *A Generation of Materialism, 1871–1900* (New York: Harper and Brothers, 1941), p. 172.

5. Glenn, *The Myth of the Common School*, p. 243.
6. Goldstein, *Console and Classify*, p. 319.
7. Rothman, *The Discovery of the Asylum*, pp. 117–21.
8. Goldstein, *Console and Classify*, p. 288.
9. Ibid., p. 281.
10. Ibid., p. 319.
11. Elizabeth Malcolm, "'Ireland's Crowded Madhouses': The Institutional Confinement of the Insane in Nineteenth- and Twentieth-Century Ireland," in Porter and Wright (eds.), *The Confinement of the Insane*, pp. 315–33.
12. Rosenberg, *The Care of Strangers*, p. 26.
13. Goldstein, *Console and Classify*, p. 345.
14. Jacalyn Duffin, *History of Medicine: A Scandalously Short Introduction* (Toronto: University of Toronto Press, 1999), p. 90.
15. Engstrom, *Clinical Psychiatry in Imperial Germany*, p. 1; emphasis in the original.
16. Dowbiggin, *Inheriting Madness*, pp. 25–26, 57.
17. Julie V. Brown, "A Sociohistorical Perspective on Deinstitutionalization: The Case of Late Imperial Russia," in Andrew Scull and Stephen Spitzer (eds.), *Research in Law, Deviance, and Social Control*, 7, 1985: 167–88, p. 170.
18. McCandless, "'Build! Build!'" p. 553.
19. Shortt, *Victorian Lunacy*, p. 26.
20. William L. Langer, "Europe's Initial Population Explosion," *American Historical Review*, 69, 1963: 1–17, p. 7.
21. Steven Hause and William Maltby, *Western Civilization: A History of European Society* (Belmont, CA: Wadsworth, 1999), pp. 650–51.
22. Shorter, *A History of Psychiatry*, p. 59.
23. Nye, *Crime, Madness, and Politics in Modern France*, p. 135.
24. Prestwich, *Drink and the Politics of Social Reform*, p. 37.
25. Ibid., p. 130.
26. Shorter, *A History of Psychiatry*, p. 60. See David Yellowlees, *Insanity and Intemperance* (Swansea: Pearse and Brown, 1874), p. 1.
27. Prestwich, *Drink and the Politics of Social Reform*, p. 37.
28. Ian Dowbiggin, "Delusional Disorder? The History of Paranoia as a Disease Concept in the Modern Era," *History of Psychiatry*, 11, 2000: 37–69.
29. Alain Corbin, *Women for Hire: Prostitution and Sexuality in France After 1850*, trans. Alan Sheridan (Cambridge, MA: Harvard University Press, 1990), pp. 387–88.
30. Shorter, *A History of Psychiatry*, pp. 57–58.
31. Dowbiggin, *Keeping America Sane*, pp. 28, 41.
32. Engstrom, *Clinical Psychiatry in Imperial Germany*, p. 30.
33. Shepherd, *Island Doctor*, p. 106.
34. David Wright, James Moran, and Sean Gouglas, "The Confinement of the Insane in Victorian Canada: The Hamilton and Toronto Asylums, 1861–1891," in Porter and Wright (eds.), *The Confinement of the Insane*, p. 124.
35. Janet Browne, "Darwin and the Face of Madness," in Bynum, Porter, and Shepherd (eds.), *The Anatomy of Madness*, vol. 1, pp. 151–65.
36. Pick, *Faces of Degeneration*, p. 131.

37. Ibid., pp. 24–27.
38. Brown, "A Sociohistorical Perspective on Deinstitutionalization," p. 171.
39. Engstrom, *Clinical Psychiatry in Imperial Germany*, p. 168.
40. Nye, *Crime, Madness, and Politics in Modern France*, pp. 244–45, 247.
41. Killen, *Berlin Electropolis*, p. 31.
42. Micale and Lerner (eds.), *Traumatic Pasts*, pp. 10–14.
43. Simon Wessely, "Neurasthenia and Fatigue Syndromes," in Berrios and Porter (eds.), *A History of Clinical Psychiatry*, p. 510.
44. F. G. Gosling and Joyce M. Ray, "The Right to Be Sick: American Physicians and Nervous Patients, 1885–1910," *Journal of Social History*, 20, 1986: 251–67.
45. Killen, *Berlin Electropolis*, pp. 66, 69.
46. Rosenberg, *No Other Gods*, p. 98.
47. Shorter, *From the Mind into the Body*, p. 205.
48. Edward Shorter, *From Paralysis to Fatigue: A History of Psychosomatic Illness in the Modern Era* (New York: Free Press), 1993, p. xi.
49. Susan E. Abbey and Paul E. Garfinkel, "Neurasthenia and Chronic Fatigue Syndrome: The Role of Culture in the Making of a Diagnosis," *AJP*, 148, 1991: 1638–46, pp. 1643, 1644.
50. Grob, *Mental Illness and American Society*, p. 53.
51. Bonnie Ellen Blustein, " 'A Hollow Square of Psychological Science': American Neurologists and Psychiatrists in Conflict," in Scull (ed.), *Madhouses, Mad-Doctors, and Madmen*, pp. 250–51.
52. Engstrom, *Clinical Psychiatry in Imperial Germany*, p. 106.
53. Grob, *The Mad Among Us*, pp. 133–34.
54. Ian Dowbiggin, " 'Midnight Clerks and Daily Drudges': Hospital Psychiatry in New York State, 1890–1905," *Journal of the History of Medicine and Allied Sciences*, 47, 1992: 130–52.
55. Hayes, *A Generation of Materialism*, pp. 176–80.
56. Torrey and Miller, *The Invisible Plague*, p. 257.
57. Peter McCandless, "Liberty and Lunacy: The Victorians and Wrongful Confinement," in Scull (ed.), *Madhouses, Mad-Doctors, and Madmen*, p. 339.
58. Norman Dain, "Psychiatry and Anti-Psychiatry in the United States," in Micale and Porter (eds.), *Discovering the History of Psychiatry*, p. 424.
59. Michael Ignatieff, "Total Institutions and Working Classes: A Review Essay," *History Workshop*, 15, 1983: 167–73, p. 172.

Chapter 3. Mental Hygiene

1. Shepherd, *Island Doctor*, pp. 88–91.
2. Suzuki, *Madness at Home*; Houston, *Madness and Society in Eighteenth-Century Scotland*.
3. James E. Moran, "The Signal and the Noise: The Historical Epidemiology of Insanity in Ante-Bellum New Jersey," *HP*, 14, 2003: 281–301.
4. Patricia Prestwich, "Family Strategies and Medical Power: 'Voluntary' Committal in a Parisian Asylum, 1876–1914," in Porter and Wright (eds.), *The Confinement of the Insane*, pp. 79–99.

5. Peter Bartlett and David Wright, "Community Care and Its Antecedents," in Bartlett and Wright (eds.), *Outside the Walls of the Asylum*, p. 6.

6. Thierry Nootens, " 'For Years We Have Never Had a Happy Home': Madness and Families in Nineteenth-Century Montreal," in Moran and Wright (eds.), *Mental Health and Canadian Society*, p. 58.

7. Akihito Suzuki, "The State, Family, and the Insane in Japan, 1900–1945," in Porter and Wright (eds.), *The Confinement of the Insane*, p. 194.

8. Prestwich, "Family Strategies and Medical Power," p. 91.

9. McCandless, " 'Build! Build!' " p. 561.

10. William Parry-Jones, "The Model of the Geel Lunatic Colony and Its Influence on the Nineteenth-Century Asylum System in Britain," in Scull (ed.), *Madhouses, Mad-Doctors, and Madmen*, pp. 201–17.

11. Waltraud Ernst, "Madness and Colonial Spaces: British India, c. 1800–1947," in Topp, Moran, and Andrews (eds.), *Madness, Architecture and the Built Environment*, p. 223.

12. Thomas Mueller, "Community Spaces and Psychiatric Family Care," in Topp, Moran, and Andrews (eds.), *Madness, Architecture and the Built Environment*, p. 180.

13. Brown, "A Sociohistorical Perspective on Deinistitutionalization."

14. Bartlett and Wright, "Community Care and Its Antecedents," p. 18.

15. Hale, *Freud and the Americans*, p. 226.

16. Gurstein, *The Repeal of Reticence*.

17. Kroker, *The Sleep of Others*, p. 111.

18. Ellenberger, *The Discovery of the Unconscious*.

19. Brower, *Unruly Spirits*, pp. 139, 140.

20. Ibid., pp. 16–17.

21. Drew Gilpin Faust, *This Republic of Suffering: Death and the American Civil War* (New York: Knopf, 2008), p. xi.

22. Pat Jalland, *Death in the Victorian Family* (Oxford: Oxford University Press, 1996), p. 375.

23. Hayes, *A Generation of Materialism*, pp. 331–32.

24. Anne Harrington, "Hysteria, Hypnosis, and the Lure of the Invisible: The Rise of Neo-Mesmerism in *Fin-de-siècle* French Psychiatry," in Bynum, Porter, and Shepherd (eds.), *The Anatomy of Madness*, vol. 3, p. 226.

25. Parker, *Mind Cure in New England*, p. 6.

26. Ellenberger, *The Discovery of the Unconscious*, p. 168.

27. Parker, *Mind Cure in New England*, p. 14.

28. Hale, *Freud and the Americans*, pp. 229, 232.

29. Parker, *Mind Cure in New England*, pp. 30, 57.

30. Raymond J. Cunningham, "The Emmanuel Movement: A Variety of American Religious Experience," *American Quarterly*, 14, 1964: 48–63.

31. Hale, *Freud and the Americans*, pp. 232, 233.

32. Barbara Sicherman, "The Paradox of Prudence: Mental Health in the Gilded Age," in Scull (ed.), *Madhouses, Mad-Doctors, and Madmen*, p. 232.

33. Sulloway, *Freud: Biologist of the Mind*, p. 206.

34. Daniel Pick, "The Id Comes to Bloomsbury," *http://www.guardian.co.uk/ books/2003/aug/16/highereducation.news*.

35. Shorter, *A History of Psychiatry*, pp. 171, 174.
36. Sulloway, *Freud: Biologist of the Mind*; Ellenberger, *Discovery of the Unconscious*.
37. John C. Burnham, "From Avant-Garde to Specialism: Psychoanalysis in America," *JHBS*, 15, 1979: 128–34, p. 130.
38. Nathan G. Hale, "From Bergasse XIX to Central Park West: The Americanization of Psychoanalysis, 1919–1940," *JHBS*, 14, 1978: 299–315, p. 307.
39. Ralph Blumenthal, "Freud Archives Research Chief Removed in Dispute over Yale Talk," *New York Times*, November 9, 1981, http://www.nytimes.com/1981/11/09/nyregion/freud-archives-research-chief-removed-in-dispute-over-yale-talk.html.
40. Burnham, "From Avant-Garde to Specialism," p. 132.
41. Nye, *Crime, Madness, and Politics in Modern France*, p. 232.
42. Ibid., pp. 326–27.
43. Robert Stephenson Smyth Baden-Powell (1857–1941), http://library.thinkquest.org/26852/people/BP.htm.
44. Lunbeck, *The Psychiatric Persuasion*, p. 112.
45. Dain, *Clifford W. Beers: Advocate for the Insane*; Grob, *Mental Illness and American Society*, p. 148.
46. Grob, *Mental Illness and American Society*, p. 154.
47. Young, *The Harmony of Illusions*, p. 41.
48. Killen, *Berlin Electropolis*, p. 160.
49. Ibid., pp. 130, 154, 160.
50. Ibid., 143.
51. Copp and McAndrew, *Battle Exhaustion*, pp. 48–49.
52. Showalter, *The Female Malady*, p. 73.
53. Carson, *The Measure of Merit*, pp. 179, 192.
54. Herman, *The Romance of American Psychology*, p. 55.
55. Pressman, *Last Resort*, pp. 23–26.
56. Ibid., p.18.
57. Ben Shephard, "'Pitiless Psychology': The Role of Prevention in British Military Psychiatry in the Second World War," *HP*, 10, 1999: 491–524; Simon Wessley, "Twentieth-Century Theories on Combat Motivation and Breakdown," *Journal of Contemporary History*, 41, 2006: 269–86.
58. Herman, *The Romance of American Psychology*, p. 95; emphasis in the original.
59. Ibid., pp. 2, 124, 176.
60. Dowbiggin, *Keeping America Sane*, pp. v–vi.
61. Christine Rosen, *Preaching Eugenics: Religious Leaders and the American Eugenics Movement* (Oxford: Oxford University Press), 2004, p. 5.
62. Connelly, *Fatal Misconception*, p. 40.
63. John Cranmer, *Asylum History: Buckinghamshire County Pauper Lunatic Asylum – St. John's* (London: Gaskell, 1990), p. 77.
64. Burleigh, *Death and Deliverance*, pp. 34, 45.
65. Rosen, *Preaching Eugenics*.
66. Ian Dowbiggin, "'A Rational Coalition': Euthanasia, Eugenics, and Birth Control in America, 1940–1970," *Journal of Policy History*, 14, 2002: 223–60.

67. Dowbiggin, *Keeping America Sane*, pp. 171–78, 223.
68. David Wright, *Down's Syndrome: The Biography* (Oxford: Oxford University Press, 2011).
69. Larson, *Sex, Race, and Science*, p. 25.
70. Steven Noll, *Feeble-Minded in Our Midst: Institutions for the Mentally Retarded in the South, 1900–1940* (Chapel Hill: University of North Carolina Press, 1995), pp. 1–2; Dowbiggin, *The Sterilization Movement*, p. 29.
71. Noll, *Feeble-Minded in Our Midst*, p. 4.
72. Shortt, *Victorian Lunacy*, pp. 143–59; Andrew Scull and Diane Favreau, "'A Chance to Cut Is a Chance to Cure': Sexual Surgery for Psychosis in Three Nineteenth-Century Societies," *Research in Law, Deviance, and Social Control*, 8, 1986: 3–39.
73. Shorter, *From Paralysis to Fatigue*, p. 87.
74. Bernhard Kuechenhoff, "The Psychiatrist Auguste Forel and His Attitude to Eugenics," *HP*, 19, 2008: 215–23, p. 218.
75. Dowbiggin, *The Sterilization Movement*, p. 56.
76. Braslow, *Mental Ills and Bodily Cures*, p. 61.
77. Burleigh, *Death and Deliverance*; Proctor, *Racial Hygiene*.
78. Dowbiggin, *The Sterilization Movement*, p. 28.
79. Ibid., p. 30.
80. Karl Pearson, "Darwinism, Medical Progress and Eugenics: The Cavendish Lecture, 1912," pp. 10–11, http://www.archive.org/details/darwinism-medical1912pear.
81. Martin Pernick, "Eugenics and Public Health in American History," *American Journal of Public Health*, 87, 1997: 1767–72.
82. Emil Kraepelin, "On the Question of Degeneration (1908)," *HP*, 18, 2007: 389–98.
83. Burleigh, *Death and Deliverance*, pp. 11, 41.
84. Proctor, *Racial Hygiene*, pp. 46, 64.
85. Dowbiggin, *The Sterilization Movement*, p. 29.
86. Frankin B. Kirkbride, "The Right to be Well-Born" (1912), *American Philosophical Society*, http://www.eugenicsarchive.org/html/eugenics/index2.html?tag=350.
87. Kuechenhoff, "The Psychiatrist Auguste Forel," p. 221.
88. Connelly, *Fatal Misconception*, pp. 103–104.
89. Ibid., 321–26.
90. Frank Dikötter, *Imperfect Conceptions: Medical Knowledge, Birth Defects, and Eugenics in China* (New York: Columbia University Press, 1998).
91. Pressman, *Last Resort*, pp. 48, 66.
92. David Crossley, "The Introduction of Leucotomy: A British Case History," *HP*, 4, 1993: 553–64.
93. Joar Tranoy and Wenche Blomberg, "Lobotomy in Norwegian Psychiatry," *HP*, 16, 2005: 107–10.
94. Rakefet Zalashik, "Last Resort? Lobotomy Operations in Israel, 1946–1960," *HP*, 17, 2006: 91–106.
95. Herman, *The Romance of American Psychology*, 243.

96. John C. Burnham, "American Medicine's Golden Age: What Happened to It?" *Science*, 215, 1982: 1474–79.

97. Pressman, *Last Resort*, pp. 127, 216.

98. Steven R. Hirsch and Michael Shepherd (eds.), *Themes and Variations in European Psychiatry* (Charlottesville: University of Virginia Press, 1974), p. 329.

99. Andrea Tone, "Listening to the Past: History, Psychiatry, and Anxiety," *Canadian Journal of Psychiatry*, 50, 2005: 373–80, p. 374.

100. Pressman, *Last Resort*, pp. 18–21.

101. As a medical author commented in 2004: "No matter what you tell a patient, if you say I'm going to give you ECT, once you explain it the patient will always say, 'Oh, shock therapy.' That will never change. Doesn't matter what you call it." Shorter and Healy, *Shock Therapy*, p. 6.

102. Ibid.

103. Andrew T. Scull, *Madhouse: A Tragic Tale of Megalomania and Modern Medicine* (New Haven, CT: Yale University Press), 2007, p. 293.

104. Valenstein, *Great and Desperate Cures*, p. 41.

105. Pressman, *Last Resort*, p. 156.

106. Ibid., p. 185.

107. Valentstein, *Great and Desperate Cures*, pp. 179–80.

108. Pressman, *Last Resort*, pp. 106, 122, 131, 143, 146.

109. Jack El-Hai, *The Lobotomist: A Maverick Medical Genius and His Tragic Quest to Rid the World of Mental Illness* (New York: Wiley, 2005), p. 1.

110. Pressman, *Last Resort*, p. 307.

111. Braslow, *Mental Ills and Bodily Cures*, p. 153.

112. Pressman, *Last Resort*, pp. 289–90.

Chapter 4. A Bottomless Pit

1. Lerner, *Hysterical Men*; Greg Eghigian, "The German Welfare State as a Discourse of Trauma," in Lerner and Micale (eds.), *Traumatic Pasts*, pp. 92–112; Wessley, "Twentieth-Century Theories on Combat Motivation and Breakdown," pp. 269–86.

2. Ben Shephard, "'Pitiless Psychology': The Role of Prevention in British Military Psychology in the Second World War," *HP*, 10, 1999: 509–10.

3. Herman, *The Romance of American Psychology*, pp. 89, 124, 125, 135.

4. Lawrence Friedman, *Menninger: The Family and the Clinic* (New York: Knopf, 1990).

5. Pressman, *Last Resort*, p. 380.

6. Grob, *The Mad Among Us*, pp. 198–99.

7. Pressman, *Last Resort*, p. 379.

8. Allan Irving, *Brock Chisholm: Doctor to the World* (Markham: Fitzhenry and Whiteside, 1998).

9. Farley, *Brock Chisholm, the World Health Organization, and the Cold War*, pp. 43–44.

10. Edward Shorter, *A History of Psychiatry: From the Era of the Asylum to the Age of Prozac* (New York: Wiley, 1998), p. 177.

11. Sommers and Satel, *One Nation Under Therapy*, p. 60. See also Kenneth E. Appel, "Nationalism, Sovereignty, and Sanity," *Proceedings of the American–Soviet Medical Society*, 1945, Abraham Stone Papers, Francis A. Countway Library of Medicine, Harvard University, Box 7, Folder 11. For the attempt to reduce conservatism as a political movement to psychiatric categories, see George H. Nash, *The Conservative Intellectual Movement in America Since 1945* (New York, Basic Books, 1976), pp. 137–139.

12. Grob, *The Mad Among Us*, 199.

13. William J. Rorabaugh, Donald T. Critchlow, and Paula Baker, *America's Promise: A Concise History of the United States*, vol. 2 (Lanham, MD: Rowman and Littlefield, 2004), 511, 512.

14. John Kenneth Galbraith, *The Affluent Society* (Boston: Houghton Mifflin), 1958.

15. Herman, *The Romance of American Psychology*, pp. 243–44, 245.

16. John C. Burnham, "The Struggle between Physicians and Paramedical Personnel in American Psychiatry," *JHMAS*, 29, 1974: 93–106, pp. 98–99.

17. Ronald W. Dworkin, "The Rise of the Caring Industry," *Hoover Institution Policy Review*, no. 161, June 1, 2010, http://www.hoover.org/publications/policy-review/article/5339?sms_ss=mailto.

18. Kristin Celello, *Making Marriage Work: A History of Marriage and Divorce in the Twentieth-Century United States* (Chapel Hill: University of North Carolina Press, 2009), pp. 58–59, 84.

19. Thomas Maier, *Masters of Sex: The Life and Times of William Masters and Virginia Johnson, the Couple Who Taught America How to Love* (New York: Basic Books, 2009); Celello, *Making Marriage Work*, p. 39.

20. Valenstein, *Great and Desperate Cures*, p. 19.

21. Grob, *The Mad Among Us*, p. 238.

22. Petigny, *The Permissive Society*, pp. 15–52.

23. Grob, *The Mad Among Us*, 239–40. See also Dworkin, "The Rise of the Caring Industry," http://historypsychiatry.wordpress.com/2010/07/31/dworkin-the-rise-of-the-caring-industry/.

24. Herman, *The Romance of American Psychology*, p. 252.

25. Jean Thuillier, "Ten Years That Shook Psychiatry," in David Healy (ed.), *The Psychopharmacologists* (London: Arnold, 2000), vol. 3, pp. 543–59.

26. Dyck, *Psychedelic Medicine*, p. 14.

27. Healy, *The Creation of Psychopharmacology*, p. 100.

28. Shorter, *A History of Psychiatry*, pp. 250–53.

29. Lane, *Shyness*, p. 3.

30. Healy, *The Creation of Psychopharmacology*, p. 354.

31. Shorter and Healy, *Shock Therapy*, pp. 164, 166, 168, 169.

32. Shorter, *A Historical Dictionary of Psychiatry*, p. 55.

33. Healy, *The Creation of Psychopharmacology*, p. 99; Tone, *The Age of Anxiety*, pp. 23, 27; emphasis in the original.

34. Tone, *The Age of Anxiety*, p. 27; Susan L. Speaker, "From 'Happiness Pills' to 'National Nightmare': Changing Cultural Assessment of Minor

Tranquilizers in America, 1955–1980," *JHMAS*, 52, 1997: 338–76, pp. 339, 341.

35. Tone, *The Age of Anxiety*, pp. 224–25.
36. Speaker, "From 'Happiness Pills' to 'National Nightmare,' " p. 349.
37. Healy, *The Anti-Depressant Era*, pp. 25–28; Tone, *The Age of Anxiety*, pp. 147–50.
38. Suzanne White Junod, "Women over 35 Who Smoke: A Case Study in Risk Management and Risk Communications, 1960–1989," in Andrea Tone and Elizabeth Siegel Watkins (eds.), *Medicating Modern America: Prescription Drugs in History* (New York: New York University Press, 2007), p. 98; Edward Shorter, "The Liberal State and the Rogue Agency: FDA's Regulation of Drugs for Mood Disorders, 1950s–1970s," *International Journal of Law and Psychiatry*, 31, 2008: 126–35.
39. Edward Shorter, *Before Prozac: The Troubled History of Mood Disorders in Psychiatry* (Oxford: Oxford University Press, 2009), p. 94.
40. John Crilly, "The History of Clozapine and Its Emergence in the U.S. Market: A Review and Analysis," *HP*, 18, 2007: 39–60.
41. Dyck, *Psychedelic Medicine*, p. 48.
42. Peter Sedgwick, *Psycho Politics* (London: Pluto Press, 1982), p. 67.
43. Dyck, *Psychedelic Medicine*, pp. 9, 11.
44. Healy, *The Psychopharmacologists*, vol. 3, p. 602.
45. Erving Goffman, *Asylums: Essays on the Social Situation of Mental Patients and Other Patients* (New York: Doubleday Anchor, 1961).
46. Dain, "Psychiatry and Anti-Psychiatry in the United States," p. 429.
47. David J. Rissmiller and Joshua Rissmiller, "Evolution of the Anti-Psychiatry Movement into Mental Health Consumerism," *Psychiatric Services*, 57, 2006: 863–66.
48. "In Tense Moment Cruise Calls Lauer 'Glib,' " http://www.msnbc.msn.com/id/8344309/.
49. Thomas Szasz, "Psychiatry's Threat to Civil Liberties," *National Review*, March 12, 1963: 191–93. For Rothbard's role in the U.S. conservative movement, see George H. Nash, *The Conservative Intellectual Movement in America Since 1945* (New York: Basic Books, 1976), pp. 313–18.
50. Thomas Szasz, *Faith in Freedom: Libertarian Principles and Psychiatric Practice* (New Brunswick, NJ: Transaction, 2004), pp. 171–76.
51. Rieff, *Triumph of the Therapeutic*, pp. 236, 242.
52. Lasch, *The Culture of Narcissism*, pp. 13–14.
53. Matt Cvetic, "The Thought Control Brigade," *American Mercury*, October 1958: 137–38.
54. "What's the Hullabaloo about Mental Health?" *Facts Forum News*, July 1956: 40–46, 64, p. 46.
55. "The Far Right's Fight Against Mental Health," *Look Magazine*, January 26, 1965: 28–32.
56. For example, see Satel and Sommers, *One Nation Under Therapy*. See also Paul R. McHugh, "How Psychiatry Lost Its Way," *Commentary*, December, 1999, http://www.commentarymagazine.com/viewarticle.cfm/how-psychiatry-lost-its-way-9101.

57. See Nikolai Krementsov, *Stalinist Science* (Princeton, NJ: Princeton University Press, 1996). See also "Medicine: Soviet Psychiatry," *Time*, June 16, 1961, http://www.time.com/time/magazine/article/0,9171,895375,00.html.

58. Ian Spencer, "Lessons from History: The Politics of Psychiatry in the USSR," *Journal of Psychiatric and Mental Health Nursing*, 7, 2001: 355–61, p. 357.

59. Tone, *Age of Anxiety*, pp. 95–97, 115.

60. Speaker, "From 'Happiness Pills' to 'National Nightmare,' " pp. 350, 355.

61. David Courtwright, *Dark Paradise: A History of Opium Addiction in America* (Cambridge, MA: Harvard University Press, 2001), pp. 175–76.

62. Speaker, "From 'Happiness Pills' to 'National Nightmare,' " pp. 355, 373.

63. Tone, *The Age of Anxiety*, p.178; Herman, *The Romance of American Psychology*, p. 294.

64. Sherry Turkle, *Psychoanalytic Politics: Jacques Lacan and Freud's French Revolution* (Cambridge: MIT Press, 1981), pp. 179, 86.

65. Jean-Paul Sartre, "Preface to Frantz Fanon's *Wretched of the Earth*," http://www.marx.org/reference/archive/sartre/1961/preface.htm.

66. Healy, *The Creation of Psychopharmacology*, p. 175.

67. Shorter, *A Historical Dictionary of Psychiatry*, p. 131.

68. Dain, "Anti-Psychiatry in the United States," p. 437.

69. Shorter, *Bedside Manners*, pp. 211–40.

70. Tone, *The Age of Anxiety*, p. 162.

71. Healy, *The Creation of Psychopharmacology*, p. 330.

72. Melvin Sabshin, "Turning-Points in Twentieth-Century American Psychiatry," *AJP*, 147, 1990: 1267–74, p. 1271.

73. David J. Rissmiller and Joshua H. Rissmiller, "Evolution of the Anti-Psychiatry Movement into Mental Health Consumerism," *Psychiatric Services*, 57, 2006: 863–66.

74. Laura D. Hirshbein, "Science, Gender, and the Emergence of Depression in American Psychiatry, 1952–1980," *JHMAS*, 61, 2006: 187–216, p. 187.

75. DeGrandpre, *The Cult of Pharmacology*, pp. 51–52; Healy, *The Creation of Psychopharmacology*, pp. 56–57.

76. Christopher Lane, "Wrangling over Psychiatry's Bible," *Los Angeles Times*, November 16, 2008, http://www.latimes.com/news/opinion/commentary/la-oe-lane16–2008nov16,0,5678764.story.

77. Healy, *The Creation of Psychopharmacology*, pp. 69, 170.

78. Gerald Curzon, Evan Hughes, Peter D. Kramer, Reply by Frederick C. Crews, "The Truth About Prozac: An Exchange," *New York Review of Books*, 55, February 14, 2008, http://www.nybooks.com/articles/21040.

79. DeGrandpre, *The Cult of Pharmacology*, pp. 54, 57.

80. Tone, *The Age of Anxiety*, p. 226.

81. David Rose, "Britain Becomes a Prozac Nation," May 14, 2007, *Times Online*, http://www.timesonline.co.uk/tol/life_and_style/health/article1784993.ece.

82. "Bottomless pit" is former APA medical director Melvin Sabshin's phrase. Mitchell Wilson interview with Sabshin, July 17, 1989. See Mitchell Wilson, "DSM-III and the Transformation of American Psychiatry: A History," *AJP*, 150, 1993: 399–410, p. 403.

83. Ian Dowbiggin, "Delusional Diagnosis? The History of Paranoia as a Disease Concept in the Modern Era," *HP*, 11, 2000: 37–69, p. 66.
84. Healy, *The Anti-Depressant Era*, p. 252.
85. Ian Dowbiggin, "Back to the Future: Valentin Magnan, French Psychiatry, and the Classification of Mental Diseases, 1885–1925," *Social History of Medicine*, 9, 1996: 383–403.
86. Wilson, "DSM-III and the Transformation of American Psychiatry," p. 403.
87. Shorter, *A History of Psychiatry*, pp. 301–302. See Ronald Bayer and Robert L. Spitzer, "Neurosis, Psychodynamics, and DSM-III," *Archives of General Psychiatry*, 42, 1985: 187–95, p. 188.
88. Wilson M. Compton and Samuel B. Guze, "The Neo-Kraepelinian Revolution in Psychiatric Diagnosis," *European Archives of Psychiatry and Clinical Neuroscience*, 245, 1995: 196–201.
89. Wilson, "DSM-III and the Transformation of American Psychiatry," p. 406.
90. Healy, *The Creation of Psychopharmacology*, p. 328. See also Ethan Watters, "The Americanization of Mental Illness," http://www.nytimes.com/2010/01/10/magazine/10psyche-t.html?pagewanted=1.
91. Lane, *Shyness*, pp. 199–200.
92. John A. Mills, "Lessons From the Periphery," *HP*, 18, 2007: 179–201.
93. Dyck, *Psychedelic Medicine*, pp. 19–26.
94. E. Fuller Torrey, *Nowhere to Go: The Tragic Odyssey of the Homeless Mentally Ill* (New York: Harper & Row, 1988), p. 33.
95. Stefan Priebe and Trevor Turner, "Reinstitutionalization in Mental Health Care," *British Medical Journal*, 326, 2003: 175–76.
96. Grob, *The Mad Among Us*, pp. 252–62, 280; Daniel Patrick Moynihan, "Promise to the Mentally Ill Has Not Been Kept," *New York Times*, May 22, 1989.
97. Healy, *The Creation of Psychopharmacology*, p. 133.
98. Saul Feldman, "Reflections on the 40th Anniversary of the Community Mental Health Centers Act," *Administration and Policy in Mental Health*, 31, 2004: 369–80, p. 372.
99. Shorter, *Historical Dictionary of Psychiatry*, p. 59.
100. Simmons, *Unbalanced*, pp. 161–62.
101. Grob, *The Mad Among Us*, p. 290.

Chapter 5. Emotional Welfare

1. Carolyn Abraham, "A Very Designed Life," http://v1.theglobeandmail.com/servlet/story/RTGAM.20080620.wmhanxiety21/BNStory/mentalhealth/.
2. Patricia Pearson, *A Brief History of Anxiety: Yours and Mine* (Toronto: Random House, 2008), p. 129.
3. Shorter, *From the Mind into the Body*, pp. 205–207.
4. James Patterson, *America in the Twentieth Century: A History* (Fort Worth, TX: Harcourt Brace, 1989), pp. 359–61; Theodore Zeldin, *France: Anxiety and Hypocrisy* (Oxford: Oxford University Press, 1981), p. 61.

5. Marlise Simons, "Gluttons for Tranquilizers, the French Ask Why?" http://www.nytimes.com/1991/01/21/world/paris-journal-gluttons-for-tranquilizers-the-french-ask-why.html; Brian Knowlton, "France Weighs Its Appetite for Booze and Tranquilizers," http://www.nytimes.com/1994/03/17/news/17iht-etopics_7.html.

6. Katharine A. Phillips, *The Broken Mirror: Understanding and Treating Body Dysmorphic Disorder* (Oxford: Oxford University Press, 2005).

7. Selye, *The Stress of My Life*, pp. 79, 81.

8. Farrell, *Freud's Paranoid Quest*.

9. Daniel Pipes, *Conspiracism: How the Paranoid Style Flourishes and Where it Comes From* (New York: Free Press, 1997); Ian Dowbiggin, *Suspicious Minds: The Triumph of Paranoia in Everyday Life* (Toronto: Macfarlane Walter and Ross, 1999).

10. Farrell, *Freud's Paranoid Quest*, p. 44.

11. Frank Furedi, *The Politics of Fear: Beyond Right and Left* (London: Continuum, 2005).

12. David Healy, "The History of British Psychopharmacology," in Hugh Freeman and German Berrios (eds.), *One Hundred and Fifty Years of British Psychiatry*, Vol. 2: *The Aftermath* (London: Athlone, 1996), p. 74.

13. Speaker, "From 'Happiness Pills' to 'National Nightmare,'" p. 346.

14. S. Grice, "It's a Crying Shame," *National Post*, May 31, 2002.

15. Kirk and Kutchins, *The Selling of DSM*, pp. 234–35.

16. Wesseley, "Twentieth-Century Theories on Combat Motivation and Breakdown," pp. 274, 279.

17. Young, *The Harmony of Illusions*, pp.107–16, 151–52.

18. Ibid., p. 113.

19. Showalter, *Hystories*, p. 144.

20. Ibid., p. 142.

21. Salerno, *SHAM*, pp. 8, 34.

22. Showalter, *Hystories*, p. 145.

23. Philip Jenkins, *Decade of Nightmares: The End of the 1960s and the Making of Eighties America* (Oxford: Oxford University Press, 2006), p. 265.

24. Hacking, *Re-Writing the Soul*.

25. Showalter, *Hystories*, pp. 157, 177.

26. Jenkins, *Decade of Nightmares*, p. 265.

27. Showalter, *Hystories*, pp. 181–82.

28. Ibid., p. 146.

29. Rorabaugh, Critchlow, and Baker, *America's Promise*, vol. 2, pp. 648–49.

30. Laura Reichenbach and Hilary Brown, "Gender and Academic Medicine: Impacts on the Health Workforce," *British Medical Journal*, 329, 2004: 792–95. See also "More Women Pull Down Big Bucks," *Washington Post*, October 7, 2010, http://www.washingtonpost.com/wp-dyn/content/article/2010/10/06/AR2010100607246.html.

31. Shorter, *From the Mind into the Body*, pp. 58–59, 71.

32. Herzberg, *From Miltown to Prozac*, pp. 181–83.

33. Frank Furedi, "Why the Politics of Happiness Makes Me Mad," *Spiked*, May 23, 2006, http://www.frankfuredi.com/index.php/site/article/36/.

34. http://www.un.org/disabilities/default.asp?navid=12&pid=150.
35. http://www.who.int/hhr/HHRETH_activities.pdf.
36. Satel and Sommers, *One Nation Under Therapy*, p. 3.
37. Frederick Crews, "Talking Back to Prozac," *New York Review of Books*, 54, December 6, 2007, http://www.nybooks.com/articles/20851.
38. Frank Furedi, *Therapy Culture: Cultivating Vulnerability in an Uncertain Age* (London: Routledge, 2003), pp. 196, 198.

Bibliography

Journals

American Journal of Psychiatry (AJP)
Bulletin of the History of Medicine (BHM)
History of Psychiatry (HP)
Journal of the History of the Behavioral Sciences (JHBS)
Journal of the History of Medicine and Allied Sciences (JHMAS)
Medical History (MH)

Books

Ackerknecht, Erwin H. *Medicine at the Paris Hospital, 1794–1848*. Baltimore: Johns Hopkins University Press, 1967.

Alexander, Franz, and Selesnick, Sheldon T. *The History of Psychiatry: An Evaluation of Psychiatric Thought and Practice from Prehistoric Times to the Present*. New York: Mentor, 1966.

Andrews, Johnathan, and Scull, Andrew T. *Customers and Patrons of the Mad-Trade: The Management of Lunacy in Eighteenth Century London*. Berkeley: University of California Press, 2003.

Andrews, Johnathan, Briggs, Asa, Porter, Roy, Tucker, Penny, and Waddington, Keir. *History of Bethlem*. London: Routledge, 1999.

Bartlett, Peter, and Wright, David (eds.). *Outside the Walls of the Asylum: The History of Care in the Community, 1750–2000*. London: Athlone Press, 1999.

Baruk, Henri. *La psychiatrie française de Pinel à nos jours*. Paris: Presses universitaires de France, 1967.

Barzun, Jacques. *From Dawn to Decadence: Five Hundred Years of Western Cultural Life*. New York: HarperCollins, 2000.

Berrios, German E. *The History of Mental Symptoms: Descriptive Psychopathology Since the Nineteenth Century*. Cambridge: Cambridge University Press, 1996.

Berrios, German E., and Porter, Roy (eds.). *A History of Clinical Psychiatry: The Origin and History of Psychiatric Disorders*. New York: New York University Press, 1995.

Bond, Earl D. *Thomas W. Salmon: Psychiatrist*. New York: W. W. Norton, 1950.

Boschma, Geertje. *The Rise of Mental Health Nursing: A History of Psychiatric Care in Dutch Asylums, 1890–1920*. Amsterdam: Amsterdam University Press, 2003.

Braslow, Joel. *Mental Ills and Bodily Cures: Psychiatric Treatments in the First Half of the Twentieth Century*. Berkeley: University of California Press, 1997.

Broberg, Gunnar, and Roll-Hansen, Nils (eds.). *Eugenics and the Welfare State*. East Lansing: Michigan State University Press, 1996.

Brower, M. Brady. *Unruly Spirits: The Science of Psychic Phenomena in Modern France*. Urbana: University of Illinois Press, 2010.

Brown, Julie V. "A Sociohistorical Perspective on Deinstitutionalization: The Case of Late Imperial Russia." *Research in Law, Deviance, and Social Control*, vol. 7, 1985: 167–88.

Brown, Thomas J. *Dorothea Dix: New England Reformer*. Cambridge, MA: Harvard University Press, 1998.

Burleigh, Michael. *Death and Deliverance: "Euthanasia" in Germany, c. 1900–1945*. Cambridge: Cambridge University Press, 1994.

Burnham, John C. *Jelliffe: American Psychoanalyst and Physician and His Correspondence with Sigmund Freud and C.G. Jung*. Chicago: University of Chicago Press, 1983.

 Psychoanalysis and American Medicine, 1894–1918: Medicine, Science, and Culture. New York: International Universities Press, 1967.

Burston, Daniel. *The Crucible of Experience: R. D. Laing and the Crisis of Psychotherapy*. Cambridge, MA: Harvard University Press, 2000.

 Erik Erikson and the American Psyche: Ego, Ethics, and Evolution. New York: Jason Aronson, 2007.

Bynum, William, Porter, Roy, and Shepherd, Michael (eds.). *The Anatomy of Madness: Essays in the History of Psychiatry*. 3 vols. London: Tavistock Publications, 1985.

Carson, John. *The Measure of Merit: Talent, Intelligence and Inequality in the French and American Republics, 1750–1940*. Princeton, NJ: Princeton University Press, 2007.

Castel, Robert. *The Regulation of Madness: The Origins of Incarceration in France*. Trans. W. D. Halls. Cambridge: Polity, 1988.

Cellard, André. *Histoire de la folie au Québec, de 1600 à 1850*. Quebec: Boréal, 1991.

Cocks, Geoffrey. *Psychotherapy in the Third Reich: The Göring Institute*. New York: Oxford University Press, 1985.

Cohen, Stanley, and Scull, Andrew T. (eds.). *Social Control and the State: Historical and Comparative Essays*. Oxford: Blackwell, 1985.

Coleborne, Catherine, and MacKinnon, Dolly (eds.). *Madness in Australia: Histories, Heritage, and the Asylum*. St. Lucia: University of Queensland Press, 2003.

Connelly, Matthew. *Fatal Misconception: The Struggle to Control World Population.* Cambridge, MA: Harvard University Press, 2008.

Cooter, Roger. *The Cultural Meaning of Popular Science: Phrenology and the Organization of Consent in Nineteenth-Century Britain.* Cambridge: Cambridge University Press, 1984.

Copp, Terry, and McAndrew, Bill. *Battle Exhaustion: Soldiers and Psychiatrists in the Canadian Army, 1939–1945.* Montreal: McGill-Queen's University Press, 1990.

Dain, Norman. *Clifford W. Beers: Advocate for the Insane.* Pittsburgh: University of Pittsburgh Press, 1980.

   Concepts of Insanity in the United States, 1789–1865. New Brunswick, NJ: Rutgers University Press, 1964.

Dale, Pamela, and Melling, Joseph (eds.). *Mental Illness and Learning Disability Since 1850: Finding a Place for Mental Disorder in the United Kingdom.* New York: Routledge, 2006.

Darnton, Robert. *Mesmerism and the End of the Enlightenment in France.* Cambridge, MA: Harvard University Press, 1968.

DeGrandpre, Richard. *The Cult of Pharmacology: How America Became the World's Most Troubled Drug Culture.* Durham, NC: Duke University Press, 2006.

Deutsch, Albert. *The Mentally Ill in America: A History of Their Care and Treatment from Colonial Times.* 2d ed. New York: Columbia University Press, 1949.

Digby, Anne. *Madness, Morality, and Medicine: A Study of the York Retreat, 1796–1914.* Cambridge: Cambridge University Press, 1985.

Doerner, Klaus. *Madmen and the Bourgeoisie.* Trans. J. Neugroschel and J. Steinberg. Oxford: Basil Blackwell, 1981.

Dowbiggin, Ian. *Inheriting Madness: Professionalization and Psychiatric Knowledge in Nineteenth-Century France.* Berkeley: University of California Press, 1991.

   Keeping America Sane: Psychiatry and Eugenics in the United States and Canada, 1880–1940. Ithaca, NY: Cornell University Press, 1997.

   The Sterilization Movement and Global Fertility in the Twentieth Century. New York: Oxford University Press, 2008.

Dumant, Sarah, and Porter, Roy (eds.). *The Age of Anxiety.* London: Virago Press, 1996.

Dwyer, Ellen. *Homes for the Mad: Life Inside Two Nineteenth Century Asylums.* New Brunswick, NJ: Rutgers University Press, 1987.

Dyck, Erika. *Psychedelic Psychiatry: LSD from Clinic to Campus.* Baltimore: Johns Hopkins University Press, 2008.

Ellenberger, Henri F. *The Discovery of the Unconscious: The History and Evolution of Dynamic Psychiatry.* New York: Basic Books, 1970.

Engstrom, Eric J. *Clinical Psychiatry in Imperial Germany: A History of Psychiatric Practice.* Ithaca, NY: Cornell University Press, 2003.

Farley, John. *Brock Chisholm, the World Health Organization, and the Cold War.* Vancouver: University of British Columbia Press, 2008.

Farrell, John. *Freud's Paranoid Quest: Psychoanalysis and Modern Suspicion.* New York: New York University Press, 1996.

Forsythe, Bill, and Melling, Joseph (eds.). *The Politics of Madness: The State, Insanity and Society in England, 1845–1914.* New York: Routledge, 2006.

Fox, Richard W. *So Far Disordered in Mind: Insanity in California, 1870–1930.* Berkeley: University of California Press, 1978.

Freeman, Lucy, and Schlaifer, Charles. *Heart's Work: Civil War Heroine and Champion of the Mentally Ill, Dorothy Lynde Dix.* New York: Paragon House, 1991.

Friedman, Lawrence J. *Menninger: The Family and the Clinic.* New York: Knopf, 1990.

Furedi, Frank. *Therapy Culture: Cultivating Vulnerability in an Anxious Age.* London: Routledge, 2003.

Gamwell, Lynn, and Tomes, Nancy. *Madness in America: Cultural and Medical Perceptions of Mental Illness Before 1914.* Ithaca, NY: Cornell University Press, 1995.

Gauchet, Marcel, and Swain, Gladys. *Madness and Democracy: The Modern Psychiatric Universe.* Trans. Catherine Porter. Princeton, NJ: Princeton University Press, 1999.

Gifford, George E. (ed.). *Psychoanalysis, Psychotherapy and the New England Medical Scene, 1894–1944.* New York: Science History Publications, 1978.

Gilman, Sander L. *Hysteria Beyond Freud.* Berkeley: University of California Press, 1993.

Glenn, Jr., Charles Leslie. *The Myth of the Common School.* Amherst: University of Massachusetts Press, 1988.

Goldstein, Jan. *Console and Classify: The French Psychiatric Profession in the Nineteenth Century.* Cambridge: Cambridge University Press, 1987.

Gollaher, David. *Voice for the Mad: The Life of Dorothea Dix.* New York: Free Press, 1995.

Gosling, F. G. *Before Freud: Neurasthenia and the American Medical Community, 1870–1910.* Urbana: University of Illinois Press, 1987.

Grob, Gerald N. *The Mad Among Us: A History of the Care of America's Mentally Ill.* Toronto: Maxwell MacMillan Canada, 1994.

   Mental Illness and American Society, 1875–1940. Princeton, NJ: Princeton University Press, 1983.

   Mental Institutions in America: Social Policy to 1875. New York: Free Press, 1973.

Gurstein, Rochelle. *The Repeal of Reticence: A History of America's Cultural and Legal Struggles over Free Speech, Obscenity, Sexual Liberation, and Modern Art.* New York: Farrar, Straus, and Giroux, 1998.

Hacking, Ian. *Rewriting the Soul: Multiple Personality and the Sciences of Memory.* Princeton, NJ: Princeton University Press, 1995.

Hale, Nathan G. *Freud and the Americans: The Beginnings of Psychoanalysis in the United States, 1896–1917.* Oxford: Oxford University Press, 1971.

Harris, Ruth. *Murder and Madness: Medicine, Law, and Society in France at the Fin de Siècle.* Oxford: Oxford University Press, 1989.

Hayes, Carlton J. H. *A Generation of Materialism, 1871–1900.* New York: Harper & Row, 1941.

Healy, David. *The Anti-Depressant Era.* Cambridge, MA: Harvard University Press, 1997.

The Creation of Psychopharmacology. Cambridge, MA: Harvard University Press, 2004.

Herman, Ellen. *The Romance of American Psychology: Political Culture in the Age of Experts.* Berkeley: University of California Press, 1996.

Herzberg, David. *Happy Pills in America: From Miltown to Prozac.* Baltimore: Johns Hopkins University Press, 2008.

Houston, R. A. *Madness and Society in Eighteenth-Century Scotland.* Oxford: Oxford University Press, 2000.

Hunter, Richard, and Macalpine, Ida (eds.). *Three Hundred Years of Psychiatry, 1535–1860: A History Presented in Selected English Texts.* Hartsdale, NY: Carlisle Publishing, 1982.

Ignatieff, Michael. *A Just Measure of Pain: The Penitentiary in the Industrial Revolution, 1750–1850.* Harmondsworth: Penguin, 1978.

Jackson, Lynette A. *Surfacing Up: Psychiatry and Social Order in Colonial Zimbabwe, 1908–1968.* Ithaca, NY: Cornell University Press, 2005.

Jackson, Stanley W. *Melancholia and Depression: From Hippocratic to Modern Times.* New Haven, CT: Yale University Press, 1986.

James, Tony. *Dream, Creativity, and Madness in Nineteenth Century France.* New York: Oxford University Press, 1995.

Jiminez, Mary Ann. *Changing Faces of Madness: Early American Attitudes and Treatment of the Insane.* Hanover, NH: University Press of New England, 1987.

Jones, Kathleen. *Asylums and After: A Revised History of the Mental Health Services: From the Early 18th Century to the 1990s.* London: Athlone Press, 1993.

Keating, Peter. *La science du mal: L'institution de la psychiatrie au Québec, 1800–1914.* Quebec: Boréal, 1993.

Killen, Andreas. *Berlin Electropolis: Shocks, Nerves, and German Modernity.* Berkeley: University of California Press, 2006.

Kirk, Stuart A., and Kutchins, Herb. *The Selling of DSM: The Rhetoric of Science in Psychiatry.* New York: Aldine de Gruyter, 1992.

Kramer, Peter D. *Listening to Prozac: A Psychiatrist Explores Antidepressant Drugs and the Remaking of the Self.* New York: Viking, 1993.

Kroker, Kenton. *The Sleep of Others and the Transformations of Sleep Research.* Toronto: University of Toronto Press, 2007.

Kühl, Stefan. *The Nazi Connection: Eugenics, American Racism, and German National Socialism.* New York: Oxford University Press, 1994.

Kushner, Howard I. *Self-Destruction in the Promised Land: A Psychocultural Biology of American Suicide.* New Brunswick, NJ: Rutgers University Press, 1989.

Kutchins, Herb, and Kirk, Stuart A. *Making Us Crazy: DSM, the Psychiatric Bible and the Creation of Mental Disorders.* New York: Free Press, 1997.

Lane, Christopher. *Shyness: How Normal Behavior Became a Sickness*. New Haven, CT: Yale University Press, 2007.

Larson, Edward J. *Sex, Race, and Science: Eugenics in the Deep South*. Baltimore: Johns Hopkins University Press, 1995.

Lasch, Christopher. *The Culture of Narcissism: American Life in an Age of Diminishing Expectations*. New York: W. W. Norton, 1979.

Lerner, Paul. *Hysterical Men: War, Psychiatry, and the Politics of Trauma in Germany*. Ithaca, NY: Cornell University Press, 2003.

Lindemann, Mary. *Medicine and Society in Early Modern Europe*. Cambridge: Cambridge University Press, 1999.

Lunbeck, Elizabeth. *The Psychiatric Persuasion: Knowledge, Gender, and Power in Modern America*. Princeton, NJ: Princeton University Press, 1994.

MacDonald, Michael. *Mystical Bedlam: Madness, Anxiety, and Healing in Seventeenth Century England*. New York: Cambridge University Press, 1981.

MacKenzie, Charlotte. *Psychiatry for the Rich: A History of Ticehurst Private Asylum, 1792–1917*. New York: Routledge, 1992.

McCandless, Peter. *Moonlight, Magnolias, and Madness: Insanity in South Carolina from the Colonial Period to the Progressive Era*. Chapel Hill: University of North Carolina Press, 1996.

McFarland-Icke, Bronwyn. *Nurses in Nazi Germany: Moral Choice in History*. Princeton, NJ: Princeton University Press, 1999.

McGovern, Constance M. *Masters of Madness: Social Origins of the American Psychiatric Profession*. Hanover, NH: New England University Press, 1985.

McLaren, Angus. *Our Own Master Race: Eugenics in Canada, 1885–1945*. Toronto: McClelland & Stewart, 1990.

Micale, Mark S. *Approaching Hysteria: Disease and Its Interpretations*. Princeton, NJ: Princeton University Press, 1995.

  (ed.). *Beyond the Unconscious: Essays in the History of Psychiatry*. Princeton, NJ: Princeton University Press, 1993.

  (ed.) *The Mind of Modernism: Medicine, Psychology, and the Cultural Arts in Europe and America, 1880–1940*. Stanford, CA: Stanford University Press, 2004.

Micale, Mark, and Porter, Roy (eds.). *Discovering the History of Psychiatry*. New York: Oxford University Press, 1994.

Micale, Mark S., and Lerner, Paul (eds.). *Traumatic Pasts: History, Psychiatry, and Trauma in the Modern Age, 1870–1930*. Cambridge: Cambridge University Press, 2001.

Midelfort, H. C. Erik. *A History of Madness in Sixteenth Century Germany*. Stanford, CA: Stanford University Press, 1999.

Miller, Judy, and Torrey, E. Fuller. *The Invisible Plague: The Rise of Mental Illness from 1750 to the Present*. New Brunswick, NJ: Rutgers University Press, 2001.

Mills, James. *Madness, Cannabis, and Colonialism: The 'Native Only' Lunatic Asylums of British India, 1857–1900*. London: Palgrave MacMillan, 2000.

Mitchinson, Wendy. *The Nature of Their Bodies: Women and Their Doctors in Victorian Canada*. Toronto: University of Toronto Press, 1991.

Moran, James. *Committed to the State Asylum: Insanity and Society in Nineteenth Century Quebec and Ontario.* Montreal: McGill-Queen's University Press, 2000.

Moran, James, and Wright, David (eds.). *Mental Health and Canadian Society: Historical Perspectives.* Montreal: McGill-Queen's University Press, 2006.

Noll, Steven. *Feeble-Minded in Our Midst: Institutions for the Mentally Retarded in the South, 1900–1940.* Chapel Hill: University of North Carolina Press, 1996.

Nye, Robert A. *Crime, Madness, and Politics in Modern France: The Medical Concept of National Decline.* Princeton, NJ: Princeton University Press, 1984.

Oppenheim, Janet. *"Shattered Nerves": Doctors, Patients, and Depression in Victorian England.* Oxford: Oxford University Press, 1991.

Paris, Joel. *Fall of an Icon: Psychoanalysis and Academic Psychiatry.* Toronto: University of Toronto Press, 2005.

Parker, Gail Thain. *Mind Cure in New England: From the Civil War to World War One.* Hanover, NH: University Press of New England, 1973.

Parry-Jones, William. *The Trade in Lunacy: A Study of Private Madhouses in England in the Eighteenth and Nineteenth Centuries.* Toronto: University of Toronto Press, 1972.

Petigny, Alan. *The Permissive Society: America, 1941–1965.* Cambridge: Cambridge University Press, 2009.

Pick, Daniel. *Faces of Degeneration: A European Disorder, c. 1848–c. 1918.* Cambridge: Cambridge University Press, 1989.

Porter, Roy. *The Greatest Benefit to Mankind: A Medical History of Humanity.* New York: W. W. Norton, 1998.

Madmen: A Social History of Madhouses, Mad Doctors and Lunatics. Stroud: Tempus, 2004.

Madness: A Brief History. New York: Oxford University Press, 2002.

Mind-Forg'd Manacles: A History of Madness in England from the Restoration to the Regency. Cambridge, MA: Harvard University Press, 1987.

(ed.). *The Faber Book of Madness.* London: Faber & Faber, 1991.

Porter, Roy, and Wright, David (eds.). *The Confinement of the Insane: International Perspectives, 1800–1965.* Cambridge: Cambridge University Press, 2003.

Postel, Jacques, and Quétel, C. (eds.). *Nouvelle histoire de la psychiatrie.* Toulouse: Privat, 1983.

Pressman, Jack D. *Last Resort: Psychosurgery and the Limits of Medicine.* Cambridge: Cambridge University Press, 2002.

Prestwich, Patricia E. *Drink and the Politics of Social Reform: Antialcoholism in France Since 1870.* Palo Alto, CA: Society for the Promotion of Science and Scholarship, 1988.

Reaume, Geoffrey. *Remembrance of Patients Past: Patient Life at the Toronto Hospital for the Insane, 1870–1940.* Toronto: Oxford University Press, 2000.

Reilly, Philip R. *The Surgical Solution: A History of Involuntary Sterilization in the United States.* Baltimore: Johns Hopkins University Press, 1991.

Reiser, Stanley Joel. *Medicine and the Reign of Technology.* Cambridge: Cambridge University Press, 1978.

Rieff, Philip. *The Triumph of the Therapeutic: Uses of Faith after Freud.* New York: Harper & Row, 1966.

Ripa, Yannick. *Women and Madness: The Incarceration of Women in Nineteenth Century France.* Trans. Catherine du Peloux Menage. Cambridge: Polity Press in association with Blackwell, 1990.

Roelcke, Volker. "Psychotherapy between Medicine, Psychoanalysis, and Politics: Concepts, Practices, and Institutions in Germany, *c.* 1945–1992." *Medical History,* 48, 2004: 473–92.

Rosen, George. *From Medical Police to Social Medicine: Essays on the History of Health Care.* New York: Science History Publications, 1974.

   Madness in Society: Chapters in the Historical Sociology of Mental Illness. Chicago: University of Chicago Press, 1980.

Rosenberg, Charles E. *The Care of Strangers: The Rise of America's Hospital System.* New York: Basic Books, 1987.

   No Other Gods: On Science and American Social Thought. Baltimore: Johns Hopkins University Press, 1976.

   The Trial of the Assassin Guiteau: Psychiatry and Law in the Gilded Age. Chicago: University of Chicago Press, 1968.

Rothman, David J. *Conscience and Convenience: The Asylum and Its Alternatives in Progressive America.* Boston: Little, Brown, 1980.

   The Discovery of the Asylum: Social Order and Disorder in the New Republic. 2d ed. Boston: Little, Brown, 1990.

Roudinesco, Elisabeth. *Jacques Lacan.* Trans. Barbara Bray. New York: Columbia University Press, 1997.

Sadowsky, Johnathan. *Imperial Bedlam: Institutions of Madness in Colonial Southwest Nigeria.* Berkeley: University of California Press, 1999.

Scull, Andrew T. *Decarceration: Community Treatment and the Deviant, A Radical View.* Cambridge: Polity Press, 1984.

   The Insanity of Place, the Place of Insanity: Essays on the History of Psychiatry. New York: Routledge, 2006.

   The Most Solitary of Afflictions: Madness and Society in Britain, 1700–1900. New Haven, CT: Yale University Press, 1993.

   Museums of Madness: The Social Organization of Insanity in Nineteenth Century England. Harmondsworth: Penguin, 1982.

   Social Order / Mental Disorder: Anglo-American Psychiatry in Historical Perspective. Berkeley: University of California Press, 1989.

   (ed.) *The Asylum as Utopia: W. A. F. Browne and Mid-Nineteenth Century Consolidation of Psychiatry.* New York: Routledge, 1990.

   (ed.). *Madhouses, Mad-Doctors, and Madmen: The Social History of Psychiatry in the Victorian Era London.* London: Athlone Press, 1981.

Selye, Hans. *The Stress of My Life: A Scientist's Memoirs.* 2d ed. New York: Van Nostrand Reinhold, 1979.

Semelaigne, René. *Les pionniers de la psychiatrie française avant et après Pinel.* 2 vols. Paris: Baillière, 1930–32.

Sheehan, Susan. *Is There No Place on Earth for Me?* Boston: Houghton Mifflin, 1982.

Shephard, Ben. *A War of Nerves: Soldiers and Psychiatrists in the Twentieth Century.* Cambridge, MA: Harvard University Press, 2000.

Shepherd, David A. E. *Island Doctor: John Mackieson and Medicine in Nineteenth-Century Prince Edward Island*. Montreal: McGill-Queen's University Press, 2003.

Shorter, Edward. *From the Mind into the Body: The Cultural Origins of Psychosomatic Symptoms*. Toronto: Maxwell MacMillan Canada, 1994.

  A Historical Dictionary of Psychiatry. Oxford: Oxford University Press, 2005.

  A History of Psychiatry: From the Era of the Asylum to the Age of Prozac. New York: John Wiley, 1997.

Shorter, Edward, and Healy, David. *Shock Therapy: The History of Electro-convulsive Treatment in Mental Illness*. New Brunswick, NJ: Rutgers University Press, 2008.

Shortt, S. E. D. *Victorian Lunacy: Richard M. Bucke and the Practice of Late Nineteenth-Century Psychiatry*. Cambridge: Cambridge University Press, 1986.

Showalter, Elaine. *The Female Malady: Women, Madness, and English Culture, 1830–1980*. New York: Pantheon, 1985.

  Hystories: Hysterical Epidemics and Modern Culture. New York: Columbia University Press, 1997.

Simmons, Harvey G. *Unbalanced: Mental Health Policy in Ontario, 1930–1989*. Toronto: Wall and Thompson, 1989.

Skultans, Vieda. *Madness and Morals: Ideas on Insanity in the Nineteenth Century*. Boston: Routledge & Kegan Paul, 1975.

Sommers, Christina Hoff, and Sally Satel. *One Nation Under Therapy: How the Helping Culture Is Eroding Self-Reliance*. New York: St. Martin's Press, 2005.

Sulloway, Frank. *Freud: Biologist of the Mind*. New York: Basic Books, 1979.

Suzuki, Akihito. *Madness at Home: The Psychiatrist, the Patient, and the Family in England, 1820–1860*. Los Angeles: University of California Press, 2006.

Szasz, Thomas S. *The Myth of Mental Illness: Foundations of a Theory of Personal Conduct*. New York: Harper & Row, 1974.

Tomes, Nancy. *The Art of Asylum-Keeping: Thomas Story Kirkbride and the Origins of American Psychiatry*. Philadelphia: University of Pennsylvania Press, 1994.

Tone, Andrea. *The Age of Anxiety: America's Turbulent Affair with Tranquilizers*. New York: Basic, 2008.

Topp, Leslie, Moran, James, and Andrews, Jonathan (eds.). *Madness, Architecture, and the Built Environment: Psychiatric Spaces in Historical Context*. London: Routledge, 2007.

Torrey, E. Fuller. *Nowhere to Go: The Tragic Odyssey of the Homeless Mentally Ill*. New York: Harper & Row, 1989.

Torrey, E. Fuller, and Miller, Judy. *The Invisible Plague: The Rise of Mental Illness from 1750 to the Present*. New Brunswick, NJ: Rutgers University Press, 2002.

Valenstein, Elliot S. *Great and Desperate Cures: The Rise and Decline of Psychosurgery and Other Radical Treatments for Mental Illness*. New York: Basic Books, 1986.

Warsh, Cheryl Krasnick. *Moments of Unreason: The Practice of Canadian Psychiatry and the Homewood Retreat, 1883–1923.* Montreal: McGill-Queen's University Press, 1989.

Weiner, Dora B. *The Citizen-Patient in Revolutionary and Imperial Paris.* Baltimore: Johns Hopkins University Press, 1993.

Weisz, George. *Divide and Conquer: A Comparative History of Medical Specialization.* Oxford: Oxford University Press, 2006.

Wright, David. *Mental Disability in Victorian England: The Earlswood Asylum, 1847–1901.* Oxford: Clarendon Press, 2001.

   Outside the Walls of the Asylum: On "Care and Community" in Modern Britain and Ireland. New Brunswick, NJ: Athlone Press, 1999.

Young, Allan. *The Harmony of Illusions: Inventing Post-Traumatic Stress Disorder.* Princeton, NJ: Princeton University Press, 1997.

Young, Robert M. *Mind, Brain and Adaptation in the Nineteenth Century: Cerebral Localization and Its Biological Context from Gall to Ferrier.* Oxford: Oxford University Press, 1970.

Index

absinthe, 52
addictions
 and asylums, 51
 Emmanuel movement and, 86
 in U.S., 3
advocacy groups, 168, 169, 172.
 See also names of specific groups
affective disorders, 172
Affluent Society (Galbraith), 140
"Age of Anxiety" (Auden), 54
aging, of population, 132. *See also* elderly
agoraphobia 185
AIDS (acquired immune deficiency
 syndrome), 54, 186
Alberta, sterilization in, 101, 111
Alcoholics Anonymous (AA), 86, 153
alcoholism, 51–53, 58, 109, 119, 153
Alexander II, Tsar of Russia, 44
Alexander, Franz, 89
alienation, mental, 32
alienism/alienists, 27, 45, 114
Allan Memorial Institute (Montréal), 153
*Allgemeine Zeitschrift für Psychiatrie und
 psychisch-gerichtliche Medicin*, 47
alprazolam, 188
Alzheimer, Aloys, 49
American Academy of Addiction
 Psychiatry, 161
American Academy of Psychiatrists in
 Alcoholism and Addictions, 161
American Association for the Study of
 Feeble Mindedness, 106
American Association of Marriage
 Counselors, 142

American Association on Mental
 Deficiency, 106, 108
American Institute for Family Relations, 143
American Journal of Insanity, 47
American Journal of Psychiatry, 47
American Medical Association, 47
American Psychiatric Association (APA),
 24, 47, 100, 113, 116, 137, 139, 166.
 *See also Diagnostic and Statistical
 Manual of Mental Disorders* (DSM)
American Psychological Association, 144
anatomical lesions, 27, 30, 34, 48
Anatomy of Melancholy (Burton), 10
Andrews, Gail, 183, 194
Angelou, Maya, 192
animal magnetism, 79, 82, 87
*Annales d'hygiène publique et de médecine
 légale*, 47
Annales médico-psychologiques, 47
anti-colonialism, 165
Anti-Insane Asylum Society, 68
anti-psychiatry movement, 65–68, 154–58,
 167, 168, 169
anxiety, 183–86, 189
 in U.S., 3
 neurasthenia and, 64
 perception of, 3
 SRHM and, 192
 and women, 194, 195–96
Appel, Kenneth, 138
*Archivio Italiano peule malattie nervose e
 più particolarmente per le alienazioni
 mentali*, 47
Aslin, Fred, 101